SOUTHERN SEED, NORTHERN SOIL

MIDWESTERN HISTORY AND CULTURE

GENERAL EDITORS

James H. Madison and Thomas J. Schlereth

SOUTHERN SEED, NORTHERN SOIL

African-American Farm Communities in the Midwest, 1765–1900

STEPHEN A. VINCENT

INDIANA UNIVERSITY PRESS

Bloomington and Indianapolis

This book is a publication of

Indiana University Press
601 North Morton Street
Bloomington, Indiana 47404-3797 USA

www.indiana.edu/~iupress

Telephone orders 800-842-6796
Fax orders 812-855-7931
Orders by e-mail iuporder@indiana.edu

Library of Congress Cataloging-in-Publication Data

Vincent, Stephen A.
    Southern seed, northern soil : African-American farm communities in the Midwest, 1765–1900 / Stephen A. Vincent.
        p. cm. — (Midwestern history and culture)
    Includes bibliographical references and index.
    ISBN 0-253-33577-9 (cl. : alk. paper). — ISBN 0-253-21331-2 (pa. : alk. paper)
    1. Free Afro-Americans—Indiana—History—19th century. 2. Afro-American farmers—Indiana—History—19th century. 3. Agricultural colonies—Indiana—History—19th century. 4. Free Afro-Americans—Southern States—History—18th century. 5. Free Afro-Americans—Southern States—History—19th century. 6. Migration, Internal—United States—History—19th century. 7. Farm life—Indiana—History—19th century. 8. Frontier and pioneer life—Indiana. I. Title. II. Series.
E185.93.I4V56   1999
307.72'089'6073077—dc21   99-27603

1 2 3 4 5 04 03 02 01 00 99

CONTENTS

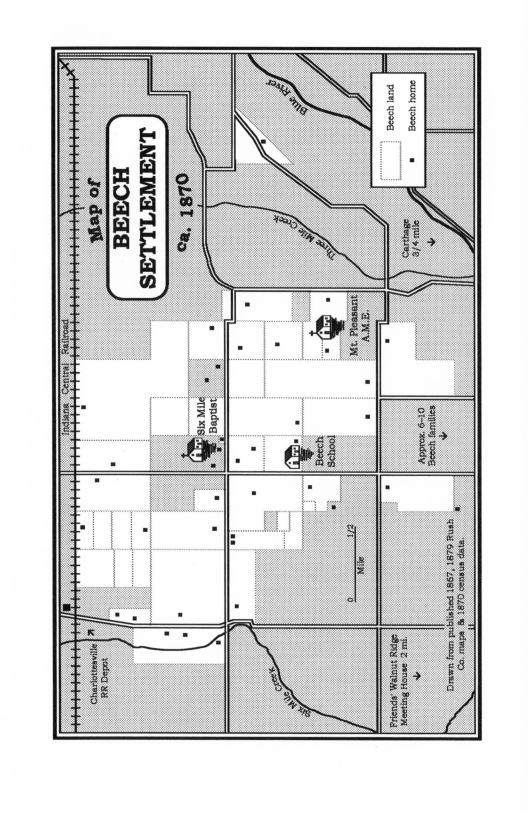

Map of
BEECH
SETTLEMENT
Ca. 1870

Indiana Central Railroad

Blue River

Three Mile Creek

Beech land
Beech home

Carthage
3/4 mile →

Six Mile
Baptist

Mt. Pleasant
A.M.E.

Beech
School

Approx. 6-10
Beech families →

Charlottesville
RR Depot

Six Mile Creek

0   1/2   Mile

Friends' Walnut Ridge
Meeting House 2 mi.
→

Drawn from published 1867, 1879 Rush
Co. maps & 1870 census data.

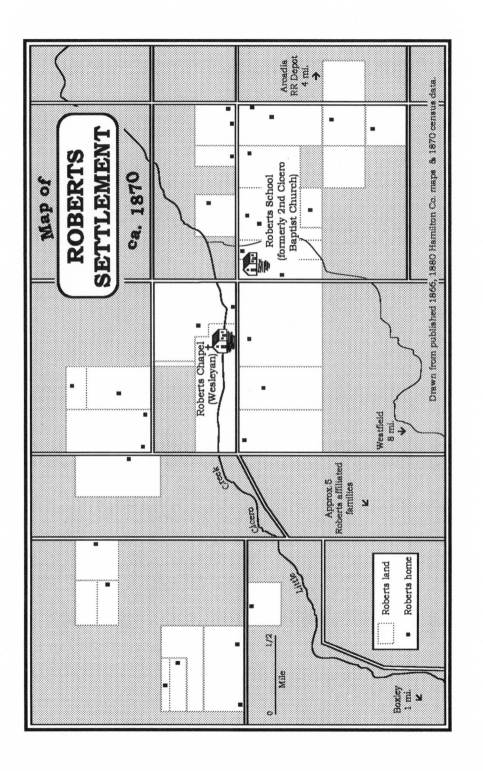

Map of
ROBERTS SETTLEMENT
ca. 1870

Arcadia
RR Depot
4 mi.

Roberts School
(formerly 2nd Cicero
Baptist Church)

Roberts Chapel
(Wesleyan)

Westfield
8 mi.

Cicero Creek

Approx. 5
Roberts affiliated
families

Little

Boxley
1 mi.

Roberts land
Roberts home

0   1/2
  Mile

Drawn from published 1866, 1880 Hamilton Co. maps & 1870 census data.

ACKNOWLEDGMENTS

This study would not have been possible without the efforts of the people of Beech and Roberts settlements. I have been guided by the pioneering work of Cyrus Roberts, Carl Roberts, and Lawrence Carter, among others, and have benefited immeasurably from the written records they have left behind. I would also like to thank the many current and recently deceased residents and descendants who shared with me their time, knowledge, and enthusiasm for the communities. Among those deserving special thanks are Jeanetta Duvall, Herbert Rice, Murphy White, Pauline Baltimore, Lawrence Carter, Ronald Tuttle, and Mildred Varnado. Hopefully this study helps repay a bit of their kindness and support. I look forward to many of our paths continuing to cross at homecoming reunions.

This project has a long history, having begun initially as an undergraduate honors thesis at Indiana University twenty years ago. Accordingly, my debts to mentors and fellow scholars are exceptionally numerous. I would especially like to thank the members of my undergraduate thesis committee—Don Carmony, Irene Neu, and Bill Harris; the members of my doctoral thesis committee at Brown University—Howard Chudacoff, Naomi Lamoreaux, and Rhett Jones; participants at Brown History Department workshops for their criticisms of chapters 1 and 3; and Jim Madison and Tom Schlereth at Indiana University Press. Because of their combined input I have become a better historian, and this manuscript is much, much better.

Debts of another sort are due to the many researchers and archivists who went well beyond the bounds of professional courtesy in their efforts to steer me to sources I otherwise would have missed. Among those whose kindness, generosity, and camaraderie deserve a special note of thanks are Coy Robbins, Robert Forest Hazel, Tom Hamm, and George Stevenson. Each has shared not just source material but an accumulation of wisdom and enthusiasm for the past as well. Our conversations have certainly been a highlight of my journey and have made me appreciate the excitement that can come with historical research.

I have also been fortunate in receiving generous funding and other forms of material support along the way. Accordingly I would like to thank the Indiana Historical Society, the National Endowment for the Humanities, Brown University, and the University of Wisconsin-Whitewater for their grants and awards. Because of their aid I was able to work in many more libraries, archives, courthouses, and other repositories than otherwise would have been possible. My mother, Mary Vincent, and brother, Rick, also deserve praise for providing me with lodging and good cheer during my research trips to the Heartland as an impoverished graduate student.

A final note of thanks goes to my wife, Linda Walton, and our two children, Claire and Matthew. Linda has offered unflagging support for my endeavors, even during the lean years of graduate school and gypsy scholarship, and has contributed to the outcome of this project in innumerable ways. Claire and Matt, meanwhile, have proven themselves to be the best of all diversions—good kids who help keep everything in perspective.

INTRODUCTION

It is not generally known that in the North there are thousands of
acres of land to which no individual white man has ever held title, and
whose only title under the Government of the United States has been in
the name of Negroes. Yet this is a fact, and a large part of this land exists
in Indiana.

—Richard R. Wright, Jr., in *Southern Workman*, 1907

Throughout the United States there are numbers of communities
of black folk, segregated, secluded, more or less autonomous, going their
quiet way unknown of most of the surrounding world. . . . there are in
Ohio and Indiana perhaps a dozen such communities, romantic in history and rich in social lessons.

—W. E. B. DuBois, in *Colored American Magazine*, 1909

Richard Wright and W. E. B. DuBois' observations remain as striking
today as they were nearly a century ago. Rural midwestern history is widely interpreted in much of the public's mind as the history of white settlers
from the time Native Americans were driven off their land in the early
nineteenth century. It is often taken as an article of faith that in the states
of the Old Northwest (today's eastern Midwest) the black population
was extremely small until the Great Migration of the twentieth century
brought southern African Americans to northern metropolises. The sturdy
pioneers of the frontier era, it is implicitly assumed, were entirely of European descent; those blacks who were free before the Civil War, in contrast,
did not have the resources, opportunity, or inclination to settle in the region's wilderness. A related impression holds that before the First World
War, midwestern African Americans lived primarily in large cities like
Chicago, Cleveland, and Detroit. In essence they were always an urban
people, without significant ties to the surrounding countryside or their
states' rural traditions and heritage.[1]

These popular perceptions do contain more than a kernel of truth. In
the nineteenth century the Old Northwest's black population was quite
small in comparison with its modern dimensions. Even though fully one-
eighth of the nation's free people of color lived in the area in the mid-
nineteenth century, their numbers were never large or concentrated. In
1860 only 63,000 were scattered across the five northwestern states, slightly less than 1 percent of the total population. And, even though the Civil

TABLE 1

Black Population of the Old Northwest States, by Size of Locations, 1860–1920

Date	Total population	Countryside/ villages under 4,000	Urban centers with 4,000+
1860	63,699	46,429 (73%)	17,270 (27%)
1880	183,298	108,718 (59%)	74,580 (41%)
1900	257,842	88,892 (34%)	168,950 (66%)
1920	514,554	72,942 (14%)	441,612 (86%)

Sources: U.S. Bureau of the Census, *Ninth Census* (Washington, 1872), 1:108–21, 123–31, 168–76, 287–95; *Tenth Census* (Washington, 1883) 1:130–55, 212–23, 285–302, 366–75, 417–25; *Twelfth Census* (Washington, 1901) 1: 613–16, 623–24, 633–36, 645–46; *Fourteenth Census* (Washington, 1922) 3: 261–69, 197–302, 488–92, 784–92, 1131–35.

War helped trigger a significant immigration of recently freed people, the black presence remained limited in most locations (see Table 1). Relative to whites in the Midwest, meanwhile, blacks were a disproportionately urban group. A majority lived in larger towns and cities as early as 1890, fully a generation or so before most whites.[2]

At the same time, as the comments by Wright and DuBois imply, there is another side to the story, one that has often been overlooked if not entirely ignored. Significant numbers of African Americans migrated to the midwestern countryside from an early point in the history of "white settlement." For most of the nineteenth century, in fact, far more lived in rural surroundings than in emerging metropolises like Chicago and De-troit. In 1860 roughly three-quarters (46,000) of the region's blacks lived either in the countryside or in small-town settings. This rural population continued to grow in absolute terms until the 1880s, when it reached well over 100,000. Thus even as the black Midwest became rapidly urbanized as the twentieth century approached, it continued to have a substantial rural element—albeit a rural element that was beginning to be overshad-owed and eclipsed even before the Great Migration.[3]

Those settling in the midwestern countryside varied considerably in terms of their pre-migration backgrounds, their ultimate destinations, and their fates once in the Old Northwest. During the period of heaviest migration, from the 1820s through the 1840s, a majority were free people of color from Virginia, North Carolina, and Kentucky who had been free for an extended length of time. Some, like legendary pioneer Free Frank McWhorter, came alone or in the company of a few friends and family.

Much larger numbers came as part of broader migrations encompassing literally hundreds of kin and neighbors. Those with longstanding histories of freedom, meanwhile, saw their ranks leavened by two other, smaller groups with more recent connections to bondage—African Americans who had been brought to the Northwest to be emancipated by their owners or their owners' agents, and fugitive slaves who clandestinely resettled in the region either independently or with the aid of the Underground Railroad.[4]

Once in the Midwest black rural immigrants tended to settle in a variety of settings. Early black pioneers, like other settlers, typically chose destinations in southern areas of Ohio, Indiana, and Illinois, often in the Miami, Whitewater, and other river valleys that were considered prime destinations. Several small, scattered neighborhoods comprising black-owned farms soon emerged. Most of these initial settlers, however, worked as casual laborers, farm hands, or farm tenants, a reflection of the greater disadvantages they faced because of poverty and overt racial discrimination. After 1820, black pioneers joined other frontier settlers in claiming land in more northerly locations. While still significantly poorer than their white neighbors, a seemingly larger proportion of these latter migrants were able to acquire their own farms upon arrival from the Old South. At least thirty well-defined neighborhoods were established between 1820 and 1850, mostly across central and south-central portions of Ohio and Indiana and, to a lesser extent, southern sections of Michigan and Wisconsin. All were "open country" rural communities: that is, following the prevailing northern pattern, all were dispersed settlements, with families residing on their own individual holdings rather than living in close proximity to one another near a nucleated village center.

The long-term fates of rural African Americans in the eastern Midwest were shaped partly by their relations with surrounding whites. At times, in fact, race relations played a determinative role in black pioneers' efforts to relocate in the countryside. Certainly this was the case with the four hundred ex-slaves of John Randolph who were set free in western Ohio in 1846, only to be driven from their land by surrounding whites. It was true in several other well documented instances as well. Generally, however, rural African Americans were left alone and allowed to fend for themselves, especially in the rural communities in the more central and northerly locations. Scattered and in small numbers, black pioneers apparently came into little direct competition with their white neighbors and therefore did little to raise whites' collective ire.

As is true of others in the countryside, black farm families' overall success or failure normally hinged upon their access to farm land, the demand for farm labor, and their abilities as farmers. During the early stages of the Northwest's settlement African-American farm communities benefited from plentiful supplies of inexpensive land and a strong demand for farm hands and farm tenants. Nonetheless the overall rural dynamic worked against them over time. Since most were poorer than surrounding whites, they tended to face diminishing opportunities sooner than most. As the rural Midwest matured, especially after the Civil War, both rental land and jobs for farm hands became more scarce, forcing many to abandon the countryside altogether. Those with land, meanwhile, typically owned less acreage than their white neighbors and thus were at a competitive disadvantage as commercial farming became more vital to the northern economy. While most midwestern farmers were forced to tighten their belts as the twentieth century approached, African American families often faced much more dire prospects. The heyday of the black rural Midwest thus was largely a memory by the time Richard Wright visited several Indiana neighborhoods in 1907.

The following study focuses on the background, founding, and development of Beech and Roberts settlements, two farm neighborhoods in central Indiana (see Map 1). The communities' founders were men and women of mixed Native American, African, and European ancestry who had been free for successive generations. Former landowners in North Carolina and Virginia, they migrated to the northern frontier of the late 1820s and early 1830s hoping to improve their economic standing and to escape increasing racial tensions in their native land. To a large extent they succeeded in their quest. Settling near the fringes of western settlement, where land was inexpensive, and near Quakers, who were known to be non-hostile, Beech and Roberts pioneers often prospered and thrived in ways they scarcely could have imagined if they had remained in the Old South. It was only in the late nineteenth century that most of the founding landowners' children and grandchildren confronted marginal prospects. Even then, Beech and Roberts residents continued to enjoy a quality of life that was arguably at least as good as, if not better than, that facing their urban black contemporaries in the Midwest.

In presenting this story I have avoided the claim that Beech and Roberts residents' experiences were typical or representative of *all* or *virtually all* rural African Americans in the Midwest. The Midwest was too varied a region, and black settlers were too diverse a people to allow such sweeping generalizations. Nonetheless, there were significant parallels and overlapping ties in the history of the two neighborhoods and those of the approximately thirty other open country neighborhoods scattered across Indiana, Ohio, Michigan, and Wisconsin. The families and larger kindreds that founded Beech and Roberts settlements came from the same areas of North Carolina and Virginia; shared the same mixed Native American, African, and European backgrounds in the Old South; migrated for similar reasons; and experienced broadly similar fates both as farmers and as African Americans attempting to create their own autonomous communities.

In addition, direct ties between the Beech, Roberts, and other rural communities were present from the very outset of settlement, and grew

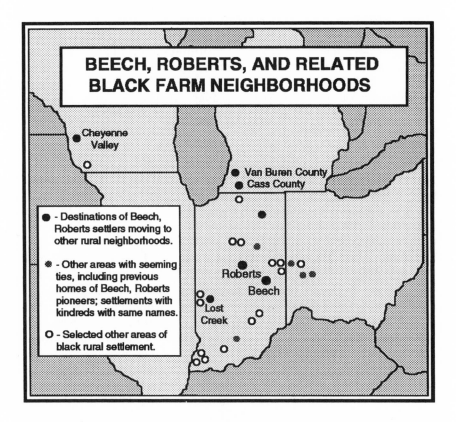

Map 1

more involved and complex over time. Members of larger kindreds often settled not just in one, but in several locations. The Roberts family, to take one of the most notable examples, was well represented not just in the Beech and Roberts neighborhoods but in more than a half dozen additional settlements ranging across four states. Other ties developed because of migration from one community to the next; marriages among men and women from different neighborhoods; residents serving as ministers and teachers at other communities; and interactions within common social, political, and military organizations such as the African Methodist Episcopal (A.M.E.) Church, Prince Hall Masonry, the Republican Party, and the Civil War–era United States Colored Troops (USCT). The experiences of Beech and Roberts residents thus may not have been typical of all African-Americans in the rural Midwest, but they did intersect with, and were representative of, a very substantial proportion of that larger world.

In the ensuing discussion I have tried to emphasize the importance of landownership for Beech and Roberts residents, their forebears in the Old South, and all Americans of African descent. Throughout American history the problems facing African Africans have frequently stemmed from economic oppression and economic discrimination. This was obviously true under slavery, itself an economic institution centered around the oppression of one people by another, but it was no less true in most other settings as well, both during and after the slave period. One need only to think of the devastating patterns associated with urban job discrimination and sharecropping to realize the severe disadvantages African Americans have faced in their efforts to control and shape their own destinies from the colonial era to the present.

Landownership, for small but significant numbers of African Americans, provided a means of circumventing this oppression and discrimination. In a revealing study of slaves who became free on Virginia's Eastern Shore in the early seventeenth century, T. H. Breen and Stephen Innes have posited that owning land was *the* critical factor in their subjects' ability to establish and maintain their freedom. Such property "provided a livelihood as well as immunity from depredation. It gave them identity before the law and security in times of trouble...." In a similar vein, Loren Schweninger has asserted that landownership among colonial blacks in the South promoted not just economic independence and autonomy, but also a sense of well-being, assertiveness, and self-confidence. Historians have echoed much the same sentiments concerning black property owners in other southern settings as well.[5]

The Beech and Roberts story amplifies and extends this basic theme. Land, quite simply, provided Beech and Roberts families with a form of power and control that was unavailable to most other African Americans. In both the Old South and the Midwest, landownership provided the communities' most prominent families with a remarkable degree of stability and security. It allowed them economic independence and elevated their status in the minds of neighboring whites, just as it did for blacks elsewhere. Yet landownership also did much more. It provided Beech and Roberts pioneers with the resources needed to escape a hostile land and to begin anew on better soil under conditions largely of their own choosing; it allowed them to create new rural neighborhoods that minimized the interference of outsiders; and it provided them with the opportunity to pass on their good fortune, at least in many instances, from one generation to the next.

I have also tried to stress, in a much more subtle and attenuated fashion, the importance of Beech and Roberts residents' identity as a people both within and outside the mainstreams of African-American as well as American societies. The communities' members, along with their immediate forebears, were not easily classified according to the prevailing racial categories of their day. While they were an African-descended people and suffered the common disabilities facing all African Americans, they were also perceptibly different from the vast majority of other blacks. Even before their migration to the Old Northwest their families had been free for several generations; they had long been independent landowners, free of white control; and their ancestry in many instances was decidedly multiracial rather than predominantly African. Some, in fact, had very little African ancestry at all. Thus both their experiences and their appearances served to set them apart from most other African Americans.

Despite these differences, surrounding whites normally refused to accept them on anything approaching an equal footing. Following the American convention that anyone with a hint of African ancestry was an African American, they were variously described as "colored," "mulatto," "Negro," and "black." These descriptive labels shifted from place to place but, in keeping with the broader trends of American race relations, generally gave increasing emphasis over time to the African element in Beech and Roberts residents' identity. The actual nature of day-to-day interactions with surrounding whites followed suit. At times Beech and Roberts residents' physical and cultural differences allowed them to escape discriminatory treatment that was common to other blacks; in most instances, especially as the nineteenth century drew to a close, it did not.

The ambiguity and ambivalence of whites' perceptions and behavior seems to have been matched by Beech and Roberts residents' own views of the world surrounding them. Time and again they identified themselves with other people of African descent, as for example in their involvement with the A.M.E. Church, the USCT, and their pursuit of careers as ministers and teachers for other African-American communities. Yet time and again they also sought to keep themselves apart. In their self-conscious decisions to seek out and settle with others like themselves, in their deliberate efforts to marry others with common heritages, in many residents' avoidance of darker-skinned African Americans with slave heritages, and in the ways they presented their heritage and history to outsiders, it is apparent that they often perceived themselves as a distinct if not unique African-descended people.

Because Beech and Roberts residents saw themselves and were seen by others as a people with varying and shifting identities, I have chosen to describe them not by one or two descriptive terms, but by several, giving primary emphasis to those that were normative for the particular time under discussion. Thus they are depicted as "free people of color" as well as "free blacks" and "free Negroes" before the Civil War, and "mixed race" as well as "black" and "African American" in the late nineteenth century and beyond. While the interchangeable use of these terms may at times slow the flow of the narrative, it more accurately conveys the multicultural heritage and fluctuating identities of those involved.

Southern Seed, Northern Soil

SOUTHERN ORIGINS,

CA. 1760–1830

IN THE WINTER OF 1828–1829, Willis Roberts was a man of mixed emotions. Mulling over prospects for moving to the Northwest frontier, the middle-aged farmer had begun taking a hard look at the world around him. A lifelong resident of Northampton County, North Carolina, he was a light-skinned free person of color whose family shared a long heritage of both freedom and landownership. His grandfather, James Roberts, had settled in Northampton more than a decade before the Revolution. Cherished memories of family and friends, white as well as non-white, came to mind when Willis thought of his native land. Still, these were troubled times. Northampton was an "old country," a long-settled region with few opportunities for its younger residents. Willis had little reason to believe that his children could follow in his footsteps by acquiring farms of their own. Even worse, relations between free blacks and local whites had deteriorated alarmingly over the course of Willis' lifetime. The group's rights and privileges were being whittled away year after year, with their status coming ever closer to that of slaves. Concerned about the future, friends of all racial backgrounds had begun urging Willis to migrate to the northern frontier. It was a suggestion he could not take lightly.[1]

Willis Roberts' thoughts in the winter of 1828–1829 apparently were matched by those of other free people of color who, like Willis, would help establish Beech and Roberts settlements in the coming years. The southern origins of two-thirds of the sixty-eight men and women listed as household heads at the settlements in the 1840 census can be traced to specific locations (see Table 2). The largest number were Willis' friends and kin from Northampton; others came from two adjacent counties, Halifax County, North Carolina and Greensville County, Virginia (see Map 2). While their backgrounds varied, most were the descendants of light-skinned free people of color whose freedom dated from at least the mid- to late eighteenth century. As the sons and daughters of small landowners they, too, found themselves trapped in the same difficult situation, surrounded by both declining economic opportunities and rising racial tensions.[2]

≈ ≈ ≈

Northampton County, North Carolina was settled by colonists of European and African descent during the decades immediately before the American Revolution. Located in the colony's northern inner coastal plain, the area attracted a mix of planters and small farmers hoping to prosper from the cultivation of tobacco, wheat, and corn. Most came from Virginia's Tidewater and Southside regions between 1740 and 1780, lured by the chance to acquire fertile lands for little more than the cost of tax payments. Large numbers of forcibly enslaved men and women, most apparently natives of western Africa, accompanied their masters and mistresses on their journeys to Northampton. By the early 1760s perhaps 5,000 individuals had settled in the county; roughly one-quarter were slaves. A generation later almost 10,000 were counted as residents by enumerators of the first U.S. Census in 1790; 44 percent were enslaved Africans and African Americans.[3]

Planters and common folk alike found ample opportunities in early Northampton County. Several large plantations were quickly established, most along the navigable Roanoke and Meherrin rivers that formed the county's western and eastern borders, respectively. By 1790 the wealthiest

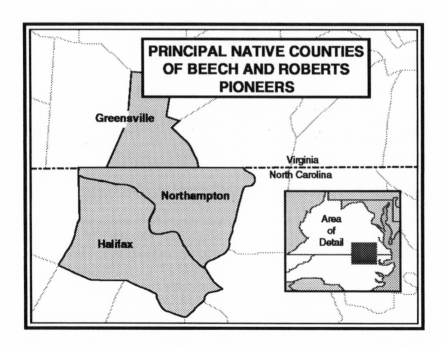

Map 2

five members of the local gentry each held more than fifty blacks in bond-age; almost fifty others owned from twenty to forty-nine slaves. Surrounding these plantations were the homesteads of several hundred small farmers whose efforts were geared more toward subsistence crops and less to tobacco. Dominating much of the countryside by their sheer numbers, most held few if any slaves. In 1790 half of Northampton's free families owned no slaves. Another fifth held only from one to three slaves. While plantation field slaves toiled under their overseers' supervision, hundreds of smaller farmers worked on more modest plots of land among family, neighbors, and perhaps a few slaves.[4]

Among the small farmers scattered across Northampton County's interior on the eve of the Revolution were perhaps two hundred free people of color, including the forebears of twenty-two Beech and Roberts pioneers. Most had migrated from Virginia during the mid-eighteenth century or were the descendants of such early settlers. While the northeastern North Carolina frontier attracted them in part for the same reason it attracted whites—good farmland was plentiful and easy to acquire—other factors also played critical roles in their decisions as free blacks to migrate to this particular area. Slavery, for one, was less concentrated in Northampton and surrounding counties during the mid- to late eighteenth century than it was in longer-settled sections of Virginia. This made the presence of free people of color, who were viewed as instigators of racial strife, less an object of special concern and/or derision among whites. The relative shortage of labor at the frontier also encouraged greater acceptance of free blacks, and allowed members of the caste more work opportunities than they might otherwise find available. And, finally, Virginia laws re-

TABLE 2

Southern Origins of 1840 Beech and Roberts Settlements Household Heads

	No. of heads	% of total heads
Northampton County, N.C.	24	35.3
Halifax County, N.C.	9	13.2
Greensville County, Va.	8	11.8
Other locations	2	2.9
Unknown	25	36.8
Total	68	100.0

Note: Appendix A provides discussion of the methods and sources used to trace the 1840 household heads.

quiring manumitted slaves to leave the colony upon gaining their freedom may have encouraged some to move just across the border into the area as well.[5]

By 1790 Northampton free blacks' heritage of freedom seemingly was more deeply rooted than that of most others of their caste. Historians have generally posited that most free people of color at the time of the first U.S. census had been manumitted either during or immediately following the American Revolution. Only a very small proportion of the nation's 56,000 free blacks in 1790, it is believed, could trace their free status back to the colonial era. Clearly this was not the case either in Northampton or in surrounding counties. As professional genealogist Paul Heinegg has painstakingly shown, scores of free people of color had deep roots in the area well before 1776. Indeed, Northampton's free blacks played a significant role in the fighting for American freedom and independence from Great Britain, thus helping to set the stage for the widespread emancipations of the 1770s and 1780s. Military records indicate that at least a dozen free black men from Northampton County served with either the Continental Army or the North Carolina militia during the fighting that swept through the South between 1779 and 1781.[6]

The most detailed evidence concerning free people of color with Beech and Roberts ties focuses on the Roberts kindred, twelve of whose members would lead their families to the Indiana settlements before 1840. James Roberts, the first identifiable family member, lived in Northampton County more than a decade before the Revolution. According to Roberts family tradition, James was the son of an African servant who was never enslaved and a Native American woman. James' father reportedly arrived in America as the personal valet of a Lord Roberts in North Carolina and acted as the nobleman's plantation overseer. Following Lord Roberts' death the Roberts family patriarch inherited his master's holdings.[7]

While local records provide little evidence that convincingly either validates or disproves this legend, it is unlikely that James' father would have arrived from Africa as either a free man or an indentured servant in the eighteenth century. Nor do North Carolina colonial records include mention of an English gentleman with the Roberts surname. The elder Roberts, however, may have been a descendent of one of the first Africans brought to the South, many of whom readily acquired both freedom and land during the early to mid-seventeenth century, before laws and customs concerning African slavery and racial boundaries were firmly defined. Such a possibility would be in keeping with the family tradition of limited direct contact with slavery itself. Or, perhaps equally plausible, the patriarch may have been the son of an interracial couple. By the mid-seventeenth century most free people of color in Virginia and North Carolina traced their free status to white servant women who cohabited with slave men.[8]

James' mother, meanwhile, may well have been a Native American.

Indians and Africans/African Americans in many ways shared a common experience throughout the colonial era—both groups were enslaved by European-American settlers, were considered to be members of subordinate castes, and generally faced inequitable, contemptuous treatment from whites. Not surprisingly, intimate social relations between the two were common throughout the southern British colonies. Native Americans, moreover, had a significant presence in Northampton County, the counties immediately surrounding Northampton, and the other areas of Virginia and northeastern North Carolina from which the Robertses may have come. Considerable numbers of three Iroquoian language tribes —the Tuscaroras, Meherrins, and Nottoways—continued to live in close proximity to white and black settlers in the greater Northampton area through the mid-eighteenth century. The first known physical descriptions of Roberts family members, from those born in the early nineteenth century, bear further testimony to the family's Indian heritage.[9]

What can be noted with even greater certainty is that James Roberts' name first appears in local land records in 1765. At that time he purchased a one-hundred-acre farm in northern Northampton County. The deed recording his transaction refers to him as "James Roberts, Northampton, planter," an indication that he had taken up residence as an area farmer before that time. Additional evidence shows that James and his wife, Ann, were parents of a large family that came of age in the last quarter of the eighteenth century. The Roberts family's growth can be surmised from a 1780 Northampton tax list that includes the names of James and four of his seven known sons among local male taxables. Three of the four sons were listed as single men at that time. Additional insight comes from the 1790 census for Northampton County, which lists six Roberts households totaling thirty-one individuals. Five of the sons, along with James, had established their own families by that time. Several of the children in these households—James' grandchildren—would ultimately play prominent roles in the founding of Beech and Roberts settlements.[10]

James Roberts, like many of his neighbors, prospered as a planter during the Revolutionary era. Extant land deed records, which are not entirely complete, provide the best measure of early landownership in Northampton County. They show that between 1765 and 1809 James purchased roughly 700 acres of farmland through four or more transactions. Between 1790 and 1797 James sold 375 acres: 215 acres to his son Jonathan for a nominal fee, presumably to provide him with a patrimony, and an additional 160 acres to neighboring whites. Despite his sales James' estate apparently was never smaller than 300 acres after 1779, and at times exceeded 500 acres. At his death in 1809 his homestead included 325 acres.[11]

James' holdings were moderately large by the general standards of the day. Studies of landownership in North Carolina during the Revolutionary era indicate that roughly half of all freeholders owned less than 200 acres, another quarter held 201 to 400 acres, and the remainder commanded plantations of more than 400 acres. The Robertses thus were planters of middling status, better situated than most of their white neighbors but not as affluent as members of the local planter elite. Even more striking, perhaps, was their favorable financial standing relative to other free people of color. A sizable proportion of James' free black contemporaries in the rural South owned land, but most apparently held much smaller, marginal acreages. Even more—perhaps the vast majority of freedmen—were landless and directly dependent upon whites for their livelihoods. Free people of color typically worked as farm laborers, rented small farms, or made ends meet plying trades such as carpentry or shoemaking.[12]

While little is known about the living conditions of James Roberts' immediate family, their ability to acquire a comfortable freehold undoubtedly provided them with a control over their financial destiny unknown to most free people of color. The family landholdings provided a large measure of economic independence and self-reliance. Together with their children, James and Ann managed the family fields, livestock, orchard, and gardens in a manner that supplied the family with its most basic food and clothing needs. The Robertses also grew a few hogsheads of tobacco each year to be sold at a nearby marketplace, probably Petersburg, Virginia, by the late 1700s. The resulting cash provided the family with the necessary means to pay the bills for many of the goods and services it could not produce. Other items and services were obtained by bartering with kin and neighbors. As a result, the Robertses did not face the poverty, uncertainty, and overt derision that typically confronted free people of color dependent upon whites for land or labor. Nor did they confront the chilling prospect of having their children indentured as servants to white masters, a fate which left many impoverished free black youngsters extremely vulnerable to illegal reenslavement.[13]

Landownership solidified the Robertses' status in several other ways as well. As T. H. Breen and Stephen Innes have perceptively noted, free blacks' standing in colonial American society was shaped to a very large extent by their access to property itself. For all British colonists, property ownership literally defined one's legal, political, and social status: the greater one's property holdings, the greater one's stake in society and, in turn, the greater one's ability to command respect and authority in virtually all matters. For free people of color, owning one's "own ground" was especially important because of the steadily encroaching view, especially after 1660, that all people of African ancestry should be enslaved. Landownership may not have made James and Ann Roberts the equals of their white neighbors, but it certainly provided them with added personal respect, enhanced their ability to defend their free status in courts of law, and distanced them from the specter of slavery itself. The Robertses were not just free people of color, but free people of color of considerable substance.[14]

Over time the Roberts family's long-term success as landholders—James and Ann's ability to add to their acreage, along with the longevity of their tenure—presumably also enhanced their reputation with their immediate neighbors. The Robertses repeatedly bought parcels of land adjacent to their original purchase, bargained and bartered with surrounding families for a variety of goods, and generally gained the trust and friendship of nearby white neighbors over succeeding generations. All of these actions, however mundane and routine they might appear on the surface, served to project an image of the Robertses as an unremarkable people who were much like other early Northampton settlers.[15]

This impression of solidity and middling status may well have been reinforced by James Roberts' ownership of two slaves. The slaves are listed in census reports from 1790 and 1800, but little else is known about them. Presumably they may have been in his possession well before 1790. The two might have been family members, perhaps the children or grandchildren of James and/or his wife. Most slaves held by free blacks in the Upper South, historians have argued, were held for fraternal rather than economic reasons. On the other hand, as the owners of more than five hundred acres of land, James and his family may very well have used the slaves as field hands and/or house servants. It is suggestive to note that James' most prosperous son, Jonathan, rented slaves on yearly contracts on at least four occasions during the 1810s. The Robertses' ownership of slaves as laborers, if that indeed was the case, would have signaled to neighbors their own acceptance of slavery as an institution and served to distance them from those free blacks who were closely identified with enslaved Africans and African Americans.[16]

A final factor favoring the Roberts family in the mid- to late eighteenth century was their mixed racial heritage. While discrimination against all people of African descent increased from the late seventeenth century as slavery spread, thereby reducing any special advantages lighter-skinned free people of color might have enjoyed, race-related boundaries nonetheless remained more fluid and ill-defined than they would become after the Revolution. Signs of the unsettled nature of the race line could be seen in both the continuation of mixed-race marriages between white servant women and African-American men into the mid-eighteenth century despite the passage of laws to prevent such miscegenation, and in the ability of some prosperous mulattoes to "pass" (that is, to be identified) as whites. The ongoing ambiguity in race relations at times favored lighter-skinned free mulattoes, especially when their mixed racial heritage went hand in hand with wealth, over those with darker complexions. It also apparently encouraged the emergence of color consciousness within the free black caste, with lighter-skinned individuals and families perceiving themselves as distinct from, and often superior to, those with darker complexions.[17]

The Robertses' mixed racial heritage *probably* fostered closer ties with neighboring whites in Northampton than otherwise would have prevailed if family members had been darker in appearance, especially before the outset of the Revolution. Family genealogical materials gathered in the early twentieth century note that the Robertses intermarried with a neighboring white family, the Ropers, in the mid- to late eighteenth century. Moreover, it seems plausible to believe that whites would have responded relatively positively to the Robertses as neighbors because their physiological features more closely matched the somatic norm image, or racial ideal, shared by white colonists. A more precise assessment of the elusive and subtle role played by skin color and heritage, however, is precluded by the limited surviving information available and the complex ways in which skin color combined with other factors to distance James and Ann Roberts' family from most Africans and African Americans in colonial Northampton County. Landholdings, long-standing residence, slaves, and mixed racial heritage—not one, but all seemingly combined to set the Robertses apart as distinctive free people of color.[18]

∽ ∽ ∽

The children of James and Ann Roberts, coming of age in the decades during and immediately after the Revolution, were able to enjoy only a portion of their parents' prosperity and acceptance. Only five of seven sons acquired substantial farms of their own in Northampton County, and their land came largely from that originally purchased by their father. Jonathan bought 215 acres from James in 1796, while Elias and Claxton each were bequeathed half of James' 325-acre estate according to instructions in his will. Land deeds suggest that the only substantial additions to the family's land came through James Junior's purchase of 100 acres in 1774, John's acquisition of 106 acres before 1797, and Jonathan's purchase of 94 acres in 1805. The holdings of each son were thus much smaller than that of the father. Only Jonathan owned more than 200 acres.[19]

Smaller holdings were only the beginning of the problems that James Senior's children faced in their struggle to stay ahead. Jonathan and Elias were probably dependent on their father for more than a decade after establishing their own families before he provided them with their land. The family patriarch waited fifteen years after the birth of Jonathan's first son, Willis, before he sold Jonathan a portion of his land; Elias had been a householder at least thirteen years before inheriting half of his father's estate, which brought with it responsibility of his mother's care. John, meanwhile, a Revolutionary War veteran, sold his farm and moved to the newly settled lands of western North Carolina in the 1790s, perhaps lured away by hopes of better farmland. James Senior's two remaining sons, Kinchen and William, do not appear to have acquired farms of their own. All of these difficulties—smaller farms, delays in the transfer of land by

TABLE 3

Population of Northampton County, N.C., 1790–1820

	1790	1800	1810	1820
Total	9,992	12,331	13,082	13,391
Whites	5,120 (51%)	5,587 (45%)	5,244 (40%)	5,254 (40%)
Slaves	4,414 (44%)	6,206 (50%)	7,258 (55%)	7,263 (55%)
Free blacks	458 (5%)	538 (4%)	580 (4%)	725 (6%)

Sources: U.S. Bureau of Census, *A Century of Population Growth from the First Census of the United States to the Twelfth, 1790–1900* (Washington, 1909), 204–205; idem, *Return of the Whole Number of Persons Within . . . the United States . . . Second Census* (Washington, 1802), 69, 74; idem, *Aggregate Amount of Each Description of Persons Within the United States . . . 1810* (Washington, 1811), 54a, 75a; idem, *Census for 1820* (Washington, 1821), 24–25.

the family patriarch, dissatisfaction with existing holdings, and the outright failure to acquire land—were common in areas of eighteenth- and nineteenth-century America where land and population pressures were beginning to mount.[20]

The decades surrounding 1800 clearly marked a turning point in the Roberts family's fortunes. Disquieting economic and demographic trends shook the foundations of Northampton County and northeastern North Carolina. New lands for expansion in the area grew increasingly scarce after the Revolution, while fields long used for tobacco were abandoned as the soil's fertility declined. After 1810 local planters and small farmers alike, including the Robertses, responded by switching away from tobacco to the more profitable production of cotton. The resulting economic boost, however, was short-lived. Northampton and adjacent counties had entered an era of prolonged financial doldrums; seemingly little could be done to stem the tide. A steady out-migration from the area began around the turn of the century and continued for more than a generation. The effect of the emigration is suggested by the fact that Northampton's white population peaked at 5,500 in 1800, then declined slightly during the decades that followed (see Table 3).[21]

Despite diminishing fortunes, most of the Roberts kindred chose to remain in Northampton County during the early nineteenth century. The group continued to expand, in fact, as the third generation began to marry and establish households of their own from about 1810 on. By 1820 eleven Roberts households totaling fifty-four members resided in the area. To some extent, those remaining may have been relatively satisfied with their individual families' holdings. While Jonathan, Elias, and Claxton owned less land than their father, they perhaps comforted themselves with the knowledge that their financial fortunes differed little from those of other early settlers' descendants. Farms throughout North Carolina generally were becoming smaller in size in the early nineteenth century due to the relative shortage of tillable land. Given James Senior's modest success, his sons may in fact have fared better than many of their neighbors. Four of Jonathan's sons, in turn, may have been somewhat mollified by their ability to acquire farms of their own. Jonathan sold each of the sons—Willis, Hansel, James, and Ransom—50- to 60-acre farms between 1813 and 1819; in his will Jonathan also named James to inherit the remainder of his estate following the death of Mary, his wife. These farms were small and "worn out" but they were freeholds nonetheless. At least five other third-generation Roberts men—Anthony, Richard, Elijah, John, and James L.—remained in the county and began raising families of their own despite owning no land. Of the five, only Richard would purchase a freehold before leaving Northampton County.[22]

The generation-to-generation slide in the Roberts kindred's financial fortunes was paralleled and exacerbated by deteriorating race relations and a precipitous drop in the status of free blacks from the early 1790s onward. In large measure, this transformation was triggered by the upsurge in slave rebelliousness associated with the Santo Domingo revolt (1791), the Gabriel Prosser (1800) and Denmark Vesey (1822) conspiracies, and the Nat Turner insurrection (1831); and by the unsettling antislavery agitation that first erupted during the Revolution and then surged again with the spread of northern abolitionism in the 1820s. Much more than before, beleaguered southern whites were forced to consider, defend, and refine their beliefs about slavery, African Americans, and free people of color. Out of this reassessment came much more sharply drawn and much more negative views of all African Americans, free as well as slave, mulatto as well as black.[23]

Free people of color became an obvious target for whites' wrath, partly because their numbers had grown significantly during the 1780s and early 1790s, when heightened humanitarian and religious concerns about the injustice of slavery led many southerners to manumit their bondmen. As slave rebelliousness festered, whites viewed free blacks with greater suspicion and derision, especially now that they were much more numerous, often only recently removed from slavery, and often dark-skinned, like the mass of bondmen. Free blacks, it was widely believed, were allies if not leaders of slaves in trying to overthrow slavery. Perhaps even more importantly, in whites' minds they had become the very symbol of whites' loss of control over southern society. In North Carolina, as elsewhere, each major challenge to slavery was followed by renewed public discussion about free people of color and efforts to restrict their legal status. While the ostensible goal of the resulting legislation was to limit slave unrest, it also served to increase anti–free black sentiment and to reduce the legal and social distance separating free people of color from slaves.[24]

The beginnings of the backlash could be seen as early as the mid-1790s. At that time the North Carolina assembly restricted the manumission of slaves, the movement of free blacks within the state, and any activity by free people of color that local officials might deem "dangerous to the peace and good order of the state and county." A period of relatively calm race relations followed after 1802, only to be shattered by an even more severe wave of anti–free black sentiment in the late 1820s. The state legislature then restricted many forms of free black–slave interaction; limited free blacks' movement across county and state lines; ordered some free black children bound out as apprentices, reducing their status closer to that of slaves; and made vagrancy a crime among free people of color, punishable by forced labor. Following the Nat Turner insurrection, additional revisions forbade free blacks from preaching the Gospel and stripped away free black men's electoral franchise. Debate began on outlawing the caste's educational opportunities, although no final action was taken.[25]

The flames of white hysteria and anti-black sentiment were fed in Northampton and surrounding northeastern counties by the growing concentration of slavery within the region. Slaves made up an ever larger proportion of the population with each passing decade. While whites outnumbered slaves by a two-to-one margin on the eve of the American Revolution, those numbers were well on the way to being reversed by the 1820s (see Table 3). With slaves now numerically dominant, and with most slaves clustered together on ever larger plantations, whites became ever more concerned with the thought they might lose control of their slaves. Slave revolt rumors swept time and again throughout northeastern North Carolina, fomenting acute fears of an impending disaster. As in other areas with large slave populations, the local courts appointed patrols to maintain order among slaves and to punish them when deemed necessary. In 1830, for example, patrollers were ordered to check slaves traveling at night for passes, search slave quarters for abolitionist and other incendiary tracts, and guarantee that religious services involving blacks were held under white supervision.[26]

The growing concentration of slaves also led to a tendency to overreact when rumors of uprisings spread, often to the detriment of free blacks. On at least two occasions several slaves and free people of color were rounded up in Northampton and neighboring counties for their alleged complicity in conspiracy plots. In 1802 widespread reports of a slave conspiracy emanating in adjacent Bertie County brought havoc to northeastern North Carolina, ultimately leading to the execution of three African Americans in nearby Hertford and Martin counties. Twenty-nine years later, two free Negro men traveling through neighboring Halifax County were shot and killed by local residents suspicious that they might be on their way to aid Nat Turner; neither man appears to have been guilty of any crime.[27]

Undoubtedly the chilling of relations between free people of color and whites, along with the degradation of the group's free status, took a heavy toll on the Roberts family. Many of those who would move to the frontier later recalled that the oppression of the early nineteenth century served as the catalyst for their migration northward. The best evidence of the frustration, fear, and anger that had built up by the late 1820s is found in a letter exchanged between two cousins, Willis and James L. Roberts, following their migration to Indiana in 1829. Both men were members of the third generation coming of age in the late eighteenth and early nineteenth century: Willis was born in 1782, "Long James" about 1790. When Willis became homesick for Northampton soon after arriving at the frontier, Long James became outraged. Writing to Willis, he asked his cousin to think "how times has altered since you could remember."[28]

Free people of color in Northampton, in James' view, had become "trapped in between two fires," with slaves and whites engulfing them in their struggles. Most slaves, on the one hand, were "very disagreeable" and thought themselves above free people of color. Living near slaves, Long Jim felt, only seemed to jeopardize their precarious quasi-free status even further. "We are always in danger of their doing us injury by some way or other," he noted. "It is well known to me that where there is slaves it is not a good place for us to live." At the same time relations with whites, in James' opinion, had become painfully strained. Appealing to Willis' parental responsibilities, he suggested to his cousin that his children would not be safe on the "best five farms" within three miles of their old home; they would be clearly at risk of losing their freedom, and might well "come under the hands of some cruel slave holder [who will] use them as bad again as [they] will one of their own slaves. . . ." Jim added with a hint of disgust that he did not know how any man would willingly bring his children to such a place. Northampton County had become a place where free people of color could not stand up for their rights in conflicts with whites. We cannot accuse whites of harming us or other Negroes, he pointed out, unless we can "prove it by a white man, and many of them will turn their backs when they think they would be [asked to bear] witness for us. . . ." Summing up the situation, Long Jim concluded that "it has been my intention ever since I had knowledge of such [that] if I lived to be a man [and] if God was willing I would leave such a place."[29]

The premigration experiences of other Beech and Roberts kindreds from Northampton and adjacent Halifax counties were broadly similar to those of the Robertses. Evidence concerning these families is less complete, but it is clear that the vast majority shared a common heritage. Like the Robertses, most were light-skinned people of Native American, African, and European backgrounds whose families could trace their free status to the colonial period. Several had members who served with the Continental Army or the patriot militia during the Revolution. Most prospered in the mid- to late eighteenth century, acquiring comfortable farms and, in a few instances, small numbers of slaves. Also like the Robertses, each family seemingly witnessed considerable economic and social decline with the passing of successive generations. Showing little favoritism for individual children, the first members of each kin group appear to have broken up their holdings into many smaller parcels. By the 1820s most of their descendants were living with reduced fortunes.

Three of the household heads at the frontier in 1840 were children or grandchildren of Drewry and Elizabeth Walden. Born of free parents in Surry County, Virginia in 1762, Drew had married Elizabeth Harris, a native-born Northampton free person of color, while serving in the North Carolina militia during the Revolution. After the war the couple settled permanently in Northampton and raised a family of nine children—six boys and three girls. Drew, neighbors would later recall, was for many years "a preacher of the Gospel of Jesus Christ" and a man of unsurpassed moral character. His early settlement in Northampton appears to have favorably affected his fate as a farmer. As early as 1780 Drew was listed in tax records as a landowner, although no indication is given of the size of his holdings at that time. In 1794 he bought a 173-acre estate, and by the early 1820s he had built up an estate of 288 acres.[30]

The issue of passing on his good fortune to his children appears to have plagued Drewry Walden as much as if not more than it did the Robertses. The Walden children came of age in the decade or so after 1810. Few, if any, were able to acquire land of their own in Northampton. Like James and Jonathan Roberts, Drew chose to divide his estate among several sons and daughters rather than pass it on to a single heir. He did not, however, apparently sell any of his land to his children for token sums as they established families of their own. Instead, he waited until his death in 1834 to divide his estate among his offspring in a generally even-handed fashion; his will stipulated that his estate, exclusive of the dower claimed by his widow and small sums given to two grandsons, was to be divided in nine equal portions and distributed among surviving children and his deceased children's heirs. Because of Drew's decision to delay the divisions of his land, each of his children was well into his or her prime before inheriting their modest portion. At least two of Drew and Elizabeth's grandchildren, in fact, had established families of their own during the elderly couple's final years. The names of at least five sons, one son-in-law, and two grandsons are listed in Northampton tax lists from the late 1820s and early 1830s; none are credited with land holdings.[31]

Seven additional 1840 heads from Northampton were members of the Bass, Byrd, Newsom, and Scott families. Each of these family groups were well represented in the county in the late eighteenth century. Among the Northampton households headed by free people of color at the first United States census were those of two Basses, four Byrds, four Newsoms, and seven Scotts; an additional three Byrd and seven Scott families resided across the Roanoke River in adjacent Halifax County. Most of those in Northampton had migrated from Virginia before the Revolution and acquired frontier farms. (The Bass kindred was descended in part from Nansemond Indians in Norfolk County, Virginia.) The eight men from the groups included in both the 1780 Northampton County tax record and the 1790 census are all listed as landholders in the former source. In addition, three members of the Byrd and Bass families, like James Roberts, were small slaveholders.[32]

Each of these four kindreds confronted fates that paralleled those of the Robertses and Waldens in the early nineteenth century. John Reddick Bass, the father of three 1840 heads, owned a 150-acre farm at his death in 1828. Like Drew Walden he chose to divide his land in a generally equitable fashion among his ten children through a will written shortly before his demise. The 223-acre estate of James Byrd, the father of Beech pioneer Asa Byrd, was partitioned into ten equitable portions for James' heirs when he died intestate in 1816. Little was inherited in either of these cases. John Bass' land was sold a few months following his death in order to meet the demands of his creditors; no funds remained to be distributed to the heirs after the estate had been settled. Asa Byrd's 24-acre legacy, meanwhile, was insufficient to support his family. He was forced to sell his land in 1827 to satisfy the demands of creditors. Three other 1840 Beech settlers—Hardy Scott along with Jesse and Turner Newsom—seem to have met similar types of fates. All were included among those without land in the Northampton tax lists of the late 1820s and early 1830s despite their ties to early, prosperous landholders.[33]

Another seven 1840 householders came from kindreds with long-standing ties to adjacent Halifax County, an area with social, economic, and demographic patterns similar to Northampton County. Six were members of the Winburn family, which had ties to the area predating the creation of the new nation. John Winburn, a free black resident of Halifax, served in the North Carolina militia during the War for Independence. In 1790 he lived near Benjamin James, probably the father or uncle of the remaining Roberts/Beech pioneer from Halifax, also named Benjamin James. Family history accounts written by descendants born in the mid-nineteenth century note that both kindreds had intermarried with local Indians while in Halifax County. Ties between the 1840 household heads and other members of the Winburn and James families in Halifax, however, are difficult to establish with certainty due to gaps in the county's public records. Surviving land deeds, however, indicate that early James and Winburn family members, like many Northampton free blacks, had acquired modest farms by the early nineteenth century. Benjamin James is listed with purchases totaling 309 acres, while brothers Thomas and David Winburn are noted with approximately 150 acres each. No additional member of the two kindreds appears to have bought land. At least two members of the Winburn family from Halifax may have migrated to Northampton County in the mid-1820s in search of better opportunities; John and Henry Winburn, brothers who would later venture to the frontier, were listed as landless taxables in Northampton in 1825 and 1827, respectively.[34]

⁓ ⁓ ⁓

The striking similarities in the Beech and Roberts pioneers' backgrounds in Northampton and Halifax counties brings into question the nature of their premigration community life. Was it merely happenstance that the pioneers had grown up in common circumstances, or were they part of a larger, cohesive free black community? If a definable community existed, what were its bounds? Did those who shared common, long-standing ties to Northampton and Halifax counties confine their associations to those of similar backgrounds and status—did their landed backgrounds lead them to form a rural counterpart to the free black elite found in antebellum cities like Charleston and New Orleans—or was their world less close-knit and constrained? Such questions have importance because little detailed study has made about community life among free people of color in the South, especially among the vast majority who resided in the countryside. Yet they are significant as well because the patterns developed in Northampton and Halifax played a crucial role in shaping the migration to, and communities at, Beech and Roberts settlements. Like other pioneers on America's nineteenth-century frontier, the founders of the two African-American communities would come to the frontier with family and friends; in starting their lives over they would rely extensively on their experiences in North Carolina.

Ties of kinship and community among many of the Beech and Roberts families were fostered by the kin groups' residence near one another in Northampton County. Tax records indicate that most of the Roberts, Walden, Bass, Byrd, Newsom, and Scott families destined for the Indiana frontier lived in two of Northampton's twelve governmental subdivisions, Militia Districts 3 and 4. Roughly three-fourths of the dozen or more families from the group were listed in the district during the 1820s and early 1830s. Included were the eldest members of the Roberts, Walden, Bass, and Byrd families, suggesting that the kindreds had lived in the vicinity from at least the late eighteenth century. Census and land records suggest that the families had not settled in a single cluster, but were scattered throughout the immediately surrounding countryside, with small groups of free black families located here and there amidst the area's somewhat swampy terrain. Thus the homesteads of farmers like Drew Walden and Jonathan Roberts were probably within a short walking distance of

TABLE 4

Marriage Bonds of 1840 Beech and Roberts Household Heads from
Northampton and Halifax Counties., N.C., 1815–1835

Date	Site	Groom	Bride	1790 Ties
1823	Northampton	Asa Byrd	Nancy Walden	Both
1829	Northampton	Turner Newsom	Martha Byrd	Both
1816	Northampton	Anthony Roberts	Elizabeth Davenport	Groom
1813	Northampton	Hansel Roberts	Priscilla Roberts	Both
1815	Northampton	James L. Roberts	Lavinia Robertson	Groom
1827	Northampton	Willis Roberts, Jr.	Wealthy Ashe	Both
1834	Halifax	Hardy Scott	Hester Mills	Groom
1817	Halifax	General Tootle	Patsey Peterson	Neither
1835	Northampton	Bryant Walden	Sarah Roberts	Both
1830	Northampton	Grey Walden	Martha Freeman	Groom
1824	Halifax	Henry Winburn	Kissiah James	Both
1830	Halifax	John Winburn	Mary Jane Curtis	Groom
1821	Halifax	Thomas Winburn	Anny James	Both

Source: North Carolina marriage bond index, NCSA.
Note: "1790 Ties" indicates member(s) of the marriage party with the surnames of 1790 free
black householders in Northampton and Halifax counties.

each other, certainly close enough to allow frequent visiting and assistance
in times of need, but were not immediately adjoining. A similar situation
seems to have prevailed in Halifax County, where the Winburn and James
families had settled near one another.[35]

Marriages, at the same time, clearly served to tie the several kindreds
into larger extended family networks. Early nineteenth century marriage
bond records, which indicate couples' plans for marriage, provide the best
gauge of how these ties had developed by the 1820s. According to the
bonds, thirteen of the household heads at Beech and Roberts settlements
in 1840 had filed their intentions to marry while living in Northampton
and Halifax counties (see Table 4). Six of the proposed marriages united
different family groups directly involved in the migration to the Indiana
frontier. Turner Newsom, for example, had married Martha Byrd; Asa
Byrd had married Nancy Walden; and Bryant Walden had married Sarah
Roberts. Those who journeyed to the frontier, it seems, knew each other

not merely as neighbors and friends but as cousins, aunts, uncles, and in-laws as well.[36]

Marriages between those migrating to Beech and Roberts settlements reveal only a small portion of the ties that had developed among North-ampton free black families before the 1830s. Additional bond records, for one thing, reveal dozens of proposed marriages uniting not only the kindreds that would venture to the settlements but also those kindreds to other free black families. A confusing array of marital alliances brought together, among others, the Haithcocks and the Byrds, the Byrds and the Scotts, the Scotts and the Turners, the Turners and the Winburns, the Winburns and the Jameses. Moreover, because not all couples filed marriage bonds, and marriage licenses were not required in North Carolina until 1850, the actual number of inter-family connections was undoubtedly much greater than the bonds indicate. A Roberts family Bible, for example, shows that the Roberts and Scott families were joined together in the 1780s through the wedding of Jonathan Roberts and Mary Scott. Similarly, inferences to marriages between members of the Roberts and Bass, Walden and James, Newsom and Byrd, and Roberts and Newsom families are found in local probate documents.[37]

A few of the pioneer householders married either relatives or members of a kin group with whom their family was closely tied. In the most notable case members of the Roberts kin group, cousins Hansel and Priscilla Roberts, married one another. Two other intra-Roberts family weddings also occurred in the early nineteenth century. While the blood relationships in all these instances are not known with certainty, they bring to mind kindred marriages among other prosperous families throughout the South. The children of the planter elite, yeomen farmers, and well-to-do urban free blacks all frequently married members of their own kin groups, at least partly to preserve their comfortable financial standings. Among the families that would migrate to Beech and Roberts settlements, however, such matches appear to have been much less common.[38]

Instead, members of the Roberts and similar families typically went outside their own immediate kin groups in choosing marriage partners. Six of the twelve 1840 heads chose partners from families other than those that would migrate to the frontier; additional marriage bonds indicate that a significant proportion of their kin did likewise. Most of the outsiders were members of free black families that shared long-standing ties to the Northampton–Halifax area. In 1827, for example, Willis Roberts, Jr., recorded his intention to marry Wealthy Ash, a Halifax resident probably related to Charles Ash, a 1790 Halifax householder. Comparable marriages involving those with late eighteenth century ties occurred between the Walden and Rowell, Byrd and Haithcock, Roberts and Sweat, James and Ash, and Roberts and Demery families.[39]

In several instances weddings brought together whites and lighter-skinned free people of color, state laws prohibiting miscegenation not-withstanding. A number of Bass and Roberts family members in North-ampton intermarried with others from local white kindreds, especially be-fore racial boundaries became more sharply drawn in the early nineteenth century. Included among such couples were Anthony Roberts and Eliza-beth ("Betsy") Davenport, the heads of an early Beech Settlement fami-ly. Betsy was of Scotch-Irish heritage. At least occasional marriages also united "old issue" families with newly freed blacks, free people of color who had recently migrated to the area, and slaves. Elijah Roberts, an early landowner at both Beech and Roberts settlements, was married to Kessiah Corbin, an ex-slave reportedly once owned by a Revolutionary War gen-eral.[40]

The generally exogamous or open pattern of these marriages was not, by itself, unusual, either among whites or African Americans. Nonethe-less, it had important ramifications for the ways in which local free blacks organized their lives and viewed their world. Because most marriages took place with other free people of color, and because there were relatively few free black families nearby, most, if not virtually all, of the free blacks were related to one another through consanguinal, or blood ties. Thus, in a vi-cinity such as Northampton's Militia District 4, a multiplicity of ties had developed among the families that would ultimately migrate to the Indi-ana frontier. At the same time, additional ties to other free black men and women throughout the surrounding countryside probably served to cre-ate an even larger sense of community among the free black population. Marriages across county lines—such as those between members of the Scott and Mills, Roberts and Ash, and Roberts and Sweat families—re-sulted in a common identity with, and an awareness of, free black families and neighborhoods throughout northeastern North Carolina and south-eastern Virginia.[41]

While little evidence remains to illustrate the specific day-to-day af-fairs of the Northampton and Halifax families involved in the frontier migration, probate records for several individuals leave little doubt about the roles played by both conjugal and extended families in times of special need. Six men and women with close ties to early Beech and Roberts pio-neers left wills in Northampton County during the early nineteenth cen-tury. Three of the six chose close family members—sons and brothers—to see that their last wishes were carried out satisfactorily. In 1803, for ex-ample, James Roberts, Sr., named his sons Jonathan and Claxton as the co-executors of his estate; when Jonathan, in turn, died seventeen years later, he called upon his own son, Willis, to execute his last wishes. In several other instances, when men and women died without leaving last wills, local courts followed North Carolina custom and appointed mem-bers of the deceased's immediate family to administer their estates. Typ-ically those chosen were widows, sons, or brothers. Lucy Roberts, for example, was appointed to administer the final matters of her husband, Kinchen, in 1816.[42]

Matters both great and small were handled by trusted kin in these and related probate proceedings. The financial dealings of a lifetime had to be untangled and resolved: inventories of personal possessions had to be taken; outstanding debts had to be assessed and settled; personal and farm goods had to be distributed and/or auctioned off; and farm lands had to be divided amongst heirs. Final wishes also had to be honored. John Bass, for example, requested that neighbors James L. and Dolphin Roberts use the proceeds from a portion of his estate to transport his four sons to the Indiana frontier following his death in 1828. Orphaned children, meanwhile, were normally assigned by courts to the custody of kin or close friends. Drew Walden thus became the guardian of David Byrd, whose father Jesse died in 1816, while James Roberts assumed the well-being of his two cousins, Turner and Harris, following the death of his uncle, Kinchen, that same year.[43]

The handling of these affairs by free blacks like Lucy Roberts and Drew Walden were at once both commonplace and noteworthy. Their actions were commonplace because they involved doing what most surviving kin did in similar situations. It was only logical that they be chosen to tie up the loose ends of their kinsmen's lives. Someone had to perform these tasks, and they were the obvious people under the circumstances. At the same time, though, the actions of Lucy, Drew, and others like them were noteworthy because they demonstrated the strength, ability, and self-determination of Northampton's free black community. In times of exceptional need, when extremely important family matters had to be addressed, individuals like James Bass knew they could turn to family and friends. Moreover, by relying upon one another, they knew their fate was more secure than if it was placed in the hands of untrusted whites.[44]

While probate records illustrate the importance of ties among the free black kindreds in Northampton County, they also point to relationships with whites as well as free people of color, and to the limits of an autonomous free black community life. Clearly most of those involved with the settling of estates, from executors to the buyers of estate items, were free black family and friends. Nonetheless, white neighbors invariably played a prominent role as well. John Bass and Drew Walden, for instance, called upon well-respected whites to act as executors of their wills, while all five of those leaving wills had whites act as the witnesses of record when drawing up their final documents. Whites also were among the purchasers at estate sales. Many of these interactions involved men who were long-standing friends, neighbors, and co-religionists of the free black testators. Lemuel Hargraves, who witnessed Jonathan Roberts' will in 1820, was a long-standing neighbor who had sold land to Jonathan and taught his children at school. William Hardee, a witness for Drew Walden, was a friend and fellow minister who would later assist Drew's survivors in their attempt to acquire pension benefits for his Revolutionary War service. Charles Kee, Drew's executor, had known him for more than thirty years prior to his death and would also support his family's efforts to claim a pension. John Jordan, who made small purchases at sales of James Roberts' estate in 1826, was apparently a member of the Jordan family that had lived adjacent to the Robertses since the 1760s. None of these men or their families apparently were tied intimately to free black families through marriage, but they all were neighbors and friends whose relationships appear to have been cordial and warm.[45]

The inclusion of so many white executors and witnesses on the wills of those with ties to Roberts and Beech settlements does not simply reflect a common feeling of personal regard among those involved. In leaving wills men like James Roberts and Jesse Byrd were acutely aware that they, as free blacks, were in a vulnerable position. In all legal dealings free people of color were at a serious disadvantage because their status before the courts was that of inferior citizens. Whites could challenge the actions of free blacks in any courtroom and free blacks would be unable to respond, barred by a mid-eighteenth-century statute that prohibited them from testifying against whites. The careful choice of whites as witnesses if not executors to wills, therefore, was necessary to insure that the last wishes of the deceased would be executed without question. Witnesses were especially important because they were bound by law to appear before the local county court following the testator's death in order to prove the will at the opening of the probate process.[46]

It is not clear whether reliance on neighboring whites in probate proceedings was actually perceived as a matter of dependency, and whether this sort of reliance was present in other areas of everyday life. Men such as Willis Roberts and Drew Walden, who clearly had cordial ties with white neighbors, may have viewed their dependence on whites in times of need as little more than requests for help among friends. Others may have turned to whites with much greater reluctance. James L. Roberts, as mentioned earlier, felt that whites in Northampton County by the late 1820s could not be trusted. What seems apparent is that restrictions placed upon families such as the Robertses, Byrds, and Waldens inhibited the full expression of their autonomy as free men and women, and that interactions with whites often took place in activities in which free blacks would have been at a disadvantage if they had acted alone. Given these circumstances, it is likely that a combination of both friendship and expediency was at the bottom of most white–free black relations.[47]

The complex nature of this interracial dynamic is further suggested by bits of conjectural evidence concerning religion and education, matters of considerable importance to all southerners. Brief references to religion found in Roberts family letters, along with the Revolutionary War pension application file of Drewry Walden, indicate that several members of the Walden and Roberts families worshipped at least occasionally with white Methodists. Walden, as noted earlier, was considered a well-respected preacher by white neighbors, while the Robertses apparently prayed regularly with white co-religionists and attended religious revivals with them in the early 1830s. That such close and intimate ties flourished among humble whites and free people of color in Northampton should hardly seem surprising. The Methodists, who prided themselves on their faith's interracial appeal and, before the mid-1780s, proclaimed blacks' basic humanity while attacking slavery, were well rooted among common folk in the neighborhood surrounding the Walden and Roberts households. The preeminent Methodist evangelist Francis Asbury made at least fifteen stops in Northampton between 1780 and 1812, preaching before congregations that combined both races on terms of much greater social and religious equality than was common at the time. Hence it would have seemed quite natural for families such as the Robertses and Waldens to have been members of interracial congregations.[48]

How comfortable they would have felt in such churches by the late 1820s and early 1830s is another matter. No direct evidence indicates that the Waldens, Robertses, or other free blacks in Northampton County considered worshipping separately from whites, or were prohibited from establishing their own congregations. It is known, however, that during the nineteenth century, slaves in the area normally worshipped with white congregations in separate church galleries set aside for them; that by 1830 local whites were so concerned about the threat posed by black religion that they forbade bondmen from attending services without white supervision; and that free people of color in North Carolina generally faced considerable difficulty in establishing independent congregations. If some free people of color in Northampton worshipped alone in the early nineteenth century they probably did so with great discretion in order to avoid the wrath of whites who viewed religion as a tool of slave insurrectionists. Certainly a free black congregation would have faced tremendous scrutiny following the slave conspiracy scares of the 1820s, and been driven underground by an 1831 statute which forbade free blacks from preaching the Gospel. Under these circumstances the Waldens' and Robertses' decision to worship with long-standing white neighbors like the Hardees and Jordans reflected a great deal of prudence, at the very least.[49]

Discretion probably also would have discouraged free blacks in Northampton County from establishing a school, another basic community institution in rural areas. As with churches, the available evidence is more suggestive than conclusive. Receipts of Jonathan Roberts from 1801 and 1804, and his son Willis, from 1828, indicate that both men sent their children to common schools taught by white neighbors. It is possible that other free black parents in the neighborhood had their children instructed at home or that a free black school existed at some time. Prevailing white sentiment in the South, however, associated literacy with an increased threat of slave unrest, and whites tended to discourage the education of free blacks, especially after the 1820s. The North Carolina legislature discussed limiting the education of free blacks in the early 1830s, though no laws were passed. As with religion, attendance with whites in neighborhood schools apparently reflected some unknown mix of personal desire and tactical caution.[50]

≈ ≈ ≈

A large plurality if not a majority of the 1840 household heads at Beech and Roberts settlements had long-standing ties to Northampton and Halifax counties. Because of their sheer numbers, and because the most complete evidence concerning the premigration backgrounds of the frontier communities' founders comes from the two counties, it is tempting to see their experiences as typical of *all* who migrated to the settlements. Such an assumption, however, would be misleading. The formation of Beech and Roberts settlements was marked by both a transplanting of extended family and community groups, and a coming together of diverse and quite different people. Free blacks from several parts of North Carolina, Virginia, and other states would arrive at Beech and Roberts settlements before 1840. Some came from families that had lived free for several generations; others had not. Mixed in with families who could say that their grandparents and great-grandparents had worked the soil as free men and women were those whose ties to freedom, land, and perhaps America itself were but thinly rooted.

A small proportion of the seemingly less established families also came from Northampton and Halifax counties. In 1840 four heads resided in the adjacent counties but appear to have had no long-standing ties connecting them to well-established kindreds such as the Robertses and Waldens. Two, General Tootle and Henry Vaughn, were listed as landless taxpayers in Northampton County during the late 1820s. Both also had ties to Halifax County; Tootle was married in Halifax in 1817, while Vaughn was listed as a resident of the county in 1830. Little additional information is available about either man. Even less is known about Isham Daniels, who was counted as a Halifax resident in 1830, and Edmund Cary, who apparently lived near Quakers in southern Northampton County. It is possible if not likely that the four were either manumitted slaves or the children of such ex-slaves. None had visible ties to free blacks living in Halifax or Northampton in the late eighteenth century.[51]

Also among those of less certain backgrounds were eight 1840 householders from Greensville County, Virginia. Adjacent to and directly north of Northampton County, Greensville apparently had patterns that were both similar to those in Northampton–Halifax and quite distinct. As in the areas directly to the north, it too was an "old country" by the early nineteenth century, saddled with a slave-based, tobacco-and-cotton economy that was stagnant at best. Free people of color in the region, meanwhile, could often trace their free heritage at least to the Revolutionary era. Common surnames among free colored families on both sides of the North Carolina–Virginia state line, in fact, suggest an intertwined lineage. On the other hand, Greensville seemingly was a much less inviting area for such families to live. Its free black population was smaller, both in absolute and proportionate terms, and more widely dispersed over neighborhoods on both sides of the Meherrin River, which bisects the county into northern and southern sections. Even in 1830 only 332 members of the caste lived in Greensville, about one-third the number then resident in Northampton, and one-sixth those in Halifax. Slavery was also more heavily concentrated—slaves outnumbered whites by a more than two-to-one margin in 1820. Presumably this greater concentration gave whites good reason to be more fearful of slave unrest and less accepting of those they considered to be "slaves without masters." Taken together, these less favorable circumstances perhaps help explain why Greensville's free colored community was less well established than its counterpart in North-ampton–Halifax; and why its overall numbers grew at a much more gradual pace.[52]

The future Beech and Roberts pioneers from Greensville County included one Hunt, two Jeffries, and five Watkins family members. All three kindreds were well represented in the local free black community by 1820. Census manuscripts from that date note the presence of thirteen households totaling eighty-five individuals from the kindreds. Earlier public records, while more fragmentary than those from Northampton–Halifax, indicate that each family had taken up residence in the vicinity by the mid- to late 1780s. They also disclose that a number of marriages had occurred between each kindred and a mix of other free people of color and local whites. There is little indication, however, of the deeply interwoven family connections and informal mutual aid networks that had developed among future Beech and Roberts kindreds from Northampton–Halifax. Jeffries family members apparently had few if any ties with the Watkinses and Hunts, and the Watkinses and Hunts seemingly had little contact with one another. This may well reflect the much smaller and more dispersed nature of Greensville's free colored population.[53]

More clearly substantiated is the area's mixed racial character, especially among those with long-standing ties to the free colored community. The Jeffries, Hunt, and Watkins families were all light-skinned people with well-documented interracial heritages. The most distinctive kindred were the Jeffrieses. Andrew and Mary (Dole) Jeffries, the maternal grandparents of three Beech pioneers, were mixed blood Occaneechi Indians, a Siouan speaking group whose remnants apparently had lived in Greensville from at least the mid-eighteenth century. Their daughter, Mourning, married or cohabited with a local white, and gave birth to future Beech founders Macklin, Walker, and Wright Jeffries. While members of the Jeffries kindred were labeled by local whites as free people of color, and are occasionally described in tax records as mulattoes and free Negroes, they seemingly had little, if any, African ancestry. Less is known about the Watkins and Hunt families, although in local records most were described as mulattoes and as individuals with "yellowish" complexions.[54]

Members of the Watkins, Jeffries, and Hunt families also shared a roughly similar economic status with the kindreds from Northampton and Halifax. The combined kindreds included several landholders, a small number of whom owned substantial farms and/or slaves. The two most prosperous, David Watkins and Andrew Jeffries, owned 380- and 112-acre estates, respectively. David Watkins also held seven slaves in the early 1830s, while three other Watkins and Hunt men owned from one to three bondmen at that time. Most of the kindreds' family heads, however, including those who came to Beech and Roberts settlements, held small amounts of land, if any, and were not slaveholders. Of the eight 1840 Beech Settlement household heads from the area, only Daniel Watkins (with 90 acres) and Goodwin Hunt (25 acres) were listed in the tax records as farm owners.[55]

All told, forty-one of the sixty-eight household heads in 1840 can be traced to Northampton, Halifax, and Greensville counties. The premigration backgrounds of the remaining twenty-seven remain largely obscured, a testimony perhaps to the generally more marginal nature of their status. Several probably came from the three counties straddling the Virginia–North Carolina line. The names of four householders appear in contemporary local records from Halifax and Greensville County, but it is uncertain whether the free blacks mentioned in these records were actually those who came to the Indiana frontier. A family history written in the early twentieth century notes that a fifth householder came from Halifax to Beech Settlement, although no readily available record remains of his presence in the former location. The names of all five of these individuals appear only fleetingly in public records. Only one owned land in either the South or at the frontier, and none is tied through marriage or probate records to others from Greensville, Northampton, or Halifax counties. If they did indeed join in the move from the Old South to the frontier they were, it seems, people of very humble if not impoverished backgrounds.[56]

For most free people of color, the half century following the Declaration of Independence was marked by unfulfilled promises and bitter disappointments. Hopes and dreams of increased acceptance and opportunity within American society, nourished by the Revolution and the widespread emancipation that followed, never lived up to expectations. Instead, as racial attitudes hardened and slavery continued to spread, free blacks found themselves increasingly characterized as an unintelligent, untrustworthy, and unwanted people. Mounting frustrations, discrimination, and hardship were the rule of the day, from northern cities like Philadelphia and New York to the countryside of Virginia, North Carolina, and beyond. In this respect the experiences of future Beech and Roberts settlements pioneers were unexceptional.[57]

What distinguished families like the Roberts, Walden, and Jeffries families was both the potential distance of their descent into the depths of near-slavery as the nineteenth century unfolded—and their ability to limit that fall. More fortunate than most free people of color, many came from families that had owned their own farms and maintained a remarkable degree of autonomy over successive generations. A large proportion of their New World forebears, moreover, had never been enslaved. The increasing restrictions facing free people of color thus did not so much threaten to return them to the sort of life they had once known, as it did threatened to engulf them in a world they could scarcely imagine.

At the same time, their resources represented an invaluable cushion that might be used to delay, diminish, or even prevent the increased suffering, dependency, and vulnerability experienced by others. Farmland was a particularly important source of strength. It provided the economic basis for a strategy of self-help and mutual aid, as well as the stake in society that encouraged relatively favorable relations with surrounding whites. For free people of color, farmland was an exceptional commodity indeed. The question was how to hold onto it and, if possible, strengthen one's standing by acquiring more and better acreage. Undoubtedly it was just this consideration that eventually helped drive Willis Roberts and dozens of his kin and friends to the northern frontier of the late 1820s and early 1830s.

2

MIGRATION TO THE FRONTIER,

CA. 1820–1840

ACCORDING TO A Beech Settlement legend, a caravan of prospective pioneers were walking to the frontier in the early 1830s when confronted by a group of white men. The whites ordered the colored travelers to stop and show their free papers. A chilling sense of apprehension immediately filled the group since they knew that unscrupulous whites might destroy their free papers, take them captive, and sell them as slaves. They ignored the command; their carts and wagons rolled on. The challengers persisted. When the caravan continued on its way, the whites gathered fence rails and placed them between the spokes of the wagon wheels. The incident had arrived at an ominous impasse. Then one of the prospective pioneers, Martha Walden, stepped forward. The light-skinned Northampton native told the assailants that she was in charge of the group and was supervising their transport to Indiana. Calmly, she ordered the free black men to take the rails from the wheels and drive on. The challengers, believing that Martha was white, let the party proceed without further protest.[1]

This story of confronting and overcoming danger is emblematic of Beech and Roberts pioneers' overall struggle to preserve their freedom by moving to the Old Northwest frontier between 1820 and 1840. The migration developed slowly during the 1820s as the first few individuals and families from the Northampton–Halifax–Greensville area resolved to accept the dangers of emigration and resettlement hundreds of miles from their native homes. Like the emigrants above, they proceeded deliberately and cautiously in order to protect their quasi-free status. This vanguard settled initially in western Ohio, some distance from the edge of the frontier itself, then moved further west into Indiana to form Beech and Roberts settlements. As their efforts demonstrated the viability of the frontier as a permanent home, and as race relations deteriorated in the Old South, the migration expanded. By the mid-1830s, when the influx began to recede, more than four hundred people had settled at the new communities. The early pioneers played critical roles in guiding later emigrants, providing aid and assistance to family and old friends who sought to rejoin them in the West. While their acts were often less dramatic than those of

Martha Walden, they too helped limit the danger associated with travel to the frontier, thereby promoting the ultimate success of the migration as a whole.

🙟 🙟 🙟

Migration to the early nineteenth century northern frontier was often a conservative undertaking. Many pioneer families traveled to the wilderness not just to improve their economic fortunes, but to preserve and maintain ways of life that were threatened in their former homes. Yeomen farmers from Kentucky's Green River Country emigrated to southern Illinois and Missouri in order to hold onto a largely self-sufficient way of life that was being jeopardized by the spread of plantation slavery; poor farmers from Norway resettled in Wisconsin in an effort to retain a folk culture that was being eroded by internal migration within Norway itself; Quakers from North Carolina moved to Ohio and Indiana so that they might pursue their religious beliefs without the tensions that had arisen from their opposition to slavery. In these and other instances, hopeful pioneers viewed the frontier as a malleable land, a place they could shape much to their own liking. Alone in the northern wilderness they could put the difficulties of their former homeland behind them and reestablish preferred patterns of farming, family, and community life.[2]

Prospective Beech and Roberts pioneers were driven by this same conservative impulse. In North Carolina and Virginia racial intolerance toward free blacks was spreading at an alarming pace, while opportunities to own farmland were becoming increasingly scarce. Their social and economic status was eroding from decade to decade, reducing their freedom and placing them in a position ever more closely akin to that of slaves. Moreover, there was little reason to believe that the process would end in the foreseeable future. Only movement to the West seemed to afford the prospect of stemming the decline. By acquiring new lands in the wilderness, families like the Robertses and Jeffrieses might regain much, if not all, of the independence they had felt slip away. The frontier held out the possibility of renewal and increased control over their destiny.[3]

Decisions on whether to migrate to the frontier, however, could not be taken lightly. Venturing to an unknown land and leaving behind familiar faces and scenes were difficult tasks for any prospective emigrant, white or black, native-born American or European. The act of leaving one's family, friends, and old neighborhood was much more arduous for free people of color. They, after all, were especially vulnerable to the capricious actions of whites. No matter how dreadful life in their rural neighborhoods might be, they were at least a world where racial customs were well known and predictable, and where friends and kin might be called upon in times of need. On the road to the frontier, and at the frontier itself, there were many more dangers to confront and many fewer allies to turn to for assistance. One of the greatest fears held by free blacks, that of being kid-

napped and sold into slavery, was much more likely to occur when traveling far from home.[4]

The fact that the prospective emigrants would be abandoning the
South for the unfamiliar North probably compounded their worries. From
the mid-seventeenth century, landowning free people of color in Virginia
and North Carolina had shown a willingness to venture to new frontiers in
order to maintain and protect their financial well-being and, by extension,
to defend the freedoms to which they had grown accustomed. Most if not
all of the future Beech and Roberts pioneers knew of family and acquaintances who had moved from one location to the next in search of better
opportunities during the late eighteenth or early nineteenth centuries. Pri-
or to the 1820s, however, the frontier had generally been associated with
areas to the south and west, areas settled by southerners like themselves.
When a member of the Roberts kindred, John Roberts, moved his family
to newly settled lands in the 1790s it was to western North Carolina; when
the families of other free blacks from Northampton and Halifax counties
headed west around the turn of the nineteenth century, it was to Tennessee. In the 1820s, as race relations deteriorated, such slaveholding regions
seemed much less desirable. The southern frontier, whether Missouri or
the Old Southwest, might offer fertile lands, but it certainly did not offer
greater freedoms. To escape the lands of slavery prospective pioneers had
to look to the Northwest. And the Northwest, for free blacks especially,
was a land of uncertain qualities.[5]

From newspaper accounts and discussions with kin and neighbors it
seemed that the frontier states north of the Ohio River had much to offer.
Rich, fertile land was abundant and easy to obtain. The federal government sold land for as little as $1.25 an acre in parcels as small as 80 acres.
For 100 dollars, an amount at least several of the prospective settlers could
muster, a new homestead could be carved out of the wilderness. The decisive defeat of Indians in much of the Northwest during and after the War
of 1812 meant that the supply of land would not be exhausted for some
years to come. Slavery, at the same time, was prohibited from the region.
The absence of slavery suggested that whites might be less worried by free
blacks' activities and hence less concerned with controlling their day to
day activities. No laws, in fact, had been passed directly limiting the movement, social institutions, or freedom of speech of free people of color.[6]

Still, the Northwest was preeminently a "white man's country." In
1820 whites outnumbered blacks in the region by more than 100 to 1,
with fewer than 8,000 blacks present. Virtually all white settlers accepted
as an article of faith the belief that blacks were mentally inferior, morally
lax, and less hardworking than whites. At best they viewed blacks with
suspicion and quiet disdain; at worst they expressed their racial antipathy
openly and, at times, violently. Adding to the volatility of the situation
were tens of thousands of southern pioneers who had migrated north of
the Ohio in order to escape the system of slavery. Having found it difficult

and degrading to compete against slave labor in their former homes, most arrived at the northern frontier with extremely negative perceptions of blacks and an ardent belief that the Northwest should be preserved for whites only.[7]

Legislation intended to restrict the rights of free people of color, and to discourage their immigration, were indeed passed within months of each state's admission to the Union. Ohio, less than a year after achieving statehood in 1803, required incoming blacks to bring proof of their freedom and register their free papers with local county clerks; three years later black newcomers were ordered to post a $500 bond upon arrival, while all blacks were forbidden from testifying in legal disputes involving whites. Indiana, which entered the Union in 1816, also moved quickly to place free people of color in an inferior position. Before the end of 1818 the state had prohibited blacks from testifying in cases involving whites, marrying whites, exercising the elective franchise, and participating in the militia. Free blacks contemplating migration to the Old Northwest had plenty of reason to pause and wonder: Would white pioneers in the region tolerate the presence of blacks? And, even if they did, would race relations in the new land soon slip into patterns all too hauntingly familiar?[8]

Despite the apparent risks a few young men and women began venturing to the Northwest in the early and mid-1820s. From Greensville County John Watkins, about twenty years old, single, and without land, packed his possessions and left for the frontier about 1822. His whereabouts over the next several years are difficult to trace, but by the early 1830s he was living in Montgomery County, Ohio, located in the state's west central region. Macklin Jeffries, also single and landless, left Greensville about 1825; Sarah Jeffries, apparently a widowed relative, also departed Greensville at that time, probably joining Macklin in his northern trek. Five years later they were each listed in the census as householders in Greene County, Ohio, adjacent to Montgomery County. In Northampton County, meanwhile, Elijah Roberts gathered his free papers from a local justice of the peace in 1820 and began planning his journey. Elijah, his wife Kessiah, and their three small children migrated to Henderson, Ohio, in 1825. The young families headed by two of Elijah's brothers, Anthony and John, either joined Elijah's family on their trip or followed shortly thereafter. Sons of Elias Roberts, who sold his farm in 1816, the three brothers ranged in age from about twenty-five to thirty-five; each had been listed as propertyless in early 1820s tax records.[9]

Undoubtedly youth itself served as a catalyst stimulating these first pioneers' northern ventures. Young men and women like John Watkins and Sarah Jeffries knew that there would be precious few opportunities for themselves and their families in the Old South, either as farmers or as free blacks. A new territory, with seemingly unlimited possibilities, had a special appeal for those with so much of their lives still ahead. Moving to the frontier, from their point of view, was less a gamble than an investment in the future. Their youth also meant that they had fewer attachments to their native land than their elders. While their parents and grandparents might have many cherished memories of the old country, theirs was a much more jaundiced view. In their short lifespans conditions in Virginia and North Carolina had only become unspeakably harsher. Turning their backs to their former neighborhoods involved little hesitation.

Yet more than youthfulness alone stirred the first migrants into action. American frontiers had long held a special appeal to the maturing adult children of landowners from areas where farm acreage was in short supply. Most faced limited prospects for obtaining land in their native regions, but had access to financial resources that would allow them to maintain their landed status if they migrated to the wilderness, where land was more plentiful and less expensive. Hence they had both the necessary means and a special motivation for moving to newly settled areas. In the nineteenth century individuals from such hard-pressed yet middling backgrounds, many with small families, were disproportionately among the first to leave long-settled communities in the East and Europe in search of better opportunities at the northern frontier.[10]

Those in the vanguard of the movement to Beech and Roberts settlements were typical in this regard. Each shared a common heritage as a member of a prominent landholding kin group. They knew, on the one hand, the security and independence that freeholds had brought their kin. Starting families of their own, farmers like Elijah, Anthony, and John Roberts felt compelled to acquire that security for their own immediate families, even if it meant moving to an unknown, unsettled region. Their farm backgrounds and kin ties, meanwhile, made their goals of landownership at the frontier seem realistic and readily obtainable. While they may not have owned land in the South, they had grown up working on family farms. Some, if not most, had rented lands on their own. Through the years they had obtained both the agricultural skills and material possessions—household goods, farm implements, livestock, and so on—that would be needed to make their dreams come true. All they lacked was the modest amount of money necessary to move to the frontier and buy land. Such funds were probably available from older, more established kin and friends who were willing to support their endeavors through personal loans.

The first pioneers' decisions to settle initially in Ohio reflected the caution that guided free people of color moving to the Northwest. Historical demographer James E. Davis has noted that between 1820 and 1840 very few free blacks were present on the cutting edge of the northern frontier, those wilderness areas most recently opened to settlement. The fringes of the frontier, which extended well into Indiana and Illinois by the mid-1820s, were often beyond the bounds of law and order. For free people of color, direct migration to such areas would greatly increase their exposure to bodily harm. Settlement a short distance from the frontier's

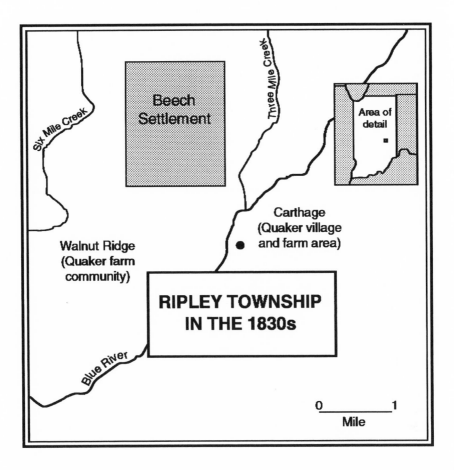

Map 3

edge, in contrast, represented a judicious compromise. While the oppor-tunities to acquire the best, first-rate land were greatly reduced in an area that had been settled for ten or twenty years, it nonetheless afforded new-comers, white and black alike, a chance to get acquainted with the frontier environment. In western Ohio, families such as those of Elijah Roberts and Macklin Jeffries were able to learn more about the possibilities for the future in the West; to profit financially by farming in an area where land was inexpensive and labor in short supply; and to begin planning for an additional move to a better location. Living near small numbers of other free blacks, they also were able to explore the possibilities of community life in the North. It was not the best of all worlds, perhaps, but it was an important start.[11]

Little is known for certain about how those in Virginia and North

Carolina reacted to the early experiences of their kin in Ohio. Circumstantial evidence, however, suggests that by the late 1820s family and friends were becoming more cautiously optimistic. The trickle of free blacks migrating to the frontier continued. Arriving in the fall of 1828 was the family of Long Jim Roberts, another of Elias' landless sons; they were followed the next spring by the family of Jim's cousin, Willis, the son of Jonathan Roberts. In contrast to those who came before them, Willis and his wife Marthaline were several years older and had a large, maturing family. They had been landowners in Northampton County for more than two decades, working a 50-acre farm Willis had inherited from his father. Among the most prosperous and well-respected members of the free black community in their old neighborhood, Willis and Marthaline seemingly had more to lose by their migration than those who had emigrated earlier, leaving behind friends and families whose company they had known for almost half a century. On the other hand, with seven children about to come of age, their family potentially had more to gain as well. If all went according to plans, their sons and daughters might enjoy a prosperity far exceeding anything they themselves had known. Willis and Marthaline Roberts' willingness to risk their family's future at the frontier undoubtedly focused new interest on the Northwest. Their experiences would provide an important measure of success or failure for others to monitor.[12]

The families of Long Jim and Willis Roberts went in separate directions once at the frontier. The family headed by Long Jim and his wife Lavinia traveled to Henry County, in east central Indiana; Willis and Marthaline's family settled several miles further south, in Ripley Township, Rush County, Indiana, the area that would become Beech Settlement (see Map 3). Both apparently found homes near Quakers, members of the Society of Friends. Despite their early divergent paths, the two families were reunited by the summer of 1830 and living near one another at the latter location. Also joining them at this time were the families of two of Long Jim's brothers, Elijah and Anthony, who apparently had lived at other frontier locations. After a number of years of searching, it would seem, the Roberts family as a kindred had begun to find a new focus in the wilderness.[13]

    ☕ ☕ ☕

Ripley Township was clearly a haven for Quakers in the 1820s and 1830s. Several kindreds of Friends originally from North Carolina had been initially drawn to the area in 1818, shortly after it was surveyed, by the presence of the Blue River. When the land was formally offered for sale two years later, members of the Holloway, Henley, Hill, and other Quaker families purchased Ripley Township's most desirable parcels of acreage, including all of those along the east side of the river. Over the course of the 1820s they added to their land holdings and founded the village of Carthage, site of the township's first grist and lumber mills and the area's principal trade center. Few non-Quakers apparently settled in the vicinity before the arrival of the first black pioneers. Friends thus controlled all aspects of Ripley Township affairs, including those pertaining to local government, politics, and other forms of public life.[14]

Free people of color such as the Robertses were drawn to Ripley Township by the presence of southern Quakers, who were well regarded because of their views concerning slavery. More than a decade before the American Revolution Friends in North Carolina had become concerned about slavery's ill effects upon slaveowners and slaves alike. Above all else, they were troubled by the way that slavery seem to interfere with their own search for the Inner Light, the religious truth that God had placed within them. As a result of their earnest, ongoing soul-searching they moved decisively to sever their immediate ties with slavery altogether between 1775 and 1800, disowning those fellow Friends who refused to follow suit. Even concerted efforts by the state of North Carolina in the late 1770s to prohibit the manumission of their slaves failed to prevent their crusade against slavery; ultimately formal ownership of Quaker slaves was simply transferred to the group's presiding body, the North Carolina Yearly Meeting of Friends, and the slaves were allowed their freedom in all but name.[15]

Because of the ongoing, protracted nature of their efforts to rid themselves of slavery's influence, the Friends' struggle in North Carolina increasingly took on an active institutional character after the turn of the nineteenth century. Standing Committees (later reorganized as the North Carolina Meeting of Sufferings) acted both as the North Carolina Yearly Meeting's agents in managing the affairs of the Meeting's nominal slaves and as vigilance committees that guarded the freedom and general welfare of slaves formerly held by Friends. The committees led legal battles to defend the rights of free people of color who had been kidnapped or were in threat of being reenslaved; helped manage their nominal slaves' financial affairs; and to a limited extent tried to improve the educational opportunities available to those they had formerly held in bondage. Perhaps most impressively of all, the North Carolina Meeting for Sufferings in the 1820s and early 1830s organized, funded, and executed the exodus of roughly 1,700 of the Yearly Meeting's nominal slaves from North Carolina to Haiti, Liberia, the Old Northwest, and other locations, permanently freeing them from slavery and delivering them from the South and its inflamed racial climate. As a result of their actions, Friends in the state developed a well-deserved reputation among free blacks as a people who were far more empathetic and tolerant than most other whites.[16]

There were, of course, limits to the Quakers' empathy and tolerance. Many North Carolina Friends viewed free people of color with considerable disdain and resentment, in part because of the heavy toll that the struggle against slavery had taken on the Quakers themselves. Quakerism as a religious force in the South had withered because of the Society of Friends' antislavery actions, with hundreds of members disowned for hold-

ing slaves and many more abandoning the faith because of related controversies. Criticism from surrounding whites added to their difficulties, and
encouraged large numbers to leave the South altogether. Many Friends
blamed blacks, both slave and free, for at least a portion of their problems,
and wished they could be entirely rid of their presence. Even the most
active members of the Standing Committees considered their efforts a
heavy burden and expressed grave reservations about the very people they
were attempting to befriend.[17]

The Friends' misgivings about free people of color were compounded
by the increasingly hostile racial climate of the early nineteenth century.
In the generations immediately following the Revolution white Americans had come to rationalize the persistence of slavery in a nation devoted
to freedom and liberty by embracing new "scientific" ideas about the racial
inferiority of African peoples. Virtually all believed that blacks inherently
were sexually promiscuous, lazy, and mentally inferior. A corollary to this
belief held that free blacks were responsible for their own degraded position in American society, and thus deserving of white contempt. Notwithstanding their opposition to slavery, Quakers generally accepted this racial
orthodoxy as an article of faith, often to the detriment of the free blacks
and nominal slaves living around them.[18]

Quakers at the western frontier shared the complex, ambivalent, and
highly varied views of their co-religionists in North Carolina. Activists in
the Quaker strongholds of western Ohio and eastern Indiana first offered
advice to those in North Carolina who were planning to relocate the Society's nominal slaves to the frontier; then, as the exodus came to fruition
in the mid-1820s and early 1830s, they provided shelter and relocation assistance to the emigrants, often at considerable personal expense and in
the face of public condemnation. At the same time, other Friends at the
frontier strongly objected to the presence of free people of color resettling
near them in the Old Northwest. After leaving the South to be rid of slavery's influence, they strongly resented their co-religionists' efforts on behalf of African Americans. "[T]here [is] as great [a] prejudice in the minds
of many of our members," one Indiana Quaker poignantly noted in 1826,
"as there is in other people[.] [T]hey will say as others do that [blacks]
ought to be free[,] but they do not want them amongs[t] us. . . . [I]t makes
it hard on those that are willing to do what they can for them[.]" A strikingly similar observation had been made by a Friend upon his arrival at the
Indiana frontier a month earlier.[19]

The Robertses and other free blacks from Northampton County were
acquainted with Quakers and probably well aware of their views before
they left for the Old Northwest. A number of Friends lived at Jack Swamp,
a few miles north of the Roberts kindred's farms, and a larger group lived
at Rich Square, several miles to the southeast. At least one farm transaction had brought the Robertses into contact with the Binfords, Friends
from Jack Swamp, although there is little evidence to suggest regular in-

teractions between the Robertses and Quakers before their migration to the Old Northwest. It is also possible that the Robertses and other Beech pioneers were at least casually acquainted with the more than one hundred nominal slaves who lived in the Jack Swamp and Rich Square areas, although again there is little to suggest extensive connections.[20]

The Roberts family's interest in Northampton Quakers probably became much stronger in the mid-1820s and may well have led to their decision to settle in Ripley Township. One source of increased attraction involved local Friends' efforts to relocate Quaker-owned slaves to the Indiana frontier. An extensive exodus from Northampton County occurred in the spring and summer of 1826 with the emigration of ninety-eight black men, women, and children to Philadelphia, Liberia, and the western frontier. At least thirty-seven and perhaps up to fifty-four of the migrants were resettled in western Wayne County, Indiana, less than a day's journey from Ripley Township; they were guided to the frontier by William Parker, a young Friend from Jack Swamp. While the Robertses and other free blacks in their neighborhood were not directly affected by these actions, they, like others in Northampton County, could scarcely have failed to notice such a bold antislavery effort near their homes, especially since members of their own families had begun migration to the same general areas of the frontier.[21]

A second source of increased attraction came at about the same time. In the spring of 1826 most of the Quaker families remaining in Jack Swamp sold their farms, settled their debts, and migrated to the West, joining a general exodus of southern Quakers to the western Ohio–eastern Indiana frontier. Included in the movement were members of the Parker family, who had been primarily responsible for the removal of the area's nominal slaves, and the Binfords. Most settled in Ripley Township. From the vantage point of prospective immigrants among the Roberts family, the Jack Swamp Friends' migration may have addressed one of their most pressing concerns: their own relative safety once at the frontier. With their sights already focused on the Northwest, the Robertses perhaps calculated that one way to minimize the danger ahead would be to settle in the same vicinity as the Binfords and Parkers, whites whom they knew and trusted. Long Jim Roberts, in fact, apparently first ventured to the frontier in the company of William Parker in the fall of 1828.[22]

⤳ ⤳ ⤳

Several other free black families came to similar conclusions about settling in Ripley Township about the same time as the Robertses. According to census reports, by the summer of 1830 fourteen black households totaling ninety-one people had taken up residence in Rush County. The census enumerators' reports do not indicate the number of black households in particular townships within the county, but it appears that that most (though not all) were clustered in the dense forests of Ripley Township.

TABLE 5

Black Landownership in Ripley Township (Beech)
and Jackson and Adams Townships (Roberts), 1831–1840

	Ripley Township		Jackson and Adams Townships	
	Landowners	Acreage	Landowners	Acreage
1831	2	180	NA	NA
1832	6	563	NA	NA
1833	9	763	NA	NA
1834	18	1,563	NA	NA
1835	22	1,713	NA	NA
1836	22	1,803	6	640
1837	24	1,804	10	920
1838	24	1,804	10	920
1839	24	1,804	10	920
1840	24	1,804	11	930

Source: Land deeds, Rush and Hamilton counties.

One family, headed by Edmund and Lucy Cary, had migrated to the area with Quakers from the Old South. Virtually no trace of information remains for the other households, excluding the four Roberts families. None bought land in the neighborhood, and all seemingly had moved on to new destinations by the end of the decade.[23]

The census taker traversed the Beech Settlement area at a time when the community's permanence was far from certain. While several families had built cabins and farmed in the area for at least a year, only one had purchased a homestead. Edmund Cary, who had bought a modest 20-acre parcel in February 1830, stood alone as the township's sole black freeholder. Others had the funds to buy land but apparently were undecided about the area's prospects. In part their hesitancy was a natural one shared by frontier farmers in general. "Squatters" often staked out a claim on public lands, grew crops for a season or so, and only then decided whether or not to stay permanently. In nearby Hamilton County, settled roughly a decade after Rush County, nearly two-fifths of the county's householders in 1840 did not own the land on which they lived. Early black pioneers in Ripley Township followed this same pattern, although it is likely that their purposes were somewhat different. In addition to judging the region's farming prospects, they apparently also used their time to assess the nature of the whites around them, looking for signs that their longterm presence was welcome.[24]

Doubts about Blue River, as the black neighborhood was first known, slowly began to fade after the fall of 1830. Having harvested his second season's crop, Willis Roberts indicated his satisfaction by purchasing a 160-acre farm from a local Quaker. Willis' cousin, Anthony Roberts, entered an 80-acre claim the following July, while three newcomers—Ann Jones along with Macklin and Walker Jeffries—made purchases of their own before the end of 1831. Three more pioneers bought homesteads in 1832, and nine others filed claims the following year. By the end of 1833, eighteen blacks had purchased 1,563 acres in the area (see Table 5). With each new transaction the community seemed more secure and attractive to prospective pioneers. Many newcomers followed the pattern of settling on their claims before making purchases, yet fewer did so out of a pressing concern for their safety. Local Friends had given little indication of open disapproval or mistrust, and by mid-decade Beech Settlement had become a bustling rural community. Although census figures are not available for the years between 1830 and 1840, it appears that most of the township's 400 black residents in 1840, along with other, less permanently rooted pioneers, had arrived by 1835.[25]

Many if not most of the first pioneers to arrive at Beech Settlement after 1830 came from areas only a short distance from the frontier. Between 1830 and 1833 the families of John Watkins, Sarah Jeffries, Macklin Jeffries, General Tootle, and John Brooks arrived from western Ohio; those of Hugh Bobson and Alex and Drew Moss, meanwhile, came from southern Indiana. All had lived in the proximity of western Friends before making their moves to Ripley Township. They apparently were attracted to the Beech neighborhood by word-of-mouth reports concerning the new outpost; few, if any, had relatives at the community. Because they were already in the West and had gained some knowledge of the frontier, the eight families were well placed to take advantage of the opportunities afforded early pioneers in a newly settled area such as the Beech. Not surprisingly, all claimed government lands at Beech Settlement before the end of 1834.[26]

A small number of additional early pioneers arrived in the company of local Friends migrating from the Old South, or came alone with the intention of settling near Friends they had known in their former homeland. Edmund Cary's family, the first to buy land in the Beech vicinity, apparently migrated with members of the Binford family from Virginia in the late 1820s. A few years later Emsley Lassiter joined the Henry Newby family from Randolph County, North Carolina when they headed to Ripley Township. The David Winslow family, also neighbors of the Newbys in the South, followed their route to the frontier in 1833 or 1834, ultimately buying land near their former acquaintances. Limited information remains about the backgrounds of these black families, although circumstantial evidence suggests that they were members of kindreds once held in bondage by Friends. They migrated to the northern wilderness knowing that their new homes would be near whites who felt a special obligation toward them.[27]

As Beech Settlement became more permanently established in the early 1830s, the nature of the influx to the community began to shift. The pace of migrations quickened and the size of the newcomers' ox-cart caravans grew larger with each passing year, ultimately peaking in 1834 and 1835. Most of these later pioneers, who formed a majority of the Beech's residents in 1840, came directly from the Northampton–Halifax–Greensville region. In journeying to Ripley Township virtually all were attempting to rejoin family and friends who had been among those settling during the late 1820s and early 1830s. Roberts, Sweat, and Walden families from Northampton; Winburn families from Halifax; and Jeffries and Watkins families from Greensville—all came seeking new farms and cabins near kin and friends already well established at Beech Settlement.[28]

To some degree the crush of newcomers in the years leading to 1835 represented a natural, predictable finale to the search for new homes in the West. Throughout the nineteenth century community-oriented migrations to the frontier typically evolved in a broadly similar fashion, building momentum as confidence in a resettlement location increased. This was clearly the case, for example, with the movement of Norwegians to Wisconsin, Germans to Missouri, and North Carolina Quakers to many locations in eastern Indiana, including Ripley Township. From this vantage point the expansion of the Beech migration in the early 1830s was hardly exceptional.[29]

Yet more was involved than a normal process of growing confidence. An almost frantic sense of urgency had been added to the migrations by the Nat Turner Rebellion, the largest slave revolt in American history. Culminating in the deaths of more than thirty blacks and fifty whites, the rebellion erupted in August 1831 in Southampton County, Virginia, which adjoins the Northampton–Greensville–Halifax area. Afterwards whites in the area were filled with much greater suspicion and animosity toward free people of color. One white resident later recalled that free blacks became "less joyous, more reticent and thoughtful" about this time, an observation that reflects the increased uneasiness among both whites and blacks. While the development of Beech Settlement and the Nat Turner uprising both had an impact on the movements of the early to mid-1830s, their confluence encouraged the settling of the Beech neighborhood in a much shorter period of time, and "pushed" more pioneers to the Beech area, than would otherwise have been the case. In Greensville County, particularly, free people of color appear to have left their homes in surprisingly large numbers following the revolt; the county's personal tax lists note the removal of twenty-six of the area's fifty-two free black taxable residents between 1833 and 1835, along with the seeming disappearance of at least eight others. Many if not most of these emigrants headed at least temporarily for Beech Settlement.[30]

Families streaming into the Beech area during the early to mid-1830s relied heavily on kin and friends at the community during every phase of their migration, from the planning of their journeys through their ultimate settlement in Ripley Township. It seemed only natural for the newcomers to seek out old neighbors and kin for help. Living in the southern countryside, they had once depended on these same people on a daily basis, sharing labor, farm equipment, and other resources in order to make ends meet. Whom could they approach with more assurance and trust than relatives and former neighbors? A willingness to utilize bonds of kinship and friendship, in fact, had been apparent from the earliest days of the migration northward. The clustering together of multiple Jeffries, Roberts, and Moss households, first in western Ohio and southern Indiana and then at Beech Settlement, suggests that even at the outset, when the movements were most likely to be made in small groups, relatives turned to one another for mutual support and aid.

As migration to Beech Settlement picked up after the early 1830s, reliance on kin and neighbors increased as well. Family and old acquaintances were now firmly established at Beech Settlement and, as a result, they had much to offer those back home. Well-respected pioneers like Willis Roberts and John Watkins took on new roles as promoters of the migration to Ripley Township, providing invaluable information about life at the frontier in general, and at Beech Settlement in particular. Glimpses of the growing reliance on frontier kin in one family, the Robertses, can be seen in nine letters sent from Northampton County to Ripley Township between 1830 and 1834. Six of the letters contained requests for information on life at the frontier. Hansel Roberts, for example, in an 1831 letter explained to his brother Willis that he was still pondering whether to come to Indiana; he then added that his family had received a letter from cousin Long Jim "which gave us great satisfaction as respects your country and we should be very glad to receive one from you." Two years later Ransom Roberts similarly noted that he was thinking of migrating to the frontier and asked his cousin, Long Jim, to "send me a letter how you are a making out and then I can judge." Requests for information became more focused as those in North Carolina prepared their moves. In April 1834 Grey Walden, anticipating migration to Ripley Township the following spring with his widowed mother, queried his Walden and Roberts kin about the prospects for buying land in the black neighborhood. "Mother wants to know," he wrote, "if there is any place in that neighborhood [that] can be got[.] . . . [S]end me word."[31]

The only surviving letter sent from Beech Settlement to Northampton County suggests that those in the wilderness were eager to comply.

Undoubtedly buoyed by the prospects of being joined by their kin at the
new setting, Willis and Long Jim Roberts offered their North Carolina
relatives an upbeat appraisal of conditions in the summer of 1831. Willis
began by providing Hansel with a description of recent weather conditions and their impact on crops. A wet spring had slowed the early growth
of his corn, Willis noted, but it now was maturing "tolerably well;" if the
weather cooperates, "I am in hopes that there will be aplenty made in this
settlement." "If you could be here," Willis boasted, "I could go with you in
some fields that would make you open your eyes." Before concluding his
message, the second-year Beech farmer went on to list the high prices
commanded by crops in the area and to describe how his stock of hogs had
increased from four to fifty in the past year. Cousin Long Jim, who arrived
at the frontier with much more modest means, included a less detailed yet
equally positive assessment. "I may inform you all that I have lived this
year like I want to live," he announced. "As to eating, . . . I have had aplenty
and some to spare and I expect to make aplenty this year for I have got
aplenty of hogs now." Closing his message, Jim rhetorically asked his landless father "if you think that I should be better off [in Northampton Coun-
ty] than I am here."[32]

Early Beech pioneers' promotional efforts went far beyond these encouraging descriptions. At considerable risk to their own safety, some ventured back to their native areas to help guide family and friends to the
frontier. Early pioneers John Watkins and Kinchen Roberts returned to
their homes in Greensville and Northampton counties, respectively, on at
least two occasions in order to pilot large caravans of kin to the Beech
neighborhood. Having spent several years in the wilderness, both men
were well acquainted with the dangers associated with free black travel to
and from the Old South. Their experience helped ease the worries of fellow travelers and assured safer journeys than would otherwise have been
possible. Comparable acts of assistance took place on a smaller scale as
well. In 1833, for example, Richard Roberts wrote to his brother Anthony
seeking his help in transporting his sons, James and Benjamin, to Ripley
Township; Richard also notified his brother that his help might be needed
to bring their widowed mother to the new settlement at a later date. Although little additional evidence remains, it is likely that many others,
particularly from larger kindreds such as the Winburns, Jeffries, and Watkins, relied on family and friends in a similar fashion. Emigrants' confidence that their Beech kin and friends could guide them safely to the
frontier undoubtedly increased the size of the Greensville–Northampton–
Halifax exodus after the early 1830s.[33]

Ironically, land in the Beech area was neither as desirable nor as plentiful as the influx of the early and mid-1830s might suggest. The best
lands in Ripley Township had been purchased by Friends within months
after it went on sale in 1820. By the early 1830s most of the unsold acreage
consisted of poorly drained soils that had been described by government

surveyors as "third rate," the lowest ranking possible. While the land was rich and fertile, the presence of damp soils and standing water, correctly associated in pioneers' minds with "ague" (malarial fever) and other wilderness illnesses, led most to avoid it during the initial stages of settlement. Black pioneers nonetheless claimed most of the remaining government held lands in the Beech vicinity, 1,503 acres in all, between 1831 and 1834. Their willingness to make such claims suggests the relative importance of settling near family, friends, and Quakers at the frontier. Other nearby frontier areas might have better soils, but they did not necessarily offer the hopes of unhindered settlement among established kin found in Ripley Township. The initial problems associated with wet lands were part of a trade-off for long term comfort and safety that many were willing to make.[34]

Free people of color arriving at Beech Settlement after the early 1830s enjoyed ever fewer options in terms of farm ownership. As the final purchases of Beech area land were made from the United States government in 1833 and 1834, opportunities to acquire homesteads became much more difficult. A few newcomers found themselves buying acreage at a considerable distance from the center of the black neighborhood. Micajah Walden in 1833 and Benjamin Winburn in 1834 bought 40-acre parcels that were more than two miles south of their kin and fellow black settlers at the Beech. On occasion farms closer to the fringe of the settlement might be bought from a white farmer, although such sales were infrequent. After Willis Roberts and David Watkins purchased tracts of 30 and 100 hundred acres, respectively, in 1835, only one additional acquisition was made by a black farmer in the immediate vicinity before 1840. The total amount of land held by black farmers in Ripley Township thus increased only marginally during the final half the 1830s, from 1,673 in 1835 to 1,843 acres in 1840 (see Table 5). The seeming scarcity of land, at the same time, was matched by escalating prices. Ripley Township land that originally had been sold by the government for $1.25 an acre in the 1820s and early 1830s was typically resold in the mid- and late 1830s for $5.00 or so per acre.[35]

Unable to acquire land at low prices, or dissatisfied with the purchases they had made, many of the free black families arriving at Beech Settlement in the mid-1830s began to look beyond the new community toward sites further north and west. In evaluating potential locations, most apparently focused on areas which were closer to the fringes of the frontier and, hence, offered greater supplies of inexpensive government lands. Significantly, they also focused on sites which were being settled by Quakers from eastern Indiana. A free black pioneer's formula for successful adaptation to northern frontier life—settlement on good land near Friends— seemingly had been acquired by many while living in the Beech neighborhood. Increasingly from the early 1830s on pioneers from the Beech put the formula into practice, moving on to help found other black farm communities in Hamilton and Vigo counties, Indiana; Cass and Van Buren counties, Michigan; and other midwestern areas.[36]

Roberts Settlement was among these second-generation communities. Its origins can be traced to the late spring or early summer of 1835, when several Beech men journeyed 40 miles northwest to examine more recently settled land. The most prosperous of the group, Hansel Roberts, had migrated from Northampton County with his family only weeks before. Like his brother Willis, Hansel had several sons and daughters who were about to come of age. Because of their late arrival, Hansel's family had little hope of finding adequate lands near the black neighborhood. Others in the Roberts Settlement contingent, mostly relatives of Hansel's, faced land-related difficulties of their own. Elijah Roberts and Micajah Walden were relatives and former neighbors from Northampton County who had been only marginally more successful in establishing themselves at Beech Settlement, having bought lands at a considerable distance from the fringes of the community in 1833 and 1834. Four of Willis Roberts' sons, meanwhile, confronted uncertain prospects in Ripley Township. Dolphin, Stephen, Jonathan, and Elias Roberts were coming of age in the mid-1830s and wanted to acquire their own farms. The scarcity and relative expense of acreage of land near Beech Settlement jeopardized their plans.[37]

Following a crude state road that had been cut out of wilderness three years earlier, the group ventured to an unsettled portion of Jackson Township, Hamilton County (see Map 4). Once there, they were able to take advantage of their early arrival in the area, claiming homestead sites that had been judged by surveyors as among the best in the vicinity. Three groups of Quakers had settled within ten miles to the south a few years earlier; the closest, at Baker's Corner, was three miles away. Another group of whites with radical abolitionist views had settled two miles southwest, at Boxley. Few, if any, other whites lived closer to the Roberts Settlement homestead sites. The black pioneers had chosen their claims well. With few immediate neighbors, land for future expansion would be available for years to come. With Quakers and other non-hostile whites present in the same general vicinity, their chances for survival were greatly enhanced.[38]

The rapid influx of immigrants from the South and the seeming scramble for land that took place at Beech Settlement found little counterpart in Hamilton County. After choosing their homestead sites, the small band of black frontiersmen at Roberts Settlement spent the summer of 1835 clearing small portions of their claims and raising cabins for their families. Three of the men—Elijah Roberts, Hansel Roberts, and Micajah Walden—also traveled back and forth to Indianapolis in late July in order to make initial land purchases totaling 400 acres. In October they returned to bring their families permanently to Roberts Settlement. After settling in at their new homes, additional trips were made to Indianapolis to add to the purchases; by the start of 1838 ten black farmers had bought

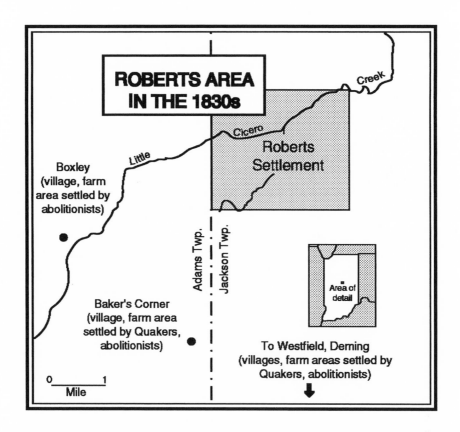

ROBERTS AREA
IN THE 1830s

Creek

Cicero

Roberts
Settlement

Boxley
(village, farm
area settled by
abolitionists)

Little

Adams Twp.

Jackson Twp.

Area of
detail

Baker's Corner
(village, farm area
settled by Quakers,
abolitionists)

To Westfield, Deming
(villages, farm areas settled by
Quakers, abolitionists)

0   1
Mile

Map 4

920 acres of public land (see Table 5 and Map 6). Despite this flurry of activity the community's population grew slowly. Census takers in 1840 counted only five black families with thirty-eight members in Jackson and Adams townships; while this estimate clearly understates that actual numbers present, it is unlikely that more than seven to ten families totaling fifty to seventy-five blacks had taken up residence at Roberts Settlement by this time.[39]

Three principal factors contributed to the slower pace of settlement in Hamilton County. The Roberts neighborhood's proximity to the Beech, first of all, provided landowners an opportunity to delay moving to the more remote and desolate site. At least three Beech residents bought land at the newer settlement while retaining their residences in Rush County, apparently intending to move only after the new community was developed further. Two of those buying land in Hamilton County in the mid-1830s, Stephen and Richard Roberts, did not migrate to Roberts

Settlement until after 1840; a third, Bryant Walden, remained at Beech Settlement until his death in the mid-1840s.[40]

The Panic of 1837 and subsequent financial difficulties also seemingly delayed the development of the Hamilton County community. The Roberts neighborhood had been settled at the height of the largest land rush of the early nineteenth century, when newcomers to the Old Northwest were at their most optimistic about the region's prospects. Land rush fever, however, quickly gave way to bust after May 1837. The national financial crisis caused by the panic forced down western farm commodity prices and reduced the amount of hard currency in circulation. At the same time, the United States government began to require that land purchases be made with gold and silver, which was far less plentiful than paper money, especially in the West. As a result the amount of acreage bought and sold in Indiana dropped to a small fraction of the volume of the peak years (1835 and 1836), never to return to its previous levels. Potential black settlers, because of their more limited resources, may well have found it especially difficult to accumulate the funds necessary to buy Jackson Township land during the depths of the downturn.[41]

Finally, the less hectic development of Roberts Settlement may also reflect the fact that the free black exodus from the South had begun to taper off by the late 1830s. While both settlements would continue to receive southern immigrants for decades to come, the relative numbers of such "latecomers" were much smaller than those arriving in the early and mid-1830s. In the Old South the heightened racial tensions of the 1820s and early 1830s dissipated somewhat, reducing the pressure to emigrate that many free people of color had felt earlier. Economic conditions in the South also became less dire for many prospective exodusters. The demand for free black laborers apparently increased over time and in Virginia, at least, the fortunes of free black landowners grew brighter as the antebellum period continued. The resulting combination of improved southern circumstances and diminished northern prospects apparently acted together as a significant drag on the northern migration's momentum.[42]

Throughout American history blacks have often turned to migration as a means of minimizing racial oppression and increasing control over their own destinies. As V. P. Franklin has argued, the quest for self-determination has been a constant, central theme of the African-American experience, with migration a critical tool in that struggle for greater autonomy and acceptance. Movement from one location to another has often served as a way to escape rising racial antipathies and gain access to greater opportunities. It is in this broader context that one finds the common meaning in such diverse sojourns as those of runaway slaves during the antebellum period, peripatetic ex-slaves within the South in the immediate aftermath of emancipation after 1865, the Kansas exodusters of the 1870s and 1880s, and the northern-bound hopefuls of the Great Migration from World War I through recent decades.[43]

The migration to Beech and Roberts settlements, in the last analysis, must be seen as one part of a related movement of free people of color from the rural South to the rural Midwest. Several hundred free black families fled the Old South for the northern frontier during the 1820s, the 1830s, and beyond, fueling a remarkable growth of the area's black population. By 1860 nearly 64,000 free people of color, over one-eighth of the nation's free black population, lived in the Old Northwest. While no comprehensive history of this migration has ever been written, it is clear that the experiences of families like the Robertses, Jeffries, and Watkinses were by no means unique or particularly exceptional. Various historians have noted particular aspects of this broader phenomenon, including the out-migration of large numbers of modest-to-middling farmers in the troubled years immediately before and after the Nat Turner Rebellion; the pronounced tendency to settle near Quakers and other non-hostile whites once in the Northwest; and the ongoing process of settling first in one location, and then another in a search for a new, permanent place amongst others of similar backgrounds. Beech and Roberts pioneers' migration thus was but one portion of a larger story—a story that itself reflects the larger experience of African Americans as a whole.[44]

3

PIONEER LIFE,
CA. 1830–1850

BEECH AND ROBERTS pioneers' first reactions to their backwoods homes are difficult to imagine. Having grown up in long-settled regions of the Old South, many must have been taken aback by the seemingly untouched, primitive nature of the world around them. Thick stands of beech, hickory, ash, oak, sugar maple, and other timber covered their homestead sites. Members of one Beech family, small children at the time, recalled that the sun's rays were so diffused by the surrounding foliage that they had to "look out through the tops of the trees to see daylight." The forest floor beneath their feet, meanwhile, was damp if not swampy, and covered in places with thick underbrush. During the autumn months malaria seemed to rise up out of the wetness and spread chills and fevers to everyone for miles around. An abundance of animal life shared the forest with the settlers and added to the neighborhoods' almost overwhelming character. Foxes and wolves, panther and bear, deer and opossums, raccoons and muskrats, turkeys and pheasant, passenger pigeons and quail— all made their homes amidst the pioneers' crude log cabins.[1]

Throughout the 1830s and 1840s Beech and Roberts pioneers engaged in a constant struggle to gain an upper hand on this forbidding wilderness. Much of their time and energy was devoted to clearing their forested claims, tackling the work associated with farm-making, and producing most of the food and other goods needed for survival. Prosperous farms and increasingly stable farm communities emerged from the settlers' backbreaking efforts, along with relatively harmonious relations with neighboring whites. Positive change and improvement nonetheless developed only at what must have seemed a glacial pace. Even at the close of the pioneer era, roughly 1850–1855, much of their woodland and its wildlife remained yet to be tamed.

Early Beech and Roberts pioneers also strove to improve the social setting surrounding them, taking advantage of the North's greater freedoms, the frontier's isolation, and their proximity to non-hostile whites. At the centers of their communities they built log cabin meetinghouses to be used as churches and schools. The resulting institutions provided residents a freedom of worship and access to education previously denied them in the Old South. Thus they clearly served as important symbols of autonomy and achievement. At the same time, Beech and Roberts pioneers used their churches and schools as vehicles for confronting and attempting to overcome the racial hostility and proscriptions they faced as people of African descent. Migration to the northern wilderness led to markedly improved opportunities, socially as well as economically, but did not erase many of the disadvantages associated with their status as free people of color.

🖎 🖎 🖎

The Indiana frontier of the 1830s attracted pioneers of all sorts. Dirt-poor squatters, well-to-do farmers whose holdings ran a mile or so in each direction, and humble homesteaders trying to make ends meet on 40-acre stakes—all found places in the wilderness landscape. In Hamilton County, site of Roberts Settlement, more than two-fifths of the area's pioneer families were landless in 1840. Of those with land, roughly a quarter held less than 80 acres, another two-fifths owned 80 to 159 acres, and the remaining third held 160 acres or more. Less is known about settlement patterns in Rush County, site of the Beech neighborhood, although it is clear that a preponderance of early landowners acquired small to moderately sized farms. More than two-thirds of those making claims between 1822 and 1831, the principal years of government land sales, purchased homesteads ranging from 60 to 100 acres.[2]

In 1840 the holdings of Beech and Roberts families were as diverse as those of the settlers around them (see Maps 5 and 6). A handful had begun clearing parcels that betokened moderate degrees of affluence. At Beech Settlement Daniel Watkins had entered 320 acres, while Willis Roberts (190 acres) and Macklin and Walker Jeffries (120 acres each) had settled on expansive claims of their own. In the more sparsely settled Roberts neighborhood, Hansel Roberts (240 acres), Micajah Walden (120 acres), and Richard Roberts (120 acres) had made similar sized entries. Surrounding them were larger numbers of small homesteaders. Twenty families at the Beech, along with eight others at Roberts, owned 119 acres or less; most held 40- to 80-acre farms. Thus clustered around the holdings of the Daniel Watkins and Hansel Roberts families were the much more modest cabins and homesteads of farmers like Goodwin Hunt (80 acres), General Tootle (40 acres), Guilford Brooks (40 acres), and Elijah Roberts (80 acres).[3]

While the acreage owned by black families varied, the Beech and Roberts settlers were generally poorer than their white neighbors. Their homesteads, for one thing, tended to be smaller than those owned by other pioneers. More than three-quarters of those who purchased land in Ham-

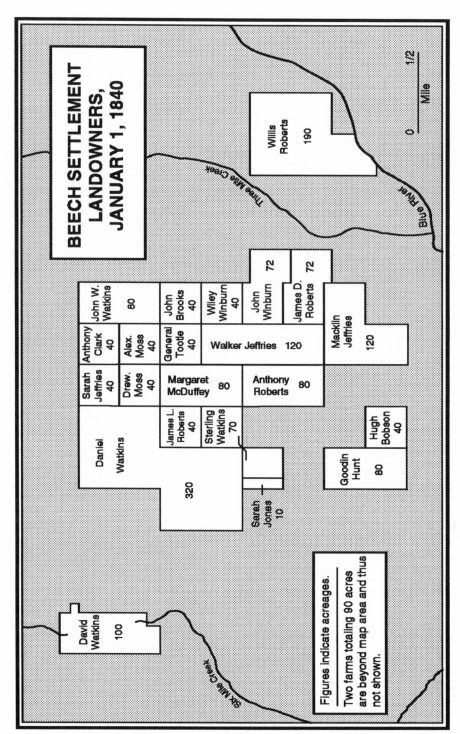

BEECH SETTLEMENT
LANDOWNERS,
JANUARY 1, 1840

Willis Roberts 190

John W. Watkins 80

Anthony Clark 40

Alex. Moss 40

John Brooks 40

Wiley Winburn 40

John Winburn 72

James D. Roberts 72

General Tootle 40

Walker Jeffries 120

Macklin Jeffries 120

Sarah Jeffries 40

Drew. Moss 40

Margaret McDuffey 80

Anthony Roberts 80

Daniel Watkins 320

James L. Roberts 40

Sterling Watkins 70

Sarah Jones 10

Goodin Hunt 80

Hugh Bobson 40

David Watkins 100

Three Mile Creek

Blue River

Six Mile Creek

0   1/2
Mile

Figures indicate acreages.

Two farms totalling 90 acres are beyond map area and thus not shown.

Map 5

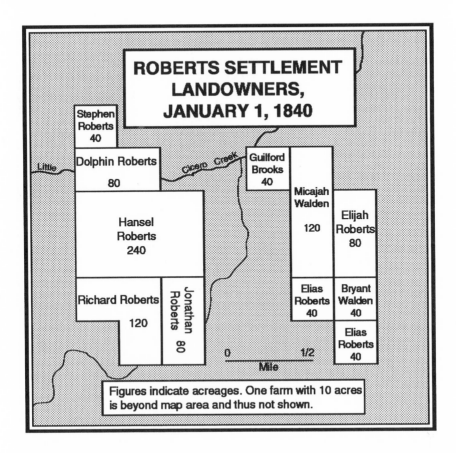

ROBERTS SETTLEMENT LANDOWNERS, JANUARY 1, 1840

Stephen Roberts 40

Dolphin Roberts 80

Little

Cicero Creek

Guilford Brooks 40

Micajah Walden 120

Elijah Roberts 80

Hansel Roberts 240

Richard Roberts 120

Jonathan Roberts 80

Elias Roberts 40

Bryant Walden 40

Elias Roberts 40

0   1/2
Mile

Figures indicate acreages. One farm with 10 acres is beyond map area and thus not shown.

Map 6

ilton County acquired 80 acres or more; in contrast, less than one-half of the black farmowners had settled on such lands. Even the largest black landowner, Beech Settlement's Daniel Watkins, was far from being the dominant farmer in his neighborhood. Six others in Ripley Township had claimed as much if not more acreage; the most affluent, Quaker Micajah Binford, held 945 acres, almost three times as much as Watkins.[4]

Landlessness, meanwhile, was more widespread among free black settlers than it was among surrounding whites. At Beech Settlement more than three-fifths of families did not own their own farms. In Hamilton County, as noted earlier, two-fifths of the householders shared this status. Landlessness by itself was neither a sure indicator of poverty nor a guarantee that a family would live its entire life scrambling to get by. Some pioneers without land had the financial resources to purchase homesteads but had not yet decided to settle permanently; others were the adult children of landowners who had not yet received their landed inheritance; and still

TABLE 6

Beech and Roberts Landowners' Holdings (in Acres)
in the Old South, 1823–1835, and at the Frontier, 1840

Name	Old South, 1823–1835	Frontier, 1840
Goodwin Hunt	26	80
Macklin Jeffries	0	120
Anthony Roberts	0	80
Dolphin Roberts	0	80
Elijah Roberts	0	80
Hansel Roberts	50–100	240
James L. Roberts	0	40
Jonathan Roberts	0	80
Richard Roberts	0–72	120
Willis Roberts	50	190
General Tootle	0	40
Bryant Walden	0	40
Micajah Walden	0	120
Daniel Watkins	80–90	320
David Watkins	380	100
John Winburn	0	72

Sources: Land deeds, Rush and Hamilton counties; land and personal property tax lists, 1820–35, Virginia State Library, Richmond; tax lists, 1823–35, North Carolina State Archives, Raleigh.

Note: Old South figures are drawn tax records, which may be less accurate than those from land deeds. Ranges are provided when the amount varied over the 1823–1835 period. No tax records are available for Halifax County, thus precluding comparison of the holdings of pioneers from that location.

others were farm laborers or renters who would successfully work their way up the "agricultural ladder" into the ranks of farmowners. Nonetheless most landless farmers faced greater hardship, dependency, and instability than those with land. The vast majority were unable to acquire farms of their own and were forced to move on, often to another frontier, within a decade of their arrival. This was especially true as settled areas matured, and opportunities for laborers and renters diminished. All things considered, the higher rate of landlessness at the Beech—50 percent above that of neighboring whites, if Hamilton County was typical—did not bode well for the neighborhood's future.[5]

While Beech and Roberts pioneers did not gain an equal footing with other farmers by moving to the frontier, those buying land nonetheless improved their financial prospects significantly. Many who had been landless in the Old South acquired homesteads for the first time, and those who had been small landholders tended to buy larger farms with richer soils. This pattern of bettered circumstances is seen vividly in a comparison of landholdings in Northampton and Greensville counties with those in the Beech and Roberts areas (see Table 6). All but one of the sixteen landowners in 1840 who had been listed previously in southern tax rolls gained larger holdings at the frontier. Goodwin Hunt, for example, increased the size of his holdings from 26 acres in Greensville County to 80 acres at the Beech; Hansel Roberts exchanged his 100-acre farm in Northampton for a 240-acre claim at Roberts; and John Winburn acquired land for the first time at Roberts.[6]

These comparisons may slightly exaggerate the opportunity afforded to men like Goodwin Hunt through their move to the Beech and Roberts neighborhoods. For one thing, their economic standing back in North Carolina and Virginia may well have improved because of changes in farming conditions after the 1830s. A combination of circumstances made it easier for free people of color to purchase land of their own. In Virginia, for example, the number of free black farmowners doubled from 1830 to 1860. Most of those acquiring land at the frontier settlements, in addition, were young men and women who had not yet received an inheritance from their elders before their exodus. Regardless of whether they lived in the Old South or Indiana, their opportunities to acquire land may well have grown over time.[7]

These qualifications should not be taken too far. Even with dramatically improved access to land, the situation of southern free people of color remained extremely difficult. In the 1850s perhaps only one in six families owned their own farms, and the quality of their acreage was often extremely poor, even by the exhausted soil standards of the surrounding region. Thus it is hard to imagine Beech and Roberts farmers prospering in the South to the extent possible at the frontier. Evidence from several Northampton County families, moreover, leaves little doubt about the very real and substantial improvement experienced by most who migrated to the frontier. Elijah, Anthony, and James L. Roberts, for instance, were the sons of a landless farmer who had few tangible assets; each managed to establish a 40- to 80-acre claim at the frontier. Micajah Walden stood to inherit only one-twelfth of the proceeds of the sale of his father's 234-acre farm when he died in 1834; at Roberts Settlement he entered a 120-acre claim. Willis and Hansel Roberts were middle-aged brothers who held a combined 100 acres of well-worn land; altogether, they and their children claimed more than 700 acres at Beech and Roberts settlements before

1840. Presumably these and similar stories from Northampton were paralleled by those of more obscure origins from Greensville, Halifax, and
beyond.[8]

To begin to turn their claims into prosperous farms, the pioneers first
had to clear their lands of underbrush and trees, a process that at times
must have seemed daunting to those raised in long-settled regions of
the Old South. At an average rate of 1 to 2 acres per year, each family
opened new fields by clearing away the underbrush and by deadening trees
through girdling, a task that involved stripping the trees of their lower
bark. Corn and wheat then were planted by hand, working around the
deadened trees and roots. After an interval of a half dozen years the pioneers, along with neighbors, joined together to cut down the dried trees
and to remove their stumps. Other tasks associated with farm-making—
cutting timbers and building fences, erecting crude log barns and cabins,
planting orchards, and the like—stole away from the time that could be
devoted to opening additional acreage. Forest gave way to farmland, but
only at a seemingly glacial pace. In 1850 farmowners at Beech Settlement
reported that 51 percent of their land (840 of 1,652 acres) had yet to be
cleared. Their counterparts at Roberts, having started a few years later,
had made even less progress by mid-century; 62 percent of their holdings
(373 of 600 acres) remained as wilderness.[9]

Transforming forest into farmland was only the start of the black pioneers' challenge. Access to the outside world was difficult and haphazard
at best. At the time of their land entries no roads crossed the sites that
would become Beech and Roberts settlements. To reach their claims the
pioneers followed Indian trails and the beginnings of early state roads, the
latter representing little more than bridle paths, to within a few miles of
their destinations; they then blazed trails of their own the remainder of
the way. During the late 1830s and 1840s a few early county roads were
started in order to provide Beech and Roberts pioneers, along with their
surrounding neighbors, with better transportation ties to one another, to
local villages, and to the world beyond. Built through the collective labor
of area residents, most were initially nothing more than stump-filled dirt
roads, difficult if not treacherous to travel during most of the year.[10]

The primitive nature of both roads and farms had important repercussions on the family and community life of early black settlers. Self-
sufficiency and reliance on family and friends became even more central to
their lives than it had been in the Old South. Farming, by necessity, emphasized clearing land and producing the foodstuffs and other goods required for the settlers' everyday existence. Fields were small and the presence of tree stumps and roots limited the use of many implements, such
as the bar share plows that they had brought from their native land. Regional markets for crops and livestock, meanwhile, could be reached only
with considerable difficulty. The journey from Beech Settlement to Cincinnati, the nearest commercial marketing center, took from ten days to

three weeks depending upon the weather and travel conditions. Roberts Settlement farmers could perhaps sell a small portion of their surplus at Lafayette, a thriving village thirty miles to the north, but had to endure an even longer trip than their Beech counterparts if they ventured to the principal western marketing hubs along the Ohio River. Not surprisingly, only limited amounts of grain were sold to outsiders by either Beech or Roberts farmers before the early 1850s.[11]

Self-sufficiency nonetheless was never complete. Black farmers, like their surrounding neighbors in Rush and Hamilton counties, apparently sold a variety of commodities at commercial markets, including pigs, sheep, eggs, and timber. Most were sold in limited quantities, however, and probably only hogs represented a steady annual source of income. Razorbacks and other pigs were fattened on mast as well as corn surpluses, then driven over crude roads to "Porkopolis" (Cincinnati) or other markets during the late fall and winter months. It was a difficult journey, one that slimmed down both hogs and potential profits. Farm census manuscripts from 1850, near the end of the frontier period, nonetheless suggest that many if not most families were able to clear at least modest sums by raising hogs. Thirty of the thirty-eight farmers listed from the combined communities owned at least ten swine; the eight largest farmers owned between forty and sixty. After setting aside small numbers for personal consumption and breeding purposes, most families probably were able to sell five or more pigs for profit.[12]

Pioneers from the two neighborhoods did not have to look far to find a place to spend their earnings. Despite the frontier's emphasis on individual initiative and mutual support among close friends, each family was deeply enmeshed in a web of financial interdependencies with others from their surrounding neighborhoods. A variety of goods ranging from apples and cider to nails, cloth, and coffee were bartered and sold on a day-in, day-out basis, often on terms of credit. Money itself, scarce throughout rural America but even more so in the West, was borrowed and lent in varying amounts in order to buy land and other goods requiring cash payments. The services of blacksmiths, coopers, sawyers, millers, and other craftsman were indispensable to all pioneers; the help of farm laborers, at the same time, was in strong demand among farmers with substantial holdings. From the most prosperous to the most humble, all were involved in a host of often small, but critical, economic exchanges with those around them. A small farmer like Wright Roberts at Roberts Settlement might work as a laborer one day; have his grain milled by a neighbor down the road a few days later; and venture to a nearby dry goods store to buy cloth and nails on credit the following week.[13]

While conducted on strict business principles—invariably interest was charged on outstanding accounts and collateral required for substantial loans—these transactions involved a strong element of personal trust and respect. The character and worth of an individual, for example, weighed heavily in a local dry goods merchant's decision to offer credit. As free blacks, Beech and Roberts pioneers undoubtedly were at a disadvantage in such dealings. Virtually all whites viewed them with greater suspicion than they would others of their own race. For Beech and Roberts families the question was not whether their transactions would be affected by the color of their skin—almost assuredly they would—but how they could minimize the amount of discrimination they faced. Their economic well-being hinged, in large measure, on their ability to gain a roughly equal footing with others in their neighborhoods.[14]

A number of factors worked in the favor of Beech and Roberts families during the frontier period. Settlement near Quakers and non-hostile whites, for one, encouraged trade with neighbors who were tolerant, trustworthy and honest. Limited evidence from probate and other local records, largely from Rush County, suggests that most dealings with whites were with just such people. Beech Settlement families during the 1830s and 1840s, for example, bought most of their dry goods from the firm of Hill and Henley, located a mile or so southeast of their farms in Carthage, a Quaker village; brought the corn and wheat for their own dinner tables to be milled by John Winslow and other Friends in the same vicinity; and solicited the services of a Carthage doctor, Owen Stratton, in times of dire need. Early Roberts Settlement pioneers, meanwhile, could similarly turn to those of less-than-antagonistic views towards blacks. The surviving, fragmentary records of Elijah Roberts and Stephen Roberts, Roberts pioneers, indicate that many if not most of their transactions took place in the nearby villages of Boxley, Deming, and Westfield, all known for their residents' ties to antislavery and abolitionist groups.[15]

The black pioneers' dealings with these hospitably inclined whites may well have been tainted at times by prejudice. Blacks of lesser means, darker skins, and/or questioned repute undoubtedly found themselves at a disadvantage when seeking goods or services from even their non-hostile neighbors. The limited evidence which survives from Ripley Township, however, provides little inkling of such discrimination. Carthage merchants, millers, and other businessmen appear to have granted both humble and prosperous Beech families credit on the same terms applied to other customers. Carthage's most prominent businessmen, in fact, appear to have carried a deep commitment to treating their black neighbors equitably. Several, including merchant Henry Henley and miller John Winslow, played active roles on the Committee on the Concerns of People of Color, the local Quaker committee charged with protecting the civil liberties of neighboring blacks from the 1840s onward.[16]

Beech and Roberts families also relied upon one another for many of their financial needs during the 1830s and 40s. In Ripley Township black farmers turned to other blacks, either at the Beech or in Carthage, to provide at least a portion of the services they needed. Emsley Lassiter hauled freight to and from Cincinnati; Uriah Bass and Farlow Lassiter worked as shoemakers; and Newsom Archey offered his services as a carpenter. Money to pay off debts and purchase new lands, at the same time, was often loaned by black farmowners to their cash-poor neighbors. David Watkins, Willis Roberts, and Daniel Watkins, the three most substantial farmers to die at Beech Settlement through the early 1850s, all left outstanding notes against other current or former Beech residents among their estate papers. David Watkins, for instance, died holding an $82 loan against Irvin Hunt; Daniel Watkins was owed $37 by Allen Brown; and Willis Roberts left notes against his sons Elias and Jonathan totaling $174. Mortgage deeds, which were recorded infrequently by local farmers during the pioneer period, detail two other early intra-community loans, including one for $135 from Elias Roberts to Dennison and Parthenia White at Roberts Settlement in 1850.[17]

Transactions within the Beech and Roberts communities did not allow black families to avoid contacts with nearby whites. Dry goods stores, mills, and many skilled trades remained largely, if not exclusively, in the hands of whites. Nonetheless, intra-community dealings lessened the pioneers' reliance on outsiders and contributed an additional element of stability to each black settlement. Large landowners, in particular, may have helped foster the growth and economic well-being of their neighborhoods. Their lending of funds at least occasionally helped facilitate the purchase of land, as when Elias Roberts provided Dennison and Parthenia White with a mortgage. They also apparently hired other blacks to provide farm labor or other services on many occasions; outstanding claims for unspecified purposes are included in each of the half dozen probate files for Beech residents who died through the early 1850s. Daniel Watkins, in one of the few identifiable cases, contracted Jonathan Roberts to build a new barn on his farm shortly before Watkins' death in 1852.[18]

The acceptance if not outright respect of many "non-friendly" whites, meanwhile, was earned by at least a portion of the early black farm families. Financial ties between such people and Beech and Roberts families are recorded in surviving estate papers from the pioneer period, although they are more difficult to discern than those with other blacks, Quakers, and abolitionists. In at least one instance the connections were quite strong. Daniel Watkins bought and sold land and borrowed and loaned funds with several of his white non-Quaker neighbors in northern Ripley Township throughout the late 1840s and early 1850s, if not earlier; at his death in 1852, he held outstanding notes against ten of these men. Evidence from another source indicates that Turner Newsom also had strong ties with a white neighbor, albeit of a contrasting nature. On three occasions between 1841 and 1857 prominent farmer John Walker provided Newsom with mortgages, increasing the amount loaned on each successive occasion. Daniel Watkins and Turner Newsom may have been unusual—insufficient evidence remains to judge their typicality one way or the other—yet their actions demonstrate that strong business relations tied at least a portion of the black pioneers to their non-Quaker neighbors.[19]

A final, related factor favoring early Beech and Roberts settlers concerned the formative nature of frontier farming. As David Schob has shown, many Northwest pioneers turned to hired help for assistance with farm-making as well as routine farm chores—building fences, clearing new fields, bringing in harvests, and chopping wood. The supply of such laborers, however, generally failed to keep up with the demand for their services. Large-scale farmers were often eager to hire any help they could find, especially during critical harvest periods. Some even felt compelled to recruit urban workers, including otherwise "undesirable" blacks, from nearby towns and villages. Others, using a different strategy, leased unimproved parcels to tenants as a means of clearing their holdings. Given these opportunities, Beech and Roberts pioneers apparently received a greater degree of acceptance and welcome than otherwise would have been forthcoming. Many, after all, were experienced farmers with small claims or no land at all. Their presence represented a reliable source of labor that could be tapped on a year-round basis.[20]

Hints of the opportunities available can be found in scattered sources. In the only detailed description of pioneer farming near either community, Thomas T. Newby noted that a number of blacks made "comfortable" livings by working for Friends in Ripley Township. Turner Newsom and Emsley Lassiter were among those cited as having reputations as hard workers. Evidence of a different sort is contained in an affidavit filed by Beech resident David Cary in 1844. About to leave Ripley Township, Cary secured the signatures of eleven Ripley Township farmers, mostly Quakers, who had hired him from time to time and recommended him as "an honest industrious young man . . . to be relied on with confidence. . . ." Unfortunately, little other evidence remains to outline the work of other Beech and Roberts laborers. Most of their employment apparently was contracted on an informal basis, thus leaving few tangible signs of such laborers' efforts.[21]

A number of Beech and Roberts families made their livings as tenants, working surplus lands held by local owners. John Roberts, for example, supplemented his work as a small farmowner near the Beech by leasing acreage from Robert Henley, a prominent Friend. Agricultural census data from 1850, near the end of the pioneer period, similarly note several others who rented farms, often of considerable size. According to the census seven Beech and two Roberts families worked as tenants on farms averaging slightly more than 100 acres each. Three of the holdings—those managed by Axsum Sweat at Roberts, and Lewis and Thomas Winburn at the Beech—were 160- to 240-acre tracts. References to fields leased by both settlements' residents in the two decades immediately following the frontier's close indicate that virtually all were leased on shares, with the owner receiving one-third of the crop and the renter the remaining two-thirds.[22]

☙ ☙ ☙

Over the course of the 1830s, 1840s, and early 1850s, Beech and Roberts pioneers did more than simply create a modest niche for themselves in the wilderness. They also transformed their fledgling communities in important ways. At each location a core of early homesteaders settled permanently, while many others—mostly those with little or no land—headed toward new and perhaps more promising sites. Small numbers of landless residents and newcomers, meanwhile, joined the ranks of the core landholders. All of these comings and goings, from one perspective, were rather mundane and unspectacular. Across the northern frontier most neighborhoods experienced a similar evolution: early landowners tended to settle permanently on their new claims, becoming the foundation upon which rural society was built; and landless families typically remained only a few years in any given neighborhood, then moved on.[23]

Beech Settlement pioneers seldom sold the initial claims they had made between 1830 and 1835. Most of the black farmowners maintained their holdings for the remainder of their lives, and many farms were kept intact by surviving heirs for many years if not decades thereafter. Three-quarters of the landholding families at the Beech in 1836 (18 out of 24) retained possession of their claims through at least mid-century. Year after year the families of Daniel Watkins, General Tootle, and Margaret McDuffey, among others, could be found struggling away on their early claims. Their persistence provided the neighborhood with a sense of identity and cohesion. In essence they *were* Beech Settlement. Largely because of the early pioneers' permanence, the boundaries of the community shifted only slightly between the initial claiming of the land and mid-century.[24]

Significantly, the fortunes of those remaining in the Beech neighborhood often improved as the frontier period wore on. Four landowning farmers increased their holdings by amounts ranging from 39 to 120 acres. Included in this group were Alexander Moss, whose acreage almost doubled from 40 to 79 acres; John Watkins (from 80 to 133 acres); Macklin Jeffries (80 to 160 acres); and Walker Jeffries (80 to 200 acres). At least six others, meanwhile, bought land at the Beech for the first time. Turner Newsom, the most successful, reportedly had arrived during the mid-1830s with less than a half dollar in his pocket. By 1850 he had established his family on an 80-acre homestead, and before his death in 1860 his holdings would total 139 acres. The five remaining new landowners acquired farms ranging from 2 to 70 acres.[25]

The advances experienced by farmowners and landless alike resulted from a variety of factors: personal initiative and hard work; early settlement in Ripley Township; large families to draw on for labor; proximity to other kin and friends to provide additional help; and so on. Certain patterns nonetheless stand out. Three of the four who increased the size of their initial claims—Watkins and the Jeffries brothers—had begun their pioneer careers with sizable, 80-acre farms. Relative to their small-farm-owning neighbors, they were able to take advantage of the larger scale of their farming operations. All three were among the largest hog producers in the neighborhood in 1850. Among the landless, meanwhile, the ability to develop strong connections with farmers beyond the Beech neighborhood may have been critical. At least four of those buying their first farms —Turner Newsom, Emsley Lassiter, David Winslow, and John Roberts —had close working ties with Ripley Township Friends. Newsom and a fifth first-time owner, Joseph Hill, had acquired funds for their purchases through mortgages offered by local whites.[26]

The Beech community also benefited from a small influx of newcomers with the resources to buy land. Four men and their families arrived after the late 1830s and purchased farms ranging from 40 to 138 acres before mid-century. William Hill, who bought a 40-acre farm in 1846, reportedly had ventured from North Carolina to Indiana a few years previous; two brothers accompanying him on the migration settled further west at Lost Creek, a black farm settlement near Terre Haute. While little is known about the origins of the other newcomers, they, like William Hill, seemingly were attracted to Beech Settlement as a promising rural area for free blacks. None had prominent ties to earlier Beech pioneers at the time of their arrival nor can their earlier homes be traced to the Northampton–Halifax–Greensville area. The largest of the new landholders, James Lowery, was a native of Kentucky.[27]

Not all Beech pioneers were so enamored with Ripley Township's prospects. Between 1836 and 1850 six of the community's landholding families sold their farms and left the area. All were small-scale homesteaders, owning 40 to 55 acres, who had held their farms at the Beech an average of more than a dozen years. Most if not all moved to locations further north and/or west, to sites in central and western Indiana and southern Michigan. The reasons behind their moves, as well as their fates, were varied and diverse. At least one, James L. Roberts, sold his land, moved to Roberts Settlement, and never became a landowner again. He lived out the remainder of his life as a farm tenant in the Roberts neighborhood. Others apparently left because better prospects lay closer to the frontier's edge. Willis Roberts, Jr., wrote to his Indiana kin in the early 1850s, boasting of the greater opportunities he enjoyed in his new home in southwestern Michigan. His profits the previous year, he ventured, were more than triple the amount he had cleared in his best year at Beech. Another emigrant, Hugh Bobson, similarly seems to have improved his fortune by moving away. After selling his 40-acre homestead in Ripley Township he purchased an 80-acre farm several miles northwest of his former home, in adjacent Hancock County.[28]

Many of Beech Settlement's landless families, meanwhile, drifted away during the final decade of the frontier period. As in other frontier locations, transiency was the rule rather than the exception among non-landowners. Roughly three-quarters (32 of 44) of such families in 1840 were not found by census takers canvassing the area ten years later; most had moved elsewhere. No simple patterns can be discerned from the paths of the few that can be followed. Jesse Newsom, for example, migrated to Roberts Settlement, where he bought a farm in the late 1850s; Grey Walden, on the other hand, moved to the urban environs of Indianapolis, where he was listed as a common laborer in 1850. Partially offsetting the departure of these poorer Beech families, meanwhile, was a smaller influx of families of similar status. Census takers in 1850 counted roughly a dozen new families in Ripley Township who were not landowners and who had no apparent ties to established Beech residents. Most, like the family of Matthew and Catherine Weaver, would stay a short while and begin the migration process anew.[29]

The constant turnover of landless families at the Beech suggests a point at which the fates of rural and urban black communities in the North converged. While farmers with the resources to acquire land enjoyed more stable and prosperous lives than most northern black city dwellers, those without either land or kinship ties to landowners experienced a much more difficult fate. At bottom they were dependent on outsiders for their livelihoods and faced steadily diminishing opportunities to move ahead as the frontier receded to the north and west. Their choices essentially were to follow the frontier, hoping to find better fortune where farm labor was in greater demand—and where their opportunities would remain limited— or migrate to surrounding towns or cities like Cincinnati, Richmond, and Indianapolis. Once in urban areas they became members of free black communities that were themselves apparently marked by extremely high rates of transiency and population turnover.[30]

Beech Settlement's evolution between the mid-1830s and the early 1850s resulted in a neighborhood with fewer black families but increased economic stability (see Tables 7 and 8). The number of blacks in Ripley Township dropped from 399 in 1840 to 349 at mid-century. Among the fifty-six households that remained, twenty-seven owned farmland. The proportion of landholders in the area thus had risen from roughly one-third to almost one-half during the 1840s. While still a poor neighborhood, the Beech clearly was less impoverished than it once had been. The total amount of land owned by black families had increased from 1,713 acres in 1835 to 2,144 acres fifteen years later, a gain of 25 percent. Residents could point to tangible signs of progress and permanence all around them. Farmers like Emsley Lassiter had not only survived for twenty years

TABLE 7

Rural Black Population of Ripley Township (Beech)
and Jackson and Adams Townships (Roberts), 1830–1850

	1830	1840	1850
Ripley Township (Beech)			
No. of households	approx. 10*	63	56
Total population	approx. 75*	399	349
Jackson and Adams Townships (Roberts)			
No. of households	NA	5	16
Total population	NA	35	111

Source: Census manuscripts, Rush and Hamilton counties, 1830–1850.

Note: Individuals and households residing in towns and villages are excluded.

*An accurate count of Ripley Towship's black population in 1830 is precluded by a census taker's error. See chap. 2, n. 15.

in the wilderness; they had financially prospered. Even the removal of several small farmers had been offset by the arrival of others with the resources to buy homesteads.[31]

Somewhat contrasting circumstances affected Roberts Settlement's initial development. Although only fifty miles from the Beech, the Roberts neighborhood was much more sparsely populated and isolated when the community's founders made their claims between 1835 and 1837. Largely because of the harsher conditions, many of the eleven early Roberts landholders chose to delay moving to their holdings. In 1840 census takers counted only four black homesteaders in Jackson and Adams townships. Despite this shaky start, the early landholders proved to be a hardy and persistent group. All four of those present in the late 1830s—Hansel Roberts, Elijah Roberts, Micajah Walden, and John Roads—staked their futures on their well-situated claims, working them profitably for the remainder of their lives. Only Elijah Roberts died before the end of the frontier period and his farm was kept intact under the guidance of his widow, Kessiah. Three others who had initially remained at the Beech, meanwhile, took up residence before the mid-1840s, settling in the same permanent manner as those who arrived before them.[32]

While Roberts Settlement attracted a strong core of founding families, uncertainty seemed to cloud the neighborhood's prospects from the late 1830s through the mid-1840s, a time of profound economic downturn and malaise throughout the West, as well as throughout the United

TABLE 8

Black Landownership in Ripley Township (Beech)
and Jackson and Adams Townships (Roberts), 1835–1850

	1835	1840	1850
Ripley Township (Beech)			
No. of black landowners	22	24	27
Total acreage held	1,713	1,844	2,144
Jackson and Adams Townships (Roberts)			
No. of black landowners	NA	11	10
Total acreage held	NA	930	800

Source: Land deeds, Rush and Hamilton counties.

States as a whole. In the Roberts vicinity, a variety of circumstances led to the disposal of much of the acreage acquired in the late 1830s: one early pioneer sold his 40 acres shortly after its purchase in 1835; another died unmarried, with his 80-acre estate sold to an outsider shortly thereafter; and two others opted to stay at Beech Settlement rather than move to the more remote Roberts location, selling their combined 80 acres to a nonresident in the mid-1840s. None of the remaining initial land purchasers, meanwhile, bought additional acreage before mid-century.[33]

Nonetheless, conditions improved gradually at Roberts Settlement. The mid- to late 1840s and, particularly, the early 1850s brought increasingly heady times. Families already firmly planted in the neighborhood, for one, began to expand their operations as their fields were cleared and modest profits developed. John Roads, an ex-slave who initially had claimed a 10-acre parcel four miles from the neighborhood, bought an 80-acre farm at the northwest corner of the settlement; Kessiah Roberts' son Peter acquired 40 acres next to her 80-acre tract; Hansel Roberts, the community's largest landowner, purchased another 80 acres; and Wade Roberts, the only landless pioneer present in 1840, acquired 80 acres from his father, Hansel. As at the Beech, those who moved ahead tended to come from families that had begun their frontier careers with entries of 80 acres or more. The sole exception, John Roads, had close ties with Owen Williams, a prominent farmer and ardent abolitionist.[34]

The Roberts neighborhood benefited as well from the purchase of additional lands by "newcomers." Included in the group were Dennison White, who bought 80 acres in 1845; Micajah Revels (80 acres, 1852); and

Anthony Roberts (40 acres, 1852). Both White and Revels, along with their spouses, were North Carolina natives. Revels had lived in at least in two earlier frontier sites in Indiana before arriving in the Roberts area. Like Beech landowners who came after 1840, the Whites and Revelses apparently had no ties to established residents but were attracted to the neighborhood by its long-term prospects. Anthony Roberts, in contrast, was a well-situated Beech homesteader whose purchase apparently was intended not for himself—he continued to struggle away on his Ripley Township farm year after year—but for his sons, William and Edward, who migrated during the 1850s.[35]

Adding a final element to Roberts Settlement's evolution during the 1840s and early 1850s was an influx of landless settlers. Several individuals and families with strong ties to the Roberts founders arrived from Beech Settlement; all were either kin or had been former neighbors in the Old South. Among those arriving before 1850 were families headed by Jesse and Charlotte Newsom, James L. and Lavinia Roberts, and Axsum and Martha Sweat. They were probably welcomed not only as kin and old friends, but as potential farm help and tenants in a labor-starved region. Jesse Newsom, Axsum Sweat, and Martha and Axsum's son John would all buy local farms of their own within a decade of the pioneer era's closing, apparently bearing further testimony to the opportunities open to well-connected landless farmers during the formative era.[36]

By the early to mid-1850s Roberts Settlement's outlook shone far brighter than ever before. The struggling band of fifty to seventy-five free people of color present in 1840 had grown into a dynamic community two to three times that size. In 1850 census takers counted 16 black households with 111 residents in Jackson and Adams townships; as the frontier period closed in the mid-1850s those numbers increased steadily. The spatial boundaries of the Roberts neighborhood had begun to expand as well. By the end of 1854 black farmers in the neighborhood owned 1,124 acres, an increase of over 200 acres when compared to the initial holdings of the mid- to late 1830s.[37]

≈ ≈ ≈

Beech and Roberts pioneers' acquisition of farms allowed for progress that extended far beyond the economic realm. In migrating to the northern frontier the settlers had hoped to reshape their lives in new and significantly different ways, free of the constant scrutiny of local whites and the concomitant restrictions that plagued them in the Old South. They wanted to build schools and churches free from outside interference, enjoy civil liberties that had been stripped away, and avoid the general harassment of whites in their daily lives. Much of the North's lure undoubtedly came in the greater social freedoms it afforded. It was in the North, after all, that the first truly independent African-American churches and other social institutions had begun to emerge; that free people of color had the greatest access to educational opportunities; and that black leaders spoke out most forcefully and openly against slavery and racial injustice.[38]

Beech and Roberts pioneers nonetheless faced formidable challenges in their efforts to gain increasing control over their destinies. The increasing democratization of nineteenth-century American culture, first and foremost, provided common whites with more and more free rein to express their dislike and hatred of free people of color. This was especially true in the Old Northwest, a region that was arguably both more democratic and more contemptuous of African Americans than the North as a whole. The perceptive French observer Alexis de Tocqueville alluded to the region's exceptional character when he noted in the early 1830s that racial prejudice in America "appears to be stronger in the states that have abolished slavery than in those where it still exists; and nowhere is it so intolerant as in those states where servitude has never been known." After 1820 states like Indiana, Ohio, and Illinois zealously sought to discourage blacks from settling within their boundaries and to severely circumscribe the rights and privileges of those who remained. In Indiana, statutes required blacks to post a bond following immigration to the state, limited their rights to court testimony, denied them the electoral franchise, excluded them from public schooling, prohibited them from serving in the militia, and outlawed intermarriage between blacks and whites.[39]

Racially based assaults on free people of color and their property also proved problematic, the increasing "civility" of the Northwest in the 1830s and 1840s notwithstanding. As the number of blacks in cities and towns rose over time, so too did competition over jobs with whites and other forms of racial tension. On a number of occasions during the pioneer period violence exploded in urban areas familiar to the settlers: in Cincinnati a riot against the local black community in 1829 left more than one hundred dead and thousands fleeing for their lives; in Indianapolis a local black resident was killed in 1845 by a gang of whites in an unprovoked attack, and the city's black Baptist church was burned to the ground under suspicious circumstances in 1851; and in Pendleton, a town located midway between the Beech and Roberts neighborhoods, black abolitionist Frederick Douglass was severely beaten in 1843 by a mob affronted by the sight of a black speaking before a white audience. Equally disturbing, several free blacks throughout Indiana were kidnapped, transported south of the Ohio River, and sold into slavery. Among those illegally abducted and sold as a slave was Eli Terry, a free person of color who had settled less than twenty miles from Roberts Settlement in a village near Indianapolis.[40]

The isolation of Beech and Roberts settlements, together with their proximity to non-hostile whites, limited the impact of much of this overt hostility and malevolence. Frontier farming, as discussed earlier, focused much of the pioneers' attention toward clearing the wilderness, building farms, and producing goods needed for survival. When pioneers like Sterling and Rebecca Watkins wanted a good or service that their family could not produce—cloth or nails, for example—they turned to others nearby whom they knew and trusted. Trips to cities and towns such as Cincinnati and Indianapolis were infrequent if not rare for most settlers. The difficult nature of both farming and travel in the wilderness, at the same time, made it unlikely that hostile whites would venture through the Beech or Roberts vicinities. Whites more than a few miles from the two settlements undoubtedly had heard of the black pioneers, but probably had had little if any contact with them directly.

Relations with surrounding Quakers and other antislavery whites remained cordial if not always warm and friendly, much as they had been during the earlier period of migration. To be sure, a combination of factors worked against a complete absence of bias in the 1830s and 1840s. Prevailing negative attitudes and stereotypes concerning free people of color adversely affected virtually all interactions to at least a limited degree. Just as important, ongoing internal controversies over doctrinal matters, opposition to slavery, and obligations to African Americans often divided Indiana Friends against one another and increased their ambivalence toward surrounding free people of color. Facing deep troubles of their own, many were inclined to see free blacks as an added burden they did not want to carry. Such racism and reluctance, however, were kept in check, in part by the Quakers' deeply rooted commitments to racial justice and to aid to free people of color (especially those Quakers themselves had held in bondage); and in part by the vigilance and actions of the Committee on the Concerns of People of Color, the formal Friends organization charged with protecting and promoting the general welfare of nearby blacks. Reports by the CCPC at the Indiana Yearly Meeting of Friends in the 1830s and 1840s occasionally chided fellow Quakers for specific acts that slighted blacks, suggesting that overt acts of discrimination among Friends were both isolated and strongly discouraged.[41]

The actions of committed antislavery whites, in fact, sometimes involved considerable self-sacrifice on behalf of Beech and Roberts residents and/or other African Americans. The most heroic and celebrated instance came through a series of events from the spring of 1844 through the spring of 1845, when Quakers and other whites near Roberts Settlements came to the assistance of the John and Luann Roads family, defending their right to freedom through a combination of both force and legal argument.

The Roadses had lived as slaves in Kentucky, Illinois, and Missouri before escaping to freedom from the latter location in 1837. Ultimately they had sought refuge on the farm of Owen Williams, a staunch abolitionist, several miles south of Roberts Settlement. During the late 1830s and 1840s they took on new lives for themselves, shedding their slave names, acquiring a small homestead with Williams' aid, and adding to their family with the birth of two children. Then in April 1844 their last slave master, Singleton Vaughan, located the family's new home. Assisted by two fellow Missourians and two local constables, Vaughan approached the family's cabin in the middle of the night and demanded their surrender. John and Luann, in response, barricaded themselves in their homes, staving off capture until early morning, when Williams and other sympathetic neighbors heard their cries and helped bring the incident to a standoff.[42]

Shortly thereafter, as 150 people came to the Roadses' aid, the two sides agreed to bring the matter before local court officials. An argument during the resulting trip, however, led to pushing and shoving, chaos, and the Roadses' escape. Vaughan responded to the event by bringing civil suit against Williams, demanding compensation for his loss. The Roadses' allies then formed the John Roads Association and raised $600 to provide for Williams' defense. The case ultimately made its way before sympathetic Justice John McClean at the United States District Court in Indianapolis in May 1845. Testimony at the trial disclosed that one of the Roadses' previous owners had resided with them in Illinois for a period of several months, an action that by virtue of the Northwest Ordinance's prohibition on slavery had inadvertently entitled them to their freedom. This action, McClean implied in his charge to the jury, protected the Roadses from being reenslaved and made the case against Williams unnecessary. The jury quickly issued judgment in Williams' favor, and in doing so validated the Roadses' claim to a permanent free status.[43]

While the Roads incident was clearly exceptional, it was not the only instance in which Quakers and other whites aided fugitive slaves. Local histories written in the twentieth century describe Friends' communities near both the Beech and Roberts neighborhoods as active stations on the Underground Railroad. And, at least in the case of the Beech, blacks as well as whites seemingly were involved in aiding slaves on their way northward. Assessing the accuracy of these stories, however, is problematic. As historian Larry Gara has noted, many if not most accounts of the Underground Railroad were written well after the antebellum period and are marked by exaggeration and a bias that elevates the heroic actions of whites at the expense of blacks. Such distortions are clearly evident in the histories under consideration as, for example, in the claims that Frederick Douglass' escape to freedom ran near Roberts Settlement and that "several thousand" fugitives passed near the Beech. Nonetheless, several detailed accounts seem plausible and the escape of the Roads family and at least one other individual can be verified with contemporary evidence.[44]

The importance of aiding fugitive slaves came less from its direct impact upon the Beech and Roberts communities—few if any settled permanently at either neighborhood, the Roads family excepted—and more from its impact upon race relations with nearby whites. Defying established authority in order to attack an institution deemed morally unjust, Underground Railroad activists demonstrated to one another and to others nearby much about their personal character and the depth of their commitment to the antislavery cause. For Beech and Roberts residents, as for free people of color in other settings, their actions served to challenge stereotypes about African Americans' docility and lack of courage, and to visibly show both their disdain for slavery and their concern for fellow blacks. Nearby whites, in turn, displayed their own resolve to fight against racial injustice, along with a willingness to back their beliefs with action. Indiana Friends sent much the same message, it should be noted, on several other occasions before 1861 when they intervened on behalf of free people of color who were kidnapped and reenslaved. While none of the kidnappings occurred at or near two neighborhoods, the Quakers' overall pattern of response to such incidents undoubtedly was well known and appreciated by free blacks throughout the state.[45]

Most efforts by surrounding whites to aid Beech and Roberts families were of a more limited character, helping the residents overcome barriers that were less daunting that those of the Roadses but significant nonetheless. One example of such assistance could be seen in county courtrooms, where free blacks were assigned an inferior legal status. As they and their forebears had in the Old South, the black pioneers repeatedly sought the assistance of trusted neighbors in settling probate matters. In six of the eight estates settled before the mid-1850s, whites were chosen either as witnesses to wills or as estate administrators. Another example could be found in local schools. As will be discussed later, Friends near Beech Settlement helped their black neighbors overcome legal handicaps concerning public education by offering assistance with schools operated by area residents.[46]

Even more important than such aid was the willingness of whites to allow their black neighbors to live alone and in peace. Quakers, for their part, felt that free people of color would rise only through their own exertions. In order for racial barriers to be surmounted direct aid was sometimes in order, especially for those recently manumitted and for the truly indigent. In most instances, however, blacks were simply encouraged to help themselves. These views reflected the Friends' faith in the values associated with the Protestant work ethic as well as their own studied efforts with philanthropy; they also meshed conveniently with most Quakers' reluctance to become involved with a people they viewed as loathsome and to a large measure responsible for their own impoverishment. Beech and Roberts pioneers, for their part, no doubt welcomed the limited nature of the benevolence extended by Friends and other whites. They were left free to shape their lives according to their own wishes, secure in the knowledge that nearby whites could be called upon to provide assistance in cases of extraordinary need.[47]

🙢 🙢 🙢

The actual process of building new communities involved the coming together of people from a variety of locations and cultural backgrounds. The

Watkins and Jeffries kindreds had migrated from Greensville; the Winburns came from Halifax; the Robertses had once resided in Northampton; a scattering of families had lived amidst Quakers in the North Carolina Piedmont; and still others came from points unknown. Differences of both experience and heritage undoubtedly separated one from another. An ex-slave like John Roads, to cite an extreme example, had grown up in a world quite removed from that known by the Robertses, themselves former slave owners, or that of the Jeffrieses, who had very little African ancestry at all.

Clearly drawn intra-group distinctions, especially concerning skin color, wealth, and heritage, were commonplace within free black communities in both the North and the South. Those with lighter skins, mixed racial heritages, and longer histories of freedom often perceived themselves as a superior people and were hesitant to intermarry with those who were different. Such standoffish behavior was certainly visible at both Beech and Roberts settlements on occasion. At the Beech at least three marriages involving couples of contrasting backgrounds triggered family feuds and hard feelings, and generally marriages bringing together those with markedly different skin colors were infrequent at both settings. For those with dark complexions, even success with farming seemingly did little to break down intracommunity color barriers at times.[48]

Early land purchasing patterns, meanwhile, may well have reinforced the tendency of many settlers to identify most closely with others from similar premigration settings. In both frontier communities newcomers typically sought farms near kin and friends from their former neighborhoods. A glance at early maps shows the prevalent pattern of kin buying land near one another. At the Beech the Watkins families settled in one area; the Mosses in another; the Winburns in a third; and the Jeffries family in a fourth. In the Roberts community a somewhat contrasting situation developed. Initially members of two related kindreds, the Robertses and Waldens, accounted for virtually all of the early pioneers. Yet ultimately a similar pattern prevailed. As the settlement grew more varied over time, those who arrived later were concentrated on the periphery, while those from the two Northampton kindreds remained in close proximity at the center.

These differences and potential conflicts were more than offset, however, by other factors which tended to encourage the development of a new, shared sense of community at each location. The pioneers' backgrounds, for one, were far more broadly similar than dissimilar. While they may not have known one another before their migrations, most of the families from Northampton, Halifax, and Greensville counties shared a common heritage that centered around mixed European, African, and Native American ancestry; and longstanding ties to landownership and freedom. Together, they comprised the vast majority of the core, stable families at each frontier neighborhood. The free black status they shared with

TABLE 9

Origins of Married Couples at Beech Settlement to 1850,
and at Roberts Settlement to 1855

Date	Site	Groom	Groom's Origins	Bride	Bride's Origins
1844	Rush	Henry Brown	Guilford	Martha Roberts	Northamp.
1841	Rush	Isham Daniels	Halifax	Mary Ann Walden	Northamp.
1843	Rush	Irvin Hunt	Greens.	Jane Roberts	Northamp.
1833	Rush	Walker Jeffries	Greens.	Sarah Winburn	Halifax
1844	Rush	Walker Jeffries	Greens.	Azariah Brown	Guilford
1849	Rush	Wright Jeffries	Greens.	Atlanta Winburn	Halifax
1841	Rush	Jesse Newsom	Northamp.	Charlotte Walden	Northamp.
1845	Rush	James A. Roberts	Northamp.	Mary Roberts	Northamp.
1848	Rush	John Roberts Jr.	Northamp.	Emeliza Winburn	Halifax
1837	Rush	Stephen Roberts	Northamp.	Mary Scott	Northamp.
1840	Ham.	Wade Roberts	Northamp.	Jane Roberts	Northamp.
1844	Rush	Miles Scott	Northamp.	Harriet Brown	Guilford
1843	Ham.	Axsum Scott	Northamp.	Martha Winburn	Halifax
1851	Ham.	John Sweat	Northamp.	Olive H. Winburn	Halifax
1839	Rush	William Sweat	Northamp.	Eliza Roberts	Northamp.
1849	Rush	Jas. W. Watkins	Greens.	Martha Roberts	Northamp.
1833	Rush	Sterling Watkins	Greens.	Rebecca Roberts	Northamp.

Source: Marriage records, Hamilton and Rush counties.

Note: Origins are based on known origins of individuals with same surnames. All Robertses, for example, are presumed to be from Northampton, all Jeffrieses from Greensville, all Browns from Guilford, and so on.

other settlers may also have encouraged a common perspective. Living in small, remote neighborhoods, the Beech and Roberts pioneers were a despised caste in the eyes of most surrounding whites. They perhaps knew that to get ahead they would have to depend on one another and keep personal disputes to a minimum. While individual differences undoubtedly lingered, they apparently did little to disrupt the neighborhoods' overall development.

The willingness to accept others from diverse backgrounds can best be seen in the ways that early pioneers chose marriage partners. Thirty-four marriages involving Beech pioneers are included in Rush County records through 1850, while another nine involving Roberts residents are found in Hamilton County through 1855. Little inclination to join families from similar backgrounds is apparent in those cases where the origins of both members of the wedding party are reasonably certain (see Table 9). In fact, pioneers tended to marry someone from a *different* native area. Walker Jeffries from Greensville married Sarah Winburn from Halifax; Isham Daniels from Halifax united with Mary Ann Walden from Northampton; and Martha Roberts from Northampton exchanged vows with James Watkins from Greensville. Couples from Northampton County, the home of a plurality of early settlers, married one another at times, and cousins within the large Roberts family were wed on two occasions. Yet these were clearly secondary patterns, more the exception than the rule, even among the Robertses.[49]

In large measure the openness of the pioneers' marriage choices paralleled a similar pattern in the Old South. In Halifax and Northampton counties (and probably other areas as well), young free black men and women sought prospective brides and grooms not from a select number of nearby kin and friends, but from a larger group that included individuals living beyond their immediate neighborhoods, generally within a day's travel—a distance of 15 to 20 miles. Beech and Roberts pioneers also did not restrict themselves to an exclusive group, but instead chose marriage partners from among all area blacks. The principal difference facing eligible men and women at the frontier was that the number of possible suitors was more restricted than in an location such as the Virginia–North Carolina border region. While more than a thousand free blacks lived within a reasonable distance from Northampton County, for example, many fewer resided at or near the wilderness communities. Even at the Beech, the larger of the two settlements, the number of prospective brides and grooms was quite limited. Only thirty-one men and twenty-seven women were unmarried and between the ages of 15 and 45 at the Beech in 1850. The pool of potential marriage partners was about half this size in the Roberts vicinity. Few free people of color, meanwhile, lived beyond each community but within a reasonable traveling distance.[50]

At Beech Settlement the open yet limited options facing unmarried pioneers resulted in the rapid development of ties among previously unrelated families. Within a generation, and often within a few years, members of the largest kindreds—the Robertses, Jeffrieses, and Watkinses—had been joined through marriage not only with one another, but with smaller family groups as well—with the Sweats, Waldens, Winburns, Lassiters, Tootles, Hills, Mabrys, and so forth. By the end of the frontier period virtually all of the core families at the Beech, like those at the Roberts, had become part of a single, broad kin network. Newcomers at both settlements, meanwhile, added another dimension to the expanding ties, often marrying within a short time of their arrival. Among those exchanging vows with the sons and daughters of well-established farmers were members of the Mabry, Brown, and Simpson families at the Beech, and the Allens, Revels, and Gilliam families at Roberts.[51]

Another symbol of the growing sense of interconnectedness at each settlement could be found in neighborhood churches. Despite having been denied religious autonomy in the Old South—or perhaps because they had been denied their religious freedom—Beech and Roberts pioneers wasted little time in building meetinghouses and beginning their own congregations. Not all settlers were devout Christians, and the nature of religious expression varied significantly from location to location. Still, churches unquestionably became the focal point of each neighborhood's community life, much as they did in other free black communities throughout the North. Church meetings addressed themselves not only to matters of religious instruction and worship, but also to the most pressing moral and racial problems of the day. Within local meetinghouse walls promises of a better world were exhorted; the evils of slavery and race laws were denounced; and the benefits of education and temperance were proclaimed. For families that had spent most of their waking hours hard at work with farm and domestic chores, these gatherings no doubt provided a welcome opportunity to visit with kin and friends as well.[52]

At Beech Settlement a large majority of families attended the Mount Pleasant Church, a Methodist Episcopal congregation in the southeast portion of the neighborhood. More than forty men and women had signed the founding agreement for the church in July 1832. Included among the founders were the area's largest landowners; homesteaders of modest means; landless squatters, tenants, and laborers; and natives from Northampton, Halifax, Greensville, and points unknown. The Mount Pleasant congregation, in short, brought together a cross section of the area's residents. During the late 1830s the congregation converted to the African Methodist Episcopal (A.M.E.) faith, probably at the urging of the Reverend (later Bishop) William Paul Quinn, a dynamic West Indian–born circuit rider who led several hundred midwestern free people of color into the A.M.E. during the 1830s and early 1840s. The Indiana Conference of the A.M.E. Church was organized at Beech Settlement in the fall of 1840.[53]

African Methodism's appeal to Beech residents came partly through its use of the larger Methodist body's "primitive simplicity." The A.M.E. relied heavily upon itinerant ministers—circuit riders— to bring the Gospel into the farthest reaches of the frontier. Circuit riders were typically poor and unlettered, but filled with a passion to deliver an earnest, heartfelt offer of salvation to all who accepted God's word. Their self-sacrificing zeal was often compared to that of Jesus Christ's early apostles. Lay preachers resident in each newly formed congregation, in turn, reinforced the itinerants' efforts and held fellow believers to high standards of self-discipline. At Mount Pleasant the mantle of early lay leadership fell to men like General Tootle, Jesse Mabry, and James McDuffey, themselves farmers of modest means and limited educations who felt a special commitment to those around them.[54]

Like the main body of Methodism, the A.M.E. stressed the importance of moral improvement among its members. As early as 1833 the Ohio Conference, the initial guiding body for the Beech congregation, had declared that "common schools, Sunday Schools, and temperance societies are the highest importance to all people; but more especially to us as a people." While limited evidence remains of Mount Pleasant's early activities, it is clear that this sentiment hit a responsive chord. Temperance was championed at Beech neighborhood meetings and schooling for both adults and children, as discussed below, was vitally important to settlement residents. In part, this stress on improvement was a reflection of contemporary evangelicals' belief in human perfectibility. Yet other, race related concerns were also involved. Through their efforts to promote temperance, education, and moral improvement, Mount Pleasant's members joined with others in the A.M.E. in both an implicit assault on prevailing stereotypes about African Americans' allegedly inferior character and an effort to demonstrate their own respectability.[55]

The Beech congregation's affiliation with African Methodism reinforced their common identity with black northerners in other ways as well. Participation with the A.M.E., on the most fundamental level, immersed Mount Pleasant members into the mainstream of African-American religious thought and action. Circuit riders brought to the Beech a form of Methodism that centered around the experiences and beliefs of African Americans as a people. Theirs was a church that emphasized not just moral improvement but black Christians' perspectives concerning such matters as deliverance and redemption; the special demands of charity and benevolence within the black community; God's fundamental opposition to slavery and racial caste; and the universal equality of all mankind. Through visiting itinerants, moreover, Mount Pleasant congregants learned more about the conditions facing free people of color in distant locations, both within the Indiana Conference and beyond, and added their own voices to that of the larger A.M.E. in its efforts to protest racial injustice and promote racial uplift.[56]

In the northern part of the Beech neighborhood two smaller Baptist churches were also active. One was organized in 1830 while the other began in 1852 as a "regular Baptist church to be styled the Six Mile Church." Neither proved to be long lasting, despite support from members of the Brown, Watkins, Jeffries, Roberts, Hill, and other families. The presence of both Baptist and Methodist congregations at the Beech suggests that religious beliefs sometimes separated one neighbor from another. Concerns about the proper degree of congregational autonomy and about doctrines of salvation—key areas of dispute among Baptists and Methodists —undoubtedly prevented some Baptist faithful from joining their Methodist counterparts for services, and vice versa. The extreme difficulties associated with traveling through the wilderness may have encouraged multiple congregations as well. The Mount Pleasant meetinghouse was a mile and a half or more from many of the homesteaders in the northern portions of the Beech. A church in that area, regardless of (or even despite) its affiliation, may have attracted some families because of its proximity. At least three of the four known trustees of the Six Mile Church—Allen Brown, Joseph Hill, and Wright Jeffries—lived close to the Baptist meetinghouse.[57]

At the even more remote Roberts Settlement, pioneers initially met with white neighbors for religious services. In March 1838 nine Roberts settlers and nine whites gathered at the home of Wilson Barker, a neighboring white, to form a Methodist congregation, also called Mount Pleasant. While the interracial character of the group probably resulted from the exigencies of frontier life—few if any additional families with similar beliefs had settled nearby—it was a situation familiar to the black settlers as well; most were members of the Roberts and Walden kindreds, who had worshipped in harmony with white Methodist neighbors in Northampton County before migrating westward. After meeting in the cabins of various Mount Pleasant members for several years, the black congregants withdrew and established their own Methodist group, their numbers apparently bolstered by the arrival of newcomers from the Beech and other locations. While the early history of the Roberts church is difficult to trace, the congregation apparently aligned itself briefly with the A.M.E. in the mid-1840s. A permanent meetinghouse was built in 1847 near the center of the community, on land donated by Elias and Mariah Roberts.[58]

In the late 1840s (probably 1848) the Roberts congregation joined the Wesleyan Methodist Connection. Established in 1843 by a small group of Methodists in protest of their denomination's refusal to condemn slavery, the Wesleyan sect had spread quickly throughout a number of antislavery areas of the West, including those in central Indiana, during the mid- and late 1840s. Congregations were organized south and west of the Roberts neighborhood in the villages of Westfield and Boxley, respectively, and a few miles to the north in a rural community. Many of the first Wesleyans around Roberts Settlements were former Quakers, apparently drawn to the emerging sect by the way it blended an antislavery emphasis similar to the Friends' with the evangelical Christianity associated with Methodism.[59]

While maintaining much of mainstream Methodism's doctrinal and organizational structure, the Wesleyans gave much greater emphasis to many aspects of the radical reform movement associated with antebellum evangelism. Embracing a "living piety," as one member put it, the sect proudly viewed itself as a "band of reformers" in its earliest days. Alcoholic beverages, tobacco, war, secret societies, Sabbath breaking, licentiousness, adultery, and excessive display were all focuses of Wesleyan attack. Most vigorous of all, however, were the group's attacks on slavery and all who refused to condemn it—slaveholders, politicians, the Methodist Church, and the American public in general. As an offshoot of their abolitionism Wesleyans decried all forms of discrimination against free people of color, claiming that "color is a physical peculiarity, to which no virtue or blame can attach. . . ." A typical expression of this view is found in a resolution for the 1849 meeting of the Indiana Conference of Wesleyans. Noting that many Indiana laws operated "unequally and partially upon citizens of the same, on account of their color," it urged the state legislature to "repeal all such laws at the earliest possible day."[60]

While Wesleyans sometimes found it difficult to live up fully to their racially egalitarian ideals, their testimonies concerning slavery and racial equality nonetheless had considerable appeal for northern free people of color, including those at Roberts Settlement. Interracial and all-black congregations were formed in at least five states, mostly in northeastern cities and western rural areas. Members of the Roberts congregation, for their part, became actively involved in the Westfield Circuit of the Indiana Conference from 1849 onward. They helped support local circuit riders who preached at the Roberts church; attended nearby revivals and quarterly meetings; and acted as hosts at their own meetinghouse for similar social–religious activities. Wade Roberts, the son of community patriarch Hansel Roberts, was ordained as an elder in the Wesleyan Connection in 1849. He preached often before both his own congregation and those of surrounding Wesleyans, developing a well-deserved reputation as a local champion of the Wesleyan faith, moral reform, and racial equality.[61]

The Beech and Roberts pioneers' churches were complemented by local schools that were organized, funded, and operated by community residents. As with religion, the drive for education was a multifaceted issue that reflected residents' overlapping identities as northerners, as evangelical Christians, and as free people of color. Undoubtedly many, if not most, shared antebellum northerners' exceptional faith in common schools, linking them in their minds with both individual advancement and America's "rising glory" as a democratic, Protestant nation. As African Americans, at the same time, Beech and Roberts residents associated education with freedom and accomplishment, the result of blacks as a people having all but been denied access to education in the South. Involuntary illiteracy was tied to racial oppression while education was seen as a tool of self-determination and a means to confront racial stereotypes. "If we ever expect to see the influence of prejudice decreased and ourselves respected," northern free black leaders declared at an 1832 convention, "it must be by the blessing of an enlightened education."[62]

Table 10

Literacy among Beech and Roberts Adults, 1850

	Aged 40 and over		Aged 21-30	
	N	Literate	N	Literate
Ripley Township (Beech)	59	23.7%	38	36.8%
Jackson and Adams Townships (Roberts)	17	5.9	16	31.2
Combined Beech and Roberts	76	19.7	54	35.2

Source: Census manuscripts, Rush and Hamilton counties, 1850.

The eldest members of the black settlements were especially sensitive to the meanings of literacy and education. They themselves had been limited in their own attainment of the basics of reading and writing before leaving the South, discouraged if not prevented from attending schools because of literacy's association with knowledge and assertiveness. In 1850 only one-fifth (20 percent) of Beech and Roberts residents 40 years of age or older—those who had grown up largely if not entirely in the Old South—could read or write (see Table 10). By comparison, the adult literacy rate for all Hoosiers at the time was roughly 80 percent. Because of their deprived backgrounds, many Beech and Roberts settlers felt a special commitment to provide their children with schooling, a commitment that went beyond the basic desire to prepare the younger generation to read, write, and know "arithmetic to the double rule of three."[63]

A number of circumstances worked against them. The harsh demands of frontier farming and the primitive conditions of pioneer life, for one, made schooling seem less than important than it would have otherwise. Early Hoosiers had a notoriously low regard for education. Illiteracy grew steadily in both absolute and relative terms during the 1830s and 40s, a reflection of the priorities most residents gave to their children's education. No comprehensive plan for public schooling was established, and only a small amount of tax money was allocated to support private subscription schools. Free blacks generally were denied access to even these meager funds; throughout the pioneer era state laws were repeatedly interpreted in a fashion that prohibited black children from schools receiving public support. The Beech and Roberts pioneers' limited resources made matters worse. Competent teachers were sometimes in short supply—a legacy of older residents' limited attainments—and many poor parents found it difficult if not impossible to scrape together the $1.00 to $1.50 a month needed to pay their children's tuition.[64]

Despite these obstacles Beech families, occasionally with Quaker support, worked doggedly toward their educational goals. School sessions for black children were held at a number of locations: in the 1830s at the Methodist and northwestern Baptist meetinghouses; from 1838 at a larger, more centrally located schoolhouse three quarters of a mile west of the Methodist church; and after 1850 or so at the Six Mile Baptist meetinghouse. During many if not most years classes were held in both northern and southern locations. The precise nature of the ties between Beech churches and the schools held within their meetinghouses is uncertain. Receipts among the personal records of Willis Roberts, an early trustee of the Mount Pleasant congregation, suggest that the Methodists sponsored the sessions held in their vicinity through at least the 1830s. One receipt, from 1835, notes payment for "teaching the poor children in the settlement of [Mount Pleasant] meetinghouse," an indication that some provision was made for educating the less fortunate. A small number of black families living south of the Beech proper, meanwhile, attended Friends schools that were closer to their homes.[65]

Teachers at the Beech schools came from the ranks of local residents whenever possible, with Quakers filling in when resident instructors were unavailable. Thus while much of the early teaching in the schools at and near the Methodist/A.M.E. meetinghouse was handled by Beech pioneers James D. Roberts, Anthony Roberts, and Henry Byrd, sessions were also led by Friends Alfred and Rebecca Gordon. As the pioneer period came to an end the need for outside instructors apparently diminished. Increasingly the one-room schools were held under the leadership of "home grown" teachers, young men and women who themselves had gained their first exposure to reading and writing at the frontier. Included among this group were at least four men and two women. All began teaching while in their late teens or early twenties, during the late 1840s and early 1850s, and most taught only a few sessions before pursuing other work, either as wives or farmers. Supplementing their ranks at mid-century were at least two newcomers, Alex McCowan and William Trail, who apparently were attracted to the area because of its demand for black teachers.[66]

The rising aspirations of Beech families could also be seen in the opening of a neighborhood subscription library in the spring of 1842. Housed in the Mount Pleasant meetinghouse, the small collection included perhaps 100 or so books on matters such as religion, philosophy, and geography; "novels, romances, [and] writings favorable to infidelity" were excluded by the library's charter. Local Quakers offered support in organizing the library, raising at least a portion of the required funds to buy the books and lending a hand with the initial chores of administration. Nonetheless, from the outset the Mount Pleasant Library, as it was known, was pri-

TABLE 11

School Attendance among Beech and Roberts Residents,
5–20 Years Of Age, 1850

	Aged 5–20	In school previous yr.	Percentage in school
Ripley Township (Beech)	170	79	46.5%
Jackson and Adams Townships (Roberts)	52	14	26.9
Combined Beech and Roberts	222	93	41.9

Source: Census manuscripts, Rush and Hamilton counties, 1850.

marily a Beech community venture. The library was operated by a board of trustees along with a secretary and librarian, virtually all of whom came from the ranks of respected Beech men. More than fifty men and women from the black neighborhood joined the library for a nominal twenty-five cents' membership fee in 1842, and a steady patronage took advantage of the collection's offerings throughout the 1840s, 1850s, and beyond.[67]

Census returns from the summer of 1850 confirm that the Beech settlers' educational and literary horizons were broadening as the frontier era came to a close (see Tables 10 and 11). The literacy rate among pioneers 21 to 30 years of age—those adults most likely to have been raised on the frontier—was almost double that of pioneers 40 or older—those raised in the South. Real, clear progress had been made in less than a generation. Reports on school attendance, meanwhile, suggested that additional improvement could be expected in the future. According to census takers roughly one-half (46 percent) of those 5 to 20 years old had attended school during the previous year, a level close to that of all children in Indiana at the time.[68]

The drive for schooling at Roberts Settlement followed a somewhat different path, one that reflected the smaller, more remote nature of the community in the 1830s and 40s. Initially Roberts children attended integrated classes at a private subscription school taught by a white instructor. Little is known about this first school, although it was probably connected with the early Mount Pleasant congregation. When black and white religionists separated in the early to mid-1840s, their children also began attending sessions divided largely along racial lines. From 1847 the log meetinghouse built near the center of the Roberts neighborhood became the focus of educational as well as religious activities.[69]

The deed transferring ownership of the meetinghouse parcel describes Hansel Roberts, Stephen Roberts, and Guilford Brooks as "trustees of school district No. One in the northwest of Jackson Township . . . the Roberts District," an indication that, at least in 1847, the Roberts school apparently was included in the public school system and received government funds. This recognition had little tangible value, given the inadequacy of local school funds, but it nonetheless suggests the cordial ties established between the pioneers and their white neighbors. Very few black schools in Indiana received even this small token of acceptance. Cyrus Roberts, who attended the Roberts school from the mid-1850s, recalled that early classes at the combination schoolhouse/church were often crude but effective. Teachers came from the ranks of "anyone who could read intelligently, write legibly and spell correctly"; their "educational fire-arms consisted of Webster's blue-black speller and McGuffey's Primer or First Reader." Backing up this arsenal were seasoned hickory switches, kept close at hand to remind young "scholars" that discipline was strictly enforced.[70]

Census reports from 1850 suggest that the early Roberts pioneers' educational accomplishments were uneven at best (see Tables 10 and 11). As at the Beech younger adults were much more likely to be literate than the neighborhood's eldest residents, an indication that those who had come of age in the Northwest were better educated. Slightly less than a third of those 21 to 30 years of age (31 percent) could read and write, while only one resident among those 40 and older (6 percent) claimed the same ability. Less dramatic results, however, were apparent among the neighborhood's children. Only about one in four (27 percent) between the ages of 5 and 20 attended school in the previous year. The more limited accomplishments of Roberts children relative to their counterparts at the Beech may have reflected the less developed nature of the Hamilton County countryside. Schooling apparently was a less pressing matter with so much of the wilderness still to tame, while difficulties with travel may have discouraged those living on the periphery of the neighborhood. None of the 14 children in Adams Township, on the community's western fringes, went to school in 1850. The absence of Quakers in the immediate vicinity—the nearest Friends Monthly Meeting was more than three miles south—may also have limited the amount of assistance extended by benevolent whites. As the pioneer era came to a close after 1850, the proportion of Roberts children in school rose slowly; at the next census in 1860 roughly one-third of the group aged 5 to 20 (27 of 88) were reported having attended sessions.[71]

Notwithstanding the obstacles placed in their paths, Beech and Roberts residents' experiences with education compare favorably with those of free people of color elsewhere in the North. Virtually everywhere the caste's members were proscribed from attending public schools and forced to rely upon themselves and a small number of Quakers and other white allies in their efforts to get ahead. Time and again they succeeded in creating their own schools, although the resulting institutions often met with considerable opposition and derision from surrounding whites. In addition, the greater economic difficulties facing other blacks, especially those in cities, often made the funding of their schools more problematic, thus adversely affecting the quality of classes, and kept many children from attending. While Beech and Roberts parents' own efforts suffered because of their disadvantaged backgrounds and isolation, they nonetheless were more successful in sending their children to school than free black parents anywhere except in New England, where the emphasis on common education generally was at its strongest. This favorable trend was apparent even in comparison with such progressive, urban-oriented states as New York and Pennsylvania.[72]

⇝ ⇝ ⇝

For northern blacks, the creation of autonomous churches, schools, and other community groups represented one of the few bright spots in an otherwise difficult and troublesome experience. These institutions were a source of "triumph" amidst the overall "tragedy" of northern race relations, to use historian Gary P. Nash's apt metaphor. While often founded partly out of necessity, the end result of racial discrimination and proscription, they quickly became vehicles for the expression of black ideals and beliefs. In essence they were nurturers of a new northern black cultural identity. Unsurprisingly, black community leaders in places like Boston and Philadelphia were almost invariably in the vanguard of efforts to establish and maintain independent black churches, schools, and fraternal associations. These same institutions also served a second critical function as centers of mutual aid and self-help. As outcasts within northern society, free people of color had a special need to work together in order to make ends meet. Churches, in particular, helped serve that function.[73]

Beech and Roberts settlements' churches and schools, like those in urban centers, acted as a bedrock of both formal community life and community identity. While formed less out of dire necessity, and apparently less deeply immersed in mutual aid activities, they too served vital needs and reflected a growing commonality among African Americans both at and beyond the rural neighborhoods. Both the A.M.E. and Wesleyan congregations, in their own ways, openly confronted the discrimination facing northern blacks and stood firmly in the forefront of efforts to end slavery and champion racial justice. Neighborhood schools, at the same time, demonstrated more than just Beech and Roberts residents' thirst for education. As in black urban communities, local schools were viewed as an important means to redress past deficiencies and as a way of proving blacks' abilities to the world. The communities' insistence on providing their own teachers and guidance suggests the importance they placed on establishing and maintaining their own separate identity as well.

Perhaps the largest difference between the Beech and Roberts neighborhoods' community institutions, on the one hand, and those in northern cities, on the other, was more a matter of context than anything else. The "triumph" of community building occurred much as it did elsewhere, but within a setting that was shaped less by the "tragedy" of contemporary race relations and more by the pioneer families' own actions. The neighborhoods' relative advantages of economic opportunity and geographic isolation had served them well during their first decades in the northern wilderness.

View from Roberts
Settlement church of
farmland purchased by
Dolphin Roberts in 1835.
This land remains in the
hands of Roberts
descendants.
*Photo courtesy of the
Indiana Historical Society
Library (negative no.
C7845).*

Beech Settlement school, ca. 1890. On far right is
teacher Robert Roberts, a Beech native.
*Photo courtesy of the Indiana Historical Society
Library (negative no. C4389).*

Peter J. Roberts, ca. 1850. The son of Beech and Roberts pioneer Elijah Roberts, Peter migrated from North Carolina as an infant. He later became one of Roberts Settlement's most successful farm owners.
Photo courtesy of Milton Baltimore, Jr.

Below: Roberts residents George (*center*) and Addie Knight (*right*), with unidentified woman, ca. 1900. George owned a small farm; Addie, his sister, became a school teacher in Terre Haute but returned each summer to the Roberts area.
Photo courtesy of Milton Baltimore, Jr.

Nathan and Mary Jane (Roberts) Rice with
daughter Lizzie, ca. 1872. Despite arriving as an
"outsider," Nathan became the Roberts area's
largest landowner; Mary was the daughter of
Roberts pioneers Wade and Mary Jane Roberts.
Photo courtesy of Jeanette Duvall.

Left: Unidentified Beech residents.
*Photos courtesy of the Indiana
Historical Society Library
(negatives no. C7844 and
C7843).*

Family of Eli N. and Laura (Mathews)
Roberts, ca. 1908. Eli achieved local
prominence as a candidate for the office
of Hamilton County recorder.
Photo courtesy of Milton Baltimore, Jr.

Eli Archey holding the reins of his
mule team, Kate and John, ca. 1910.
Archey was among the last
Beech farmers.
*Photo courtesy of the Indiana
Historical Society Library
(negative no. C4595).*

The adult children of William P. Roberts, 1912.
From left: Maggie Harvey, Lucetta Gilliam,
Luther, and William C. ("Willie"). Only Lucetta,
who married Willard Gilliam, would remain in the
Roberts neighborhood. Willie became a
prominent Wesleyan evangelist.
Photo courtesy of Milton Baltimore, Jr.

Jessie P. Q. and Almary (Roberts) Wallace family, ca. 1907.
Almary was the only child of Peter and Mary Jane Roberts.
Jessie was a prominent A.M.E. minister and
president of Edward Waters College.
Photo courtesy of Milton Baltimore, Jr.

George and Ida (Gee) Winslow with daughter and unidentified
man, ca. 1910. George, the grandson of Beech pioneers, grew
up at the rural settlement but moved to Indianapolis as a
young man. He later returned to live in nearby Carthage.
Photo courtesy of the Indiana Historical Society Library
(negative no. C7842).

Roberts Settlement homecoming, 1947.
Photos courtesy of Joseph Roberts.

A group photograph from the 1950 Roberts Settlement
reunion. Dr. Carl G. Roberts is seated in the second
row, holding a hat and cane.
*Photo courtesy of the Indiana Historical Society
Library; photograph by M325.*

Roberts Settlement homecoming, 1987.
Photo courtesy of Joseph Roberts.

Left: Lawrence Carter in front of the Mount Pleasant
A.M.E. (Beech) Church, ca. 1980, apparently a
few hours before a homecoming celebration.
*Photo courtesy of the Indiana Historical Society
Library (negative no. C7841).*

Roberts Settlement church, ca. 1980.
*Photo courtesy of the Indiana Historical Society
Library; photograph by M325.*

Community cemetery behind Roberts
Settlement church, 1982.
*Photo courtesy of the Indiana Historical
Society Library; photograph by M325
(negative no. C7847).*

Tombstones of Roberts Settlement's most affluent
early pioneers, Hansel and Priscilla Roberts.
*Photos courtesy of the Indiana Historical Society
Library; photograph by M325.*

4

FROM FRONTIER TO MATURE
FARM SETTLEMENTS,
1850–1870

"HARRY [WINBURN] has been writing to [his son] Joe about buying
a share or two of the Roads farm," Junius B. Roberts wrote to his family
at Roberts Settlement in September 1865. "If I succeed in getting out [of
the Union Army] as soon as I think I will, I will give him a race for it
myself." It is easy to understand Junius' enthusiasm. Having spent almost
two years in the 28th U.S. Colored Regiment, much of it near or in heavy
fighting, he was eager to "race" lifelong companion Joe Winburn for a
piece of a neighbor's estate and start a farming career of his own. In many
ways the future seemed especially promising to the 25-year-old son of a
small farmer: slavery had been abolished, race relations were improving,
and, not least of all, farming was more profitable than ever. Still, beneath
the surface, a bit of unease could be felt in his determination to challenge
his friend. Junius Roberts knew that farmland at Roberts Settlement was
no longer as cheap or as plentiful as it had been when he was a child. Land
supplies were dwindling; land prices were escalating. Even if he won the
race to get home the rewards would likely be small. Given his family's
modest means he might buy a share of the Roadses' 80-acre homestead,
perhaps, but not the entire farm.[1]

Junius Roberts' predicament paralleled that of all families at Beech
and Roberts settlements during the Civil War era (1850–1870). Life in
many ways was better than ever. Farming prospects improved steadily with
the advent of railroads and country turnpikes, while the privations of frontier life slowly faded away. Even the status of northern blacks, although
still deplorable, seemed to be more positive in the immediate afterglow of
the Civil War. Yet everything was not as sanguine as it appeared. The
"golden age" of the Midwest countryside was also a time of coming to
grips with ever more limited natural resources. The land could simply not
support all of the children and grandchildren of the region's pioneers as
the younger generations matured and set out on their own. Thus the decades after mid-century were both a time of prosperity and a time to learn

to live with less, a time when financial well being and circumspect hopes went hand in hand.

⁓ ⁓ ⁓

The arrival of railroads helped hasten the end of the pioneer era in the Whitewater Valley of eastern Indiana. Hundreds of miles of railroad track were laid through the region from the late 1840s, thus providing farmers with much more direct, convenient, and inexpensive access to farm markets. No longer did hogs have to be herded down country roads for days and weeks on end in order to be sold at Cincinnati; instead, they could be consigned or sold at nearby railroad depots, often only a few hours away. Perhaps even more importantly, corn and wheat could be marketed in large quantities for the first time. Sharply rising livestock and grain prices, made possible by a rapid expansion in the market for western farm products, added even further to the potential for new profits. Prices for corn, for example, rose from 16 to 25 cents per bushel during the 1840s to 46 to 69 cents per bushel during the late 1860s, roughly a threefold increase over the period. (The cost of cotton cloth, cooking utensils, and other "store bought" goods rose as well, but at a much less brisk pace.[2])

Families at Beech Settlement, located on the western fringe of the Whitewater Valley, were among the first to benefit from these new developments. The Knightstown and Shelbyville Railroad (K & S), completed in 1850, ran from Knightstown, two miles northeast of the black neighborhood's center, to Shelbyville, twenty-six miles southwest; from there the Shelbyville Lateral line connected with the Madison and Indianapolis, the state's first major railroad, which had had begun service three years earlier (see Map 7). Beech residents had convenient access to K & S depots in both Knightstown and Carthage, a mile or so southeast of the Beech center. A second line with more direct connections to market centers, the Indiana Central, began operating nearby in 1853 and soon drove the K & S out of business. Depots for the Indiana Central were located at Knightstown and Charlottesville, two miles northwest of the neighborhood's center.[3]

The resulting changes had both positive and negative implications for Beech families. On the one hand, residents of the black community took advantage of their growing profits and improved their living standards in modest but important ways. They bought lard and coal oil lamps along with an increasing number of domestic goods; acquired corn cultivators, chilled iron plows, and other new pieces of farm equipment; and had wells drilled and hand pumps installed. Like their surrounding white neighbors, they were able to enjoy greater comforts while suffering fewer hardships. Such improvements, however, were not without their cost. Increased spending for household and farm items, most importantly, brought residents into more frequent contact with the world beyond their neigh-

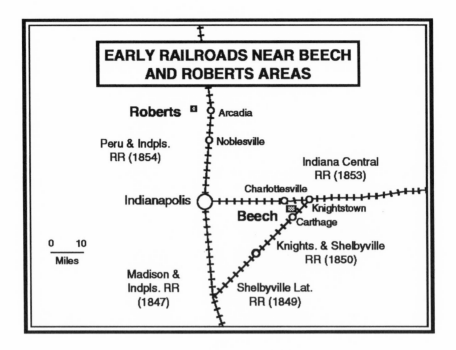

EARLY RAILROADS NEAR BEECH
AND ROBERTS AREAS

Roberts ◻ ○ Arcadia

Peru & Indpls.
RR (1854)

○ Noblesville

Indiana Central
RR (1853)

Charlottesville

Indianapolis ○

Knightstown

Beech ⊠
Carthage

0   10

Miles

Knights. & Shelbyville
RR (1850)

Madison &
Indpls. RR
(1847)

Shelbyville Lat.
RR (1849)

Map 7

borhood. The spread of commercial agriculture led unevenly but inex-orably to declining self-sufficiency and greater contact with local grain and livestock dealers, retail merchants, and craftsmen. Prosperous farmers especially, because of their larger surpluses and greater profits, became much more active in their dealings with surrounding whites. When Allen Brown died in 1870, for example, he left outstanding debts totaling rough-ly $1,500 with more than twenty individuals and firms in nearby villages. Among his creditors were five dry goods establishments, five physicians, two wagon repair shops, a contractor, a carpenter, a wallpaperer, a shoe-maker, a tailor, a seamstress, and a lumber supplier.[4]

Beech residents had good reason to be troubled by any increased in-volvement with surrounding whites. Race relations throughout Indiana during the 1850s and 1860s, as will be discussed below, were marked by escalating white–black conflicts. Traveling more often to villages like Knightstown and Charlottesville to buy and sell goods, families from the black neighborhood were exposed to more racial contempt and acts of deliberate discrimination than they had been during the frontier era. The extent and nature of these slights are difficult to determine. Beech Settle-ment residents apparently were treated with derision but, even in non-

Quaker Knightstown and Charlottesville, escaped the most severe types of abuse and overt hostility experienced by blacks in larger, more impersonal urban centers. The well-established nature of the Beech community, along with the respect accorded many of its residents, apparently helped mitigate at least a portion of the resentment that black residents might otherwise have faced.[5]

Some Beech families, at the same time, faced less exposure to white hostility than others because their financial affairs with outsiders grew at a more gradual pace. Small farmers in the black neighborhood, like farmers of similar status in other areas of the North, gave relatively greater emphasis to self-sufficiency than did their more affluent neighbors. They produced only limited surpluses of grain and livestock to sell at market, the spread of commercial farming notwithstanding. While a farmer like Allen Brown or Macklin Jeffries might be involved in dealings with several outside merchants and craftsmen on a regular basis, those of more modest means were involved in far fewer transactions. Estate papers for two small farmers who died in 1860, William Sweat and Richard Roberts, suggest just how limited their outside affairs might be. Both Beech residents died with only one commercial creditor, the Quaker-owned dry goods establishment of Hill and Henley; neither man owed the firm more than fifty dollars.[6]

The intrusions of the outside world were also limited by the continuation of earlier patterns of reliance on neighboring blacks and non-hostile whites. Networks of mutual aid, trade, and finance established during the frontier era were neither destroyed nor appreciably undermined by the changes after 1850. Estate papers from prosperous and humble Beech residents alike attest to the fact that black families continued to turn repeatedly to one another and to nearby Quakers for many of their most important needs. Turner Newsom, for example, died in 1860 holding outstanding notes against Jordan Freeman, David Winslow, and three other nearby blacks; most owed Newsom amounts ranging from $2.00 to $25.00. Allen Brown, similarly, was owed money by at least nine relatives and black neighbors when he passed away. The names of several Friends, other trusted whites, and their firms—John D. Hill, Daniel Hastings, John C. Clark, John Walker, and Hill and Henley, among others—also appear repeatedly as creditors and/or debtors in the estate records of the five Beech men who died between 1850 and 1870. The advent of commercial farming led to an erosion of the black neighborhood's isolation but did not suddenly thrust area residents into an overwhelmingly hostile world.[7]

Much more pressing were concerns about the future prospects of farming itself. By mid-century the Whitewater Valley had been settled for more than a generation and the area's rural population had begun to level off. The amount of remaining uncleared land was limited—in many sections more than half of the acreage had been brought into production

by 1850—and growing smaller with each passing year. Faced with diminishing prospects to become farm owners, more and more of the pioneers' children either left the region or settled for smaller farms than those
claimed by their elders. Farm prices, already high by the standards of the
Old Northwest, were forced even higher, partly due to the rising demand
for land and partly because of the growing profitability of western farming
in general. According to census reports, the value of farmland in the counties immediately surrounding Beech Settlement increased from roughly
$15 an acre in 1850 to more than $50 an acre in 1870. In contrast, the
average value of all farmland in Indiana advanced at a more modest pace,
from $11 an acre at mid-century to $28 an acre in 1870.[8]

Beech Settlement families were not exceptional. Only about half of
the land owned by black farmers in Ripley Township had been cleared by
mid-century; two decades later almost two-thirds had been brought under
cultivation. While considerable stretches of woodland remained, it was
clear that the days of planting crops in virgin fields were limited. Land
prices in the Beech neighborhood, meanwhile, rose as rapidly as those
in the surrounding countryside. Farms that pioneers like Alex Moss and
Goodwin Hunt had acquired from the United States government at $1.25
an acre were sold and resold for ever larger amounts: $5 an acre in the early
1840s, $15 to $20 an acre in the early 1850s, and $30 to $40 an acre in the
early 1860s. Forty-acre homesteads that had been purchased for $50 in
the early 1830s were typically being resold for $50 *per acre* by 1870.[9]

While making farm expansion more difficult, such sharply rising
prices added to the financial well-being of all landowners, at least on paper. Opportunities for the children of early pioneers might be diminishing, but the fortunes of the pioneers themselves were never more secure.
Not surprisingly most Beech farm owners, like landholders in other maturing regions of the northern countryside, continued to work their increasingly valuable estates, regardless of any concerns they shared about
their sons and daughters' prospects (see Map 8). Continuity and stability
remained hallmarks of the neighborhood's core of landholding families,
much as they had in decades previous. Roughly two-thirds (16) of the 25
families with land at mid-century maintained their farmowning status
through the entire 1850–1870 period, if not longer. Several Beech homesteads were passed through inheritance to a new generation of farmers,
but much of the neighborhood's land remained in the hands of its early
pioneers. In 1870 six residents—Goodwin Hunt, Macklin and Walker
Jeffries, Anthony Roberts, General Tootle, and Sterling Watkins—continued to hold homesteads they had acquired from the federal government
in the early 1830s; another, Fanny Watkins, maintained a significant portion of her deceased husband Daniel's initial government claim; and an
eighth, John Watkins, continued his nearly forty-year career as the owner
of various Beech farms. As the world of farming changed around them,

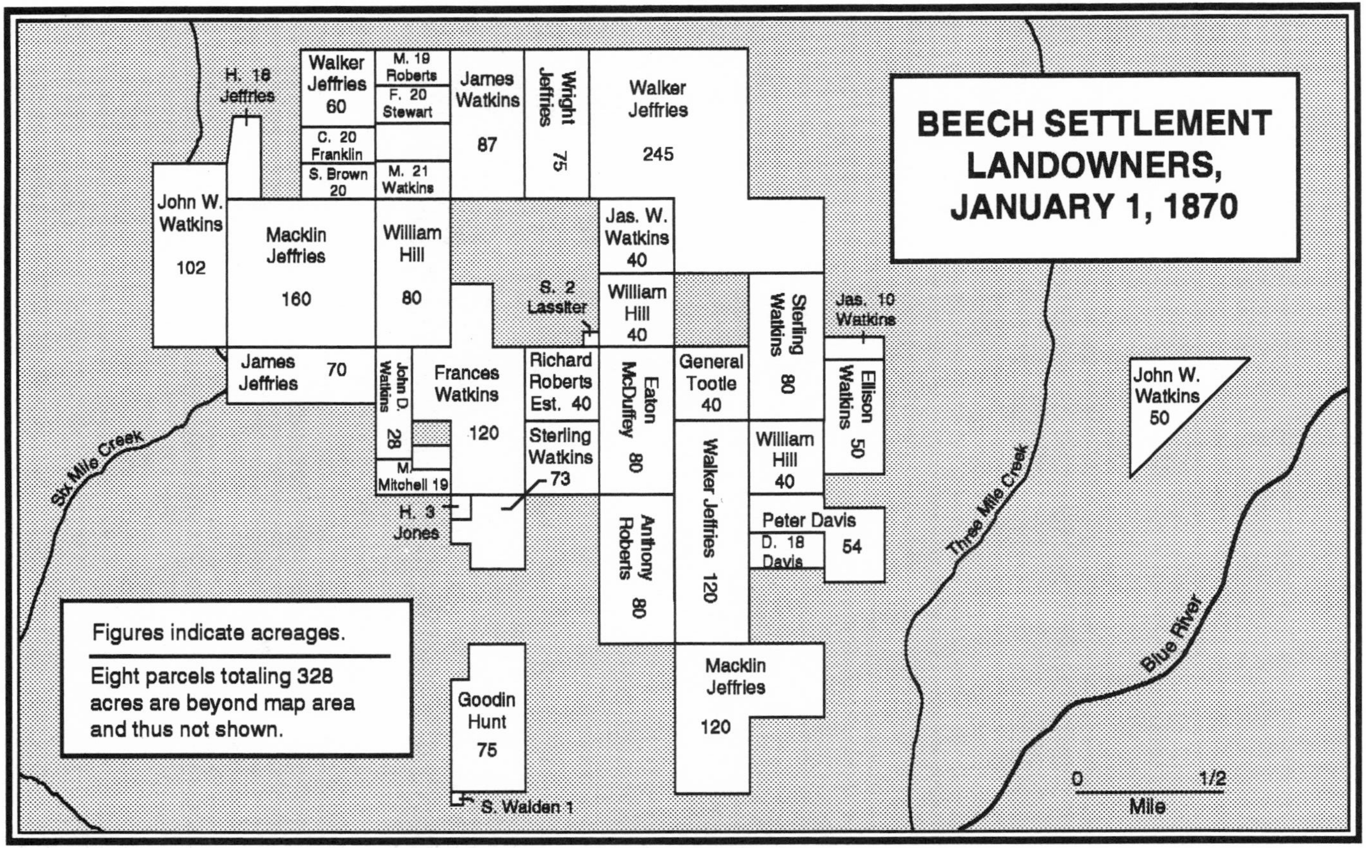

BEECH SETTLEMENT LANDOWNERS, JANUARY 1, 1870

John W. Watkins 50

Three Mile Creek

Blue River

0 — 1/2
Mile

Jas. 10 Watkins

Ellison Watkins 50

Sterling Watkins 80

William Hill 40

Peter Davis 54

D. 18 Davis

Walker Jeffries 245

Jas. W. Watkins 40

William Hill 40

General Tootle 40

Walker Jeffries 120

Macklin Jeffries 120

Wright Jeffries 75

S. 2 Lassiter

Eaton McDuffey 80

Anthony Roberts 80

James Watkins 87

Richard Roberts Est. 40

Sterling Watkins 73

M. 19 Roberts

F. 20 Stewart

Frances Watkins 120

Goodin Hunt 75

Walker Jeffries 60

C. 20 Franklin

S. Brown 20

M. 21 Watkins

William Hill 80

John D. Watkins 28

M. Mitchell 19

H. 3 Jones

S. Walden 1

H. 18 Jeffries

Macklin Jeffries 160

James Jeffries 70

John W. Watkins 102

5th Mile Creek

Figures indicate acreages.

Eight parcels totaling 328 acres are beyond map area and thus not shown.

Map 8

these old-timers and their holdings provided Beech Settlement with an ongoing sense of permanence and place.[10]

At the same time, the maturation of the farm economy helped re-shape the Beech neighborhood in significant ways. Farmowners with large holdings, like other well-positioned farmers throughout the Northwest, tended to prosper the most in both absolute and relative terms as new marketing opportunities opened before them. All four of the area's black farmers with 160 acres or more in 1850 added to their families' acreages, repeatedly investing new profits into additional fields near their original claims. Walker Jeffries, the most successful, bargained with neighboring farmers for tracts ranging from 40 to 80 acres on five separate occasions between 1852 and 1869; as a result the size of his family's estate more than doubled, growing to include 423 acres altogether. His brother Macklin expanded his operations from 160 to 282 acres, while Daniel Watkins added 80 acres to his 260-acre spread before his death in 1853. John W. Watkins, the final member of the group, increased his holdings from 171 acres to 231 acres during the 1850s, then sold a portion of his holdings to his son Ellison in 1864.[11]

The ability of Beech Settlement's largest farmers to move ahead was directly tied to the scale of their operations. Even before the arrival of rail-roads their farms were producing healthy, marketable surpluses. In 1850, for example, Walker Jeffries' family was working 100 acres of cleared land, had 40 hogs on hand, and, in the previous year, had grown 600 bushels of corn and 90 bushels of wheat. When access to commercial markets im-proved, families such as the Jeffrieses were ready and able to take advan-tage of the situation. Like other Whitewater Valley farmers, they devoted much of their new acreage to the production of wheat, a profitable grain, while continuing to market hogs as they had in the past. They also ap-parently invested in new forms of horse-powered machinery—threshers, reapers, corn cultivators, and the like—as they were introduced and adapt-ed by prosperous Northwest farmers during the Civil War era. The value of farm machinery reported by Beech farmers in agricultural census re-ports more than tripled between 1850 and 1870.[12]

Beech families with smaller farms, meanwhile, experienced a more mixed fate, much as families of similar status did elsewhere in the North-west. Only four of the twenty-one black landowners with holdings under 160 acres increased their acreages between 1850 and 1870; most simply maintained the homesteads they had purchased earlier, neither buying nor selling land. Their fortunes gradually improved as crop and livestock prices rose and as they cleared additional timber from their land. Like other small farmers, however, they found it extremely difficult to acquire additional acreage. Land prices in the Whitewater Valley, already among the highest in the Northwest, escalated at a faster pace than prices for corn, wheat, and pork. Thus most families' hopes of buying larger homesteads remained unrealizable, their greater profit margins notwithstanding. Those who did manage to increase their holdings seemingly did so with the help of nearby kin. Two of the four small farmers who bought more land, Sterling Watkins and Wright Jeffries, were closely related to the neighborhood's affluent Watkins and Jeffries families. Another had married Edith Tootle, daughter of landholder General Tootle.[13]

While most small farmers in the Beech neighborhood held onto their farms, six of the twenty-one families with less than 160 acres sold their homesteads and moved away. All but one owned less than 80 acres. Although decisions to dispose of Beech farms undoubtedly were guided by a variety of factors, financial distress seems to have played only a minor role. While one family apparently sold their land after suffering a setback, none had mortgages foreclosed during the Civil War era. Families most frequently were encouraged to sell out because of the growing disparity between land prices in Ripley Township and less developed farm regions of the Northwest. With farm prices rising much more rapidly near the Beech than elsewhere, small owners increasingly found themselves tempted to resettle in newer neighborhoods where they could buy at least twice as much land for a given amount of money. Certainly that was the case with Benjamin and Sarah Winburn. Selling their 40-acre homestead in 1857 for $1,600, they subsequently relocated at Roberts Settlement and acquired an 82-acre farm for $1,500. Two other families that bought small farms at the Beech in the early 1850s apparently employed a similar strategy when they pulled up stakes and resettled near other Beech emigrants in Van Buren County, Michigan, a decade later.[14]

The escalation of land prices from $20 an acre during the early 1850s to $50 an acre by 1870 also affected Beech Settlement's ability to attract new residents. Prospective black immigrants seeking to buy farms seemingly bypassed the neighborhood for other destinations, deterred by land prices that were often double those at other black farm communities in Indiana, Michigan, and Wisconsin. Only one family migrated to the Beech with the resources to buy land after mid-century, and their case was exceptional. Rose Davis and her four children had been slaves in Halifax, North Carolina before they arrived in early 1851 in order to be emancipated according to the instructions of their owner's last will. With funds set aside for the purpose, the group purchased a 72-acre farm shortly thereafter. Several other families resettled at the Beech during the 1850s and 1860s, but none were able to join the ranks of black landowners.[15]

At the same time the children of the neighborhood's black pioneers, coming of age mostly during the Civil War era, confronted farming prospects shaped largely by their parents' economic status. A half dozen of the sons, sons-in-law, and other close kin of the community's most affluent patriarchs proved themselves able to buy their own farms, apparently with their families' assistance; none of the sons of small farmers, in contrast, made such purchases. The most successful, James W. Watkins, had arrived at the frontier as the ward of Daniel Watkins; setting out on his own in the early 1850s, he had built up an estate totaling 137 acres by 1870. Others acquired between 27 and 70 acres. Their farms did not rival those of their elders but provided them with a considerable degree of autonomy, an autonomy that would be enhanced when they received the remainder of their inheritances later in life.[16]

Yet even the children of prominent farmers were not always enamored with agricultural opportunities in the Beech neighborhood. Several eventually settled well beyond Ripley Township, following in the footsteps of the area's small owners who ventured to areas further north and west in search of less costly acreages. During the late 1850s and 1860s Irving and Robinson Jeffries, along with Napolean Watkins, migrated to Van Buren County; and Lafayette McCowan, son-in-law of Micajah Jeffries, resettled at Roberts Settlement. At least three of the four had purchased farmland at their new homes by 1870. Two of the Beech's second-generation landowners, meanwhile, sold their homesteads and joined the exodus as well.[17]

More than a dozen other members of this maturing group acquired farms in Ripley Township during the 1860s through another means—inheritance. Two of the neighborhood's largest family farms, those headed by Daniel Watkins and Turner Newsom, were partitioned following the deaths of their owners. Watkins, who died intestate in 1853, left holdings comprising 340 acres; Newsom held 139 acres at his passing in 1860. Their surviving widows, Fanny Watkins and Patsey Newsom, were granted dowers yet continued to manage their family holdings as single entities for several years, until the last of their children reached maturity. When the estates were settled in the mid-1860s each of the surviving heirs received modest parcels of land. Each of Daniel Watkins' twelve children was granted 18 to 21 acres, while Turner Newsom's six sons and daughters each received 17 to 19 acres.[18]

For the Watkins and Newsom heirs, the transformation of their parents' farms into many smaller holdings was a bittersweet process. Each acquired title to a landholding, thus gaining financial independence and a chance to establish families of their own. The size of the inheritances, however, was small and capable of producing only marginal profits; given the high price of nearby land by the mid-1860s, their hopes for buying additional acreage were limited at best. Understandably, reactions to this predicament varied considerably. Of the combined families' eighteen heirs, three sold their interests to non–family members before the estates were divided formally; two sold portions of their shares to siblings; and seven kept their inheritances but migrated to other locations, probably renting their land to the brothers and sisters they left behind. Only seven remained on their Ripley Township farms at the end of the decade.[19]

Opportunities for propertyless families in the Beech neighborhood, meanwhile, although always limited, grew even more scarce after 1850. As in other maturing farm regions of the North, tightening land supplies and rising prices tended to favor farm owners, especially those with large acreages, over those without land. Fewer aspiring individuals of humble origins were able to move up the agricultural ladder into the ranks of landholders, and a larger proportion of the landless were forced to move on as the children of landowners came of age and started farms of their own. Opportunities for those without kinship ties to established landowners were especially limited. At the Beech only two farmers without such connections acquired land between 1850 and 1870. Both made their purchases early in the period and sold their holdings shortly after the Civil War. Clearly neither managed to sink his roots as deeply into the soil as those who had purchased land during the frontier era.[20]

Landless farmers continued to find work opportunities in Ripley Township, but on much less favorable terms than before. Agricultural census manuscripts suggest that the number of Beech families renting farms decreased from nine in 1850 to four in 1860; and that the average size of leased acreages diminished from 106 acres to 63 acres. The impression given by census records, however, varies somewhat from that provided by another source. Scattered chattel mortgage records from the 1850s and 1860s indicate that it was common for propertyless farmers to lease small parcels of land, often 15 to 20 acres in size, from surrounding landowners; few if any of the individuals renting such acreages were listed in the agricultural census in 1860 and 1870. Regardless of these discrepancies, it seems clear that opportunities to rent sizable farms dissipated as the commercial era advanced. A farmer such as Reddick Brooks or Peterson Hunt might rent an 18-acre parcel here and a 15-acre field there, but few farms with 80 acres or more could be found by families intent on moving into the ranks of owner-operators.[21]

The marginal prospects facing poorer Beech residents could be seen in other ways as well. A growing number of young men and women, for one, began working as farm laborers and household servants on the estates of prosperous farmers. Some found jobs with Beech farmers, especially aging patriarchs like Macklin Jeffries and John Watkins, but most were employed by white households. The number of blacks living with whites in rural Ripley Township increased from three in 1850 to seventeen in 1860, then dropped to twelve in 1870. Virtually all were young, usually in their late teens or twenties, and came from families with little if any land. Most left Ripley Township after working for a few years, unable to acquire a permanent farm of their own. Twenty-two-year-old Zeno Winslow, for example, labored for Quaker John Clark in 1860; the son of David and Huldah Winslow, owners of a modest 30-acre farm, Zeno apparently migrated from the neighborhood during the 1860s, seemingly never to return.[22]

The village of Carthage also provided alternative means of employ-

TABLE 12

Rural Black Population of Ripley Township (Beech)
and Jackson and Adams Townships (Roberts), 1850–1870

	1850	1860	1870
Ripley Township (Beech)			
Number of households	56	58	51
Total population*	349	320	280
Jackson and Adams Townships (Roberts)			
No. of households	16	31	35
Total population**	112	194	206

Source: Census manuscripts, Rush and Hamilton counties, Indiana, 1850–1870.

*Includes the following number of individuals living in households headed by whites: 3 in 1850;
17 in 1860; and 12 in 1870.

**Includes the following number of individuals living in households by whites: 1 in 1850; 0 in
1860; and 1 in 1870.

ment for those unable to make a go of farming. Carthage's population
doubled during the 1850s and 1860s, increasing from 250 at mid-century to 481 in 1870, with several new businesses opening their doors to
meet the burgeoning demands of the surrounding countryside. The number of blacks living in the Quaker community grew at an especially brisk
pace, from twelve in 1850 to sixty-five at the end of the 1860s; like other
residents, most had lived previously in rural Ripley Township. Carthage
seemed especially attractive to newcomers from the Beech for a number
of reasons—the dominating presence of Friends, the village's expanding
commercial prospects, and its proximity to the Beech were all important
factors. And, in fact, nine of the village's sixteen black householders in
1870 found employment in semi-skilled or skilled trades. David Watkins,
for example, worked as a shoemaker; his cousin Wash Watkins plied the
carpentry trade; and William Harris was a blacksmith. A few were at least
modestly successful at their callings. The most prosperous, barber John J.
Roberts and shoemaker Uriah Bass, reported owning property valued at
$1,500 and $1,000, respectively.[23]

Whether the vast majority of Carthage's black residents lived comfortably, however, is another matter. Most appear to have held jobs with
limited prospects. Five of the nine craftsmen worked in a single field,
shoemaking, which offered only modest remunerative reward; three of the

TABLE 13

Black Landownership in Ripley Township (Beech)
and Jackson and Adams Townships (Roberts), 1850–1870

	1850	1860	1870
Ripley Township (Beech)			
No. of black landowners	25	25	34
Total acreage held	2,141	2,788	2,496
Jackson and Adams Townships (Roberts)			
No. of black landowners	10	18	25
Total acreage held	800	1,484	1,738

Source: Land deeds, Rush and Hamilton counties.

Note: Holdings totaling less than 10 acres are not included.

five reported owning no personal or real property in 1870, while a fourth estimated his worth at just $300. Other black workers experienced similar fortunes. While nine of the village's sixteen black householders were listed with real estate in 1870, only four held property valued at more than $500. Moving from the Beech to Carthage allowed families to remain in a relatively hospitable setting, but apparently offered them little hope for improving their financial status. Their economic opportunities, in fact, were probably as bleak in the local Quaker village as they would have been in a larger city such as Indianapolis or Cincinnati.[24]

Improving fortunes for well-to-do families, out-migration among small farmers and the younger generation, diminishing prospects for the propertyless—all of these trends combined to transform Beech Settlement over the course of the Civil War era. The end result was a farm neighborhood that was at once both smaller and larger. The number of blacks living in Ripley Township's countryside gradually declined, continuing the steady drop that had begun decades before (see Table 12). By 1870 only 268 African Americans remained in the area, a quarter fewer than had been present two decades earlier. The amount of land owned by Beech families, meanwhile, expanded rapidly during the 1850s, then began to decline thereafter (see Table 13). In 1870 black farmers owned 2,500 acres, 350 acres more than at mid-century, but 300 acres less than in 1860.[25]

Landholding and population changes, in turn, helped reshape the Beech neighborhood in significant ways. The vicinity became less thickly settled as families with little or no land pulled up stakes and moved away. At mid-century Beech Settlement's population density had been more than double that of Ripley Township as a whole; by 1870 it came close to equaling that of the surrounding countryside. Those who remained increasingly were either landowners or their kin; half of the neighborhood's black householders owned their own farms by the close of the Civil War era, while another quarter were closely related to propertyholders. Grudgingly little room remained, it seems, for those who did not have ties to farm owners. With fewer families moving into the area, and with many of the landless having left, the Beech also took on the trappings of a more stable community. As in other long-settled farm regions, the proportions of householders who continued to reside in the area from one census to the next steadily rose over time. While only one family in three had persisted from 1840 to 1850, more than half remained between 1860 and 1870.[26]

Among those who persisted, none were more prosperous than the kith and kin of the Jeffries and Watkins families. Members of the two groups had owned a large share of the community's land even before the first railroad arrived in Ripley Township; in 1850 seven Jeffries and Watkins houesholders held a total of 1,000 acres, or slightly less than half of the township's black-owned acreage. As many of the area's small farmers sold their homesteads, and as members of the two kindreds benefited from the larger scale of their operations, the size and proportion of their holdings steadily advanced. By 1870 the Jeffries and Watkins families (including close relatives) owned 1,800 acres, almost three-quarters of the Beech total. Virtually all of the neighborhood's largest landowners came from their ranks—six of the seven black farmers with more than 100 acres were members of the kin groups—while another dozen held parcels ranging from 18 to 80 acres.[27]

Control over Beech Settlement farmland also was increasingly concentrated in the hands of aging men and women. By 1870 a quarter of the neighborhood's households were headed by men and women 60 years of age or older, mostly pioneers who had claimed homesteads before 1835. Included in this group were farmers with small and moderate holdings, like Anthony Roberts and Goodwin Hunt, along with those much more substantial estates. Together they owned more than 1,500 acres. While a few had helped establish their children with farms, most continued to work the estates they had built up over the previous four decades, choosing to manage their own affairs and delay the process of dividing their land among their heirs until some future date. Some, to be sure, had begun thinking of retirement. In the late 1860s Allen Brown began building a house in Charlottesville, while Macklin Jeffries purchased a lot on the village's outskirts. Others had begun to depend more on kin or farmhands to help with their work as their strength and stamina failed. Nonetheless, as they reached their late 60s and early 70s, men and women like Anthony

Roberts and Macklin Jeffries controlled an ever larger share of the neighborhood's landed resources.[28]

≈ ≈ ≈

In Hamilton County, families at Roberts Settlement experienced a considerably different fate. Railroads, to be sure, were operating within a comfortable day's journey of the neighborhood not long after they began running near the Beech. In 1851 the Peru and Indianapolis Railroad opened service between the state capitol and Noblesville, twelve miles southeast of the Roberts farms, and, two years later, reached Arcadia, four miles east of the settlement. Access to livestock and grain markets thus became little more than a few hours' walk or ride away. What set Roberts Settlement apart was the matter of available farmland. Although only forty miles from the Beech, the area surrounding Roberts Settlement had been settled later and at a markedly slower pace. At mid-century only about a third of the land owned by Roberts farmers had been cleared, and much of the area immediately to the neighborhood's west, in Adams Township, remained largely unsettled.[29]

Gradually farmers at and near Roberts Settlement brought more of their acreage under cultivation; by 1870 about three-fifths of the area's farmland had been transformed into productive fields and pasturage. The relatively greater supply of land for expansion, coupled with the area's more sparse settlement, nonetheless combined to keep land prices at a more reasonable level than in the Whitewater Valley. Roberts farmers bought and sold parcels of farmland for $5 to $10 an acre during the early 1850s, $10 to $20 during the late 1850s and Civil War years, and $20 to $30 an acre in the years leading up to 1870. With the cost of farmland still within reach of individuals with modest resources, the neighborhood remained an attractive location for prospective free black immigrants as well as families already present. Only in the mid- to late 1860s, as land prices soared above $25 an acre, did the community's expansion taper off.[30]

Roberts Settlement's early landholding families continued to form a stable group around which the neighborhood evolved (see Map 9). Eight of the ten black families with land in 1850 held onto their farms through at least 1870. This group included seven families whose members had been among Jackson Township's first pioneers. Micajah Walden and Hansel, Stephen, and Elias Roberts had purchased much of the surrounding area from the federal government during the mid-1830s, while Dicey Brooks along with Mary Jane and Kessiah Roberts were widows who continued to maintain their deceased husband's early claims. Relatively few early landowners, meanwhile, sold their farms and moved away. Among those with land in 1850 only Nancy Chavis, who had bought land a few years earlier, and Jonathan Roberts, who inherited a larger farm at the Beech, disposed of their holdings after mid-century.[31]

The limited number of total farmowners at Roberts Settlement makes

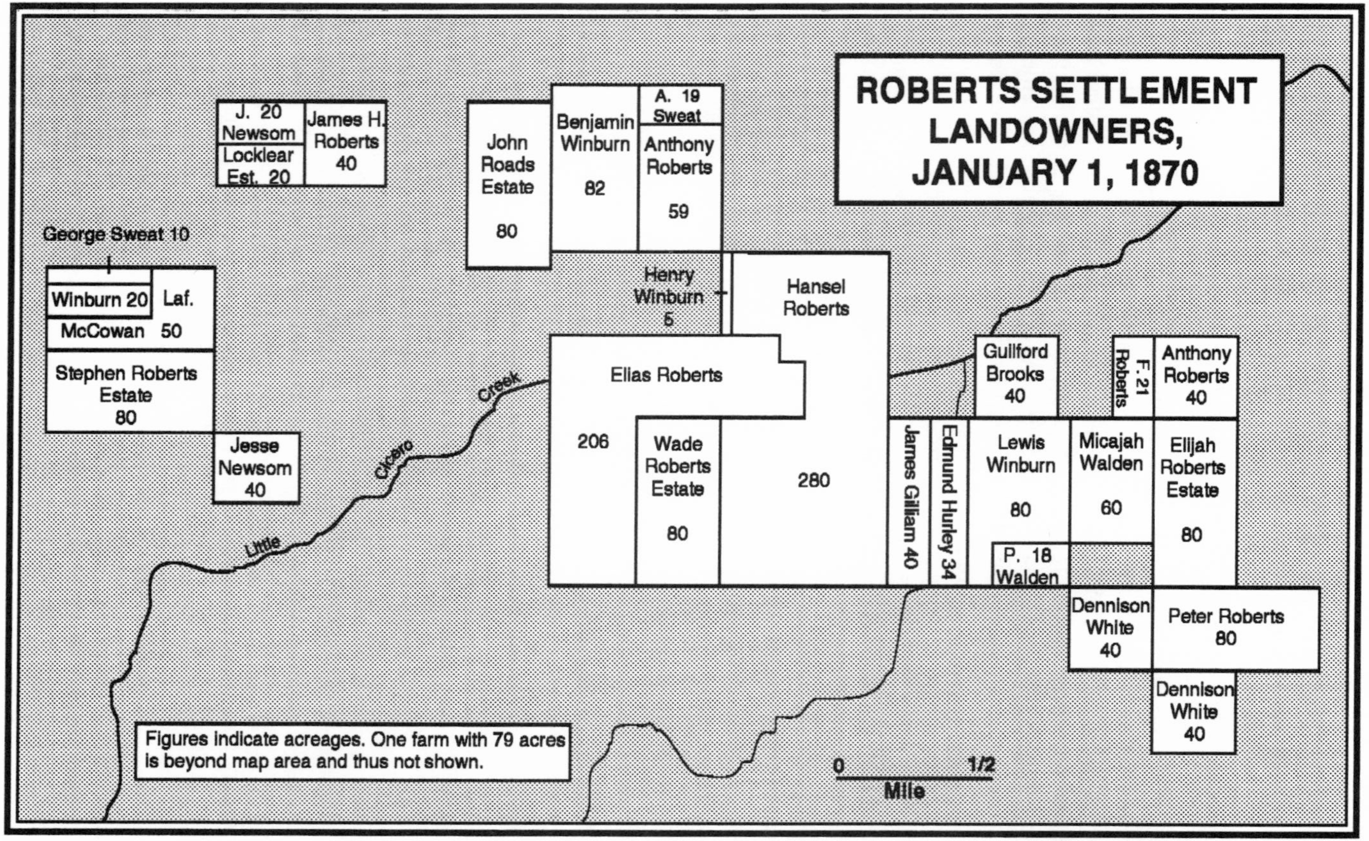

ROBERTS SETTLEMENT LANDOWNERS, JANUARY 1, 1870

J. 20 Newsom	James H. Roberts 40				
Locklear Est. 20					

George Sweat 10

| Winburn 20 | Laf. McCowan 50 | | Anthony Roberts 40 | F. 21 Roberts | Anthony Roberts 40 |
| Stephen Roberts Estate 80 | | John Roads Estate 80 | Benjamin Winburn 82 | A. 19 Sweat | Guilford Brooks | Micajah Walden 60 | Elijah Roberts Estate 80 |

Jesse Newsom 40

Little Creek

Hansel Roberts

Ellas Roberts 206

Wade Roberts Estate 80

Anthony Roberts 59

Henry Winburn 5

280

Edmund Hurley 34

James Gilliam 40

Lewis Winburn 80

P. 18 Walden

Dennison White 40

Micajah Walden 60

Peter Roberts 80

Dennison White 40

Figures indicate acreages. One farm with 79 acres is beyond map area and thus not shown.

0 ——— 1/2 Mile

Map 9

it difficult to generalize about patterns among farmers with holdings of different sizes; no sharp contrasts, for example, can be drawn between farmers with 10-to-79-acre homesteads and those with 80 acres or more. A handful increased the size of their holdings, both as the frontier period came to an end in the early 1850s and following the arrival of railroads thereafter. Hansel Roberts, the most prosperous of the early pioneers, increased the size of his holdings from 160 acres to 280 acres through a series of ten transactions scattered over the course of the 1850s. His nephews, Elias and Stephen Roberts, also expanded their operations, probably aided in part by an inheritance from their bachelor brother, Beech farmowner Jonathan Roberts. Elias added 40 acres to his 80-acre claim during the 1850s and an additional 88 acres in 1862. Stephen sold his original 40-acre claim in 1864, a year after buying an 80-acre farm a mile further west in Adams Township.[32]

Illness and death may well have prevented other Roberts families from expanding their holdings after 1850. As at the Beech, the demise of a landholder generally led to the maintenance of the family estate under the widow's care until all of the children had reached the age of majority. Thus the deaths of seven farmers—Elijah Roberts (died 1848), Wade Roberts (1855), John Roads (1863), Axsum Sweat (1863), Guilford Brooks (1867), Dennison White (1867) and Stephen Roberts (1868)—resulted in their farms being managed by surviving wives during at least a portion of the Civil War era. None were partitioned before 1870, thereby avoiding the fragmentation of holdings that occurred at the Beech.[33]

(The ability and willingness of women like Kessiah Roberts and Dicey Brooks to step in and take control of their family's holdings was not particularly exceptional. In the nineteenth century countryside farmers' widows, with the cooperation and assistance of their eldest sons, frequently maintained family farms in the fashion found at Beech and Roberts settlements. Their actions were merely a highly visible extension of their responsibilities as central figures within the household economy. Contemporaries and historians alike, however, have tended to overlook or downplay women's roles in such instances, in part because inheritance laws restricted married women's rights to their deceased husband's real property to a lifetime interest.)[34]

Ample supplies of moderately priced land near Roberts Settlement, meanwhile, attracted several black families with the resources to buy farms and resettle at or near the community. As noted earlier, the influx of land-purchasing newcomers began in the early 1850s with the arrival of the Micajah Revels family and the purchase of acreage by a Beech farmer, Anthony Roberts, for his sons. It continued for several years thereafter as six other families acquired farms in the vicinity through the early 1860s, mostly in less densely settled areas to the west and northwest of the neighborhood's center. The arrivals included two families headed by brothers of Henry Winburn, an early pioneer, and a third led by Anthony Roberts' son-in-law. Two others, meanwhile, had owned farms elsewhere in central Indiana before resettling in the Roberts vicinity in 1859.[35]

Ten members of Roberts Settlement's second generation, mostly sons and sons-in-law of early farmowners, bought farms in the Roberts neighborhood between 1850 and 1870. Opportunities to buy land favored those from families with moderate-to-large sized holdings—eight of the ten came from families with 80 acres or more—although, in contrast to the Beech, their ranks were not limited exclusively to those from the area's most prosperous households. Among the purchasers, for example, was Flavius Roberts, the son of landless farmer William H. Roberts. The resulting holdings tended to be small if not marginal, a reflection of the fact that most of the new owners set out on their own during the 1860s, when land prices were above $25 per acre. Only Peter Roberts, who made his first purchase in 1853, owned more than 40 acres in 1870. Perhaps not surprisingly, four of the ten sold their farms before the end of the 1860s.[36]

The gradual tightening of opportunities in the Roberts neighborhood during the 1850s and 1860s affected all propertyless farmers, not simply the sons and daughters of landowners. To be sure, African-American families continued to migrate to the countryside surrounding the community in the hope of finding farm work. Census takers in 1860 and 1870 recorded the names of a half dozen or so families that had moved to Jackson and Adams townships during each previous decade—the Hendersons and Spencers in the 1850s, the Sweats and Cottons in the 1860s, and so on. Only a small number, however, found permanent homes at Roberts or acquired farmland. The most successful families were headed by Jesse Newsom, Axsum Sweat, and Jesse Locklear, who began their careers as farm laborers and/or tenants and later purchased land. The three cumulatively acquired 99 acres between 1857 and 1863.[37]

The small size of the formerly landless farmers' purchases, along with the fact that no propertyless farmer bought land between 1863 and 1870, suggests the difficulties facing those arriving without the means to acquire a farm. Opportunities to buy even marginal parcels of land diminished as land prices escalated, especially after 1860. And, as at the Beech, limited access to rental land may have dampened the prospects of many newcomers. While the number of black farmers renting land increased, according to census manuscripts, the sizes of their farms grew smaller. In 1850 two black renters managed farms averaging 111 acres; twenty years later, eight Roberts tenants operated holdings averaging 33 acres. Farmers like Johnson Brady and William Henderson perhaps made ends meet by working 14-acre parcels, as they tried to do in 1860, but they could scarcely have done much better. Both men and their families were gone from the Roberts neighborhood before 1870.[38]

Small signs of shifting fortunes could be found in other areas as well. A few members of Roberts Settlement's second generation sought work in local villages. In 1870 Charles Roberts, the son of prominent farmowner Elias Roberts, was working in Noblesville, the county seat, as a barber; his cousin, Dudley Roberts, had found similar employment in nearby Arcadia. A scattering of others worked as farmhands for surrounding landowners. And two families with small holdings sold their acreage in the early 1860s and moved to Vernon County, Wisconsin, where a former Roberts pioneer, Micajah Revels, had relocated a few years earlier. Still, families at Roberts Settlement seem to have been less hard pressed than their counterparts at the Beech. There were no significant movements to newer farm regions or nearby urban centers, and the number taking work as laborers and servants remained limited.[39]

Located in a less thickly settled and more affordable region, most families at Roberts Settlement clearly thrived as the surrounding countryside matured. Both the population and the amount of black-owned land in the neighborhood doubled between 1850 and 1870 (see Tables 12 and 13). By the latter date 35 families totaling more than 200 individuals resided in rural Adams and Jackson townships; African-American farmers held more than 1,700 acres. During much of the Civil War era the numbers of families coming and going from the area increased each year, giving the neighborhood a dynamic appearance. Unlike the Beech, the Roberts area remained a popular destination for families both with and without financial resources. Yet by the end of the 1860s even Roberts Settlement's growth had tapered off and the neighborhood had taken on the trappings of a long-settled region. High acreage prices and tight land supplies effectively slowed the influx of immigrants and made additional purchases prohibitively difficult. And, as in Ripley Township, the community's farmland increasingly came under the control of an elderly cohort. In 1870 three-fifths of the black-owned acreage was held by men and women 55 years of age or older.

The maturation of Beech and Roberts settlements in the mid-nineteenth century occurred against a backdrop of escalating racial tension. As the Civil War approached northern free people of color found themselves victimized time and again by controversies over slavery and the place of African Americans in American life. In the early 1850s the group's precarious hold on freedom was weakened by a revision of the federal Fugitive Slave Law that simplified the requirements for recapturing escaped slaves. The new provisions eliminated the accused's right to a jury trial, thereby emboldening aggrieved masters and potential kidnappers while leaving free people of color more vulnerable to false enslavement. A much-publicized case involving a free person misidentified as a fugitive, in fact, unfolded in 1853 not far from the Beech and Roberts communities, in nearby Indianapolis. African Americans' legal and social standing was made even more tenuous in the late 1850s by the Supreme Court's Dred Scott decision, which declared blacks inferior and unworthy of United States citizenship rights.[40]

Western whites were particularly notorious for their harsh treatment of blacks during the late antebellum era. Fearing that large numbers of African Americans might migrate to their areas if slavery were to be ended, officials in several midwestern states mounted vigorous new campaigns to discourage black settlement. In Indiana anti-black sentiment came to the fore at a constitutional convention in the fall and winter of 1850–51. Delegates gave disproportionate attention to the state's "Negro problem," debating proposals to promote Liberian colonization, restrict black landownership, and bar newcomers from settling within the state's boundaries. Article XIII of the resulting State Constitution of 1851, together with its enabling legislation, prohibited free blacks from entering the state after November 1851 and declared invalid any legal contracts created with blacks arriving thereafter. Additional restrictions followed, including an 1853 law prohibiting African-American testimony in court cases involving whites.[41]

Northern free people of color responded to this escalating hostility in a variety of ways. At one end of the spectrum prominent race leaders like Frederick Douglass urged blacks to defend themselves, with force if necessary, in order to place all northerners on notice about their rightful place in American society. Increasing assertiveness, in turn, could be seen in both the stepped-up activism of black abolitionists, especially in trying to prevent the new Fugitive Slave Law from being enforced, and in the calling of more than a dozen state and national black protest conventions. At the other end of the spectrum, those African Americans most threatened and/or disillusioned by the changes after 1850 often fled their northern homes for safer locations. Both fugitive slaves and, to a lesser extent, legally free blacks sought refuge in more remote sections of the North, Canada, and beyond. The lure of exodus was nowhere stronger than in Indiana. The state's black population grew at the slowest pace of any in the North, with movement away from Indiana outpacing in-migration by a significant margin.[42]

Beech and Roberts residents responded to the gathering storms of the 1850s with increased caution and concern along with restrained protest. Neither settlement sent delegates to a statewide gathering of blacks that convened in Indianapolis in August 1851 to protest the pending exclusion clause of the new Indiana State Constitution. Nor did the settlements' residents seemingly play any other prominent part in opposing anti-black developments as the Civil War approached. Yet Beech and Roberts residents were active in several groups that were vocal in condemning the rising tide of racial injustice, including state-level associations of African Methodist Episcopals, black Baptists, and Prince Hall Masons. Moreover, at least a small number of Beech community members apparently felt threatened enough by the turn of events to take legal steps to safeguard their personal liberty. Between October 1851 and late 1854 three families from the neighborhood filed sworn statements and documents attesting to their free status with the Rush County Clerk. None had felt compelled to take such precautions in the preceding twenty-five years.[43]

All in all, however, the external events of the 1850s played only a limited role in the overall transformation of the two farm neighborhoods. At Beech Settlement out-migration to more desirable locations had begun during the early 1830s, well before state officials stepped up efforts to drive blacks away at mid-century, and continued even after the public harangues began to die down; rising hostility towards blacks probably added to the disenchantment of many families, but was not the primary impetus behind most moves. The doubling of Roberts Settlement's population in the 1850s, meanwhile, was made possible because few families moved away and several newcomers settled nearby. At least one family, the Dempseys, had immigrated to Indiana after the state's exclusion law went into effect. Economic trends more than shifts in white attitudes shaped the comings and goings of families at the two farm settlements.[44]

Relations between Beech and Roberts residents and their immediately surrounding neighbors, ironically, may actually have been strengthened by the rise of anti-black sentiment during the final antebellum years. The commitment of both Quakers and Wesleyans to black equality remained firm despite the antipathy expressed toward blacks during the 1850s and, if anything, became even more resolute. While Hoosiers overwhelmingly supported the exclusion provision of the Indiana constitution of 1851, Wesleyans denounced the article as "contrary to the Constitution of the United States, . . . an outrage upon humanity and a direct interference with the government of God." Interracial Wesleyan revivals and quarterly meetings were held at the Roberts church throughout the early and mid-1850s and the congregation joined their co-religionists in attacking the iniquities of slavery. When the neighborhood's resident minister, the Reverend Wade Roberts, died in 1855 he was praised on the front page of the sect's national newspaper as "a faithful and zealous advocate of human rights" who was "well respected at home, and abroad." No attention was drawn to the color of his skin.[45]

Friends, meanwhile, developed a renewed interest in the conditions at the Beech and Roberts communities. Out of concern for the welfare of free blacks, local Quaker committees had kept an eye on the development of the two neighborhoods, especially the Beech, from the earliest days of black settlement; their benevolent actions, however, involved little direct contact between the groups before mid-century. The Friends' own records from the 1830s and 1840s provide little mention of helping blacks, noting only the small amounts spent assisting Beech educational efforts each year. After 1850 the basic pattern of aid remained unchanged, but the Quakers began making lengthier and more frequent visits to both neighborhoods. They met with many of the area's families, dropped in on school sessions, and on occasion attended black religious meetings—all in an effort combining neighborly good will, the promotion of "moral progress," and a growing desire to learn about the problems facing nearby blacks. Although the visits had paternalistic and judgmental overtones they nonetheless affirmed a sincere concern for the settlements' residents at a point when most whites were decidedly more antagonistic.[46]

With the outbreak of the Civil War in April 1861 northern race relations became even more problematic. The war was unpopular among many whites, especially as the fighting in the South claimed the lives of thousands of young men and emancipation began to emerge as one of the North's war aims. Northern blacks frequently became scapegoats for those opposed to serving in the Union Army as well as those upset with the course of the war itself. Race riots flared up in several cities, including New York, Detroit, and Cincinnati. In the Midwest racial tensions were further heightened by exaggerated fears that emancipation would lead to an "invasion" of the region by southern freedmen. In several successive political campaigns Democratic leaders constantly warned voters of the impending "catastrophe" that would result from a black influx.[47]

Beech and Roberts residents were not directly involved in any serious confrontations with outsiders—or at least local histories have failed to record such incidents—but they had ample reason to be worried. Quakers near the Beech suffered personal assaults because of their abolitionist beliefs, and in 1864 the Walnut Ridge meetinghouse, two miles southwest of the Beech, was burned by southern sympathizers. Intolerance of a different sort flared up near Roberts Settlement. In the spring of 1864 a recently freed slave was threatened by an angry group of men at Boxley, a mile from the Roberts neighborhood. George Knox, while visiting the village as the guest of a fellow Union soldier, was told that the war "was done 'to free the niggers' [and] they did not intend to have any 'niggers' come into [Boxley] to stop." The crowd backed down when addressed by Knox's host, an army officer, but its message remained clear: blacks, especially those with recent ties to slavery, were a despised and unwelcome people, even in an area noted for racial tolerance.[48]

As the Civil War unfolded, northern African Americans like those at Beech and Roberts settlements came to interpret the war's meaning in markedly different ways from surrounding whites. From the very outset blacks viewed the conflict as an opportunity to both end slavery and more firmly establish their rights as United States citizens. Many clamored to join the Union Army as a way to help hasten slavery's demise, to prove they deserved a full place in American society, and to dispel any doubts about their character as individuals and as a people. White northerners, in contrast, initially tried to downplay if not completely deny the connections between the Civil War, slavery, and matters of race. Blacks were refused a place in the Union Army until the spring of 1863, as the North's war effort grew more desperate and white volunteers became fewer and farther in between. Even then, many states like Indiana continued to resist enrolling black soldiers, relenting only near the very end of 1863.[49]

When given the chance, northern African-American men joined the Union Army in numbers proportionately similar to their white counterparts, if not in even greater numbers. Many Beech and Roberts men were among those most eager to sign up. At least one Beech resident, Alexander Moss, enrolled with the Massachusetts 54th Regiment of the United States Colored Troops (USCT) when the regiment's recruiting agents came to Indianapolis in May 1863, at a time when Indiana still refused to establish its own black troops. Later, as Indiana organized its own 28th Regiment (USCT) from late November 1863 through February 1864, at least an additional eleven men from Beech and Roberts settlements were among the first to enlist. All were young—their ages ranged from 18 to 26—and most were the sons of Beech and Roberts pioneers with modest means. Roughly a dozen additional men from the neighborhoods, most from similar backgrounds, joined the ranks of the 28th when a subsequent recruiting drive was held in early 1865.[50]

Black Union troops, including the 28th Regiment, quickly proved their mettle in combat and played a pivotal role in determining the war's final outcome. The 28th was rushed into the thick of fighting in eastern Virginia not long after its arrival for duty in May 1864. The regiment first helped provide diversionary support as the Army of the Potomac shifted its operations from Cold Harbor to the outskirts of Petersburg in mid-June, then took up position at the siege of Petersburg that pinned down Robert E. Lee's Confederate forces during the last nine months of the war. Along with other black troops, the 28th played a central role in the heavy fighting at the Battle of the Crater, an ill-fated attempt by Union forces to break through the rebel fortifications at the end of July. More than 5,000 Union troops were killed or wounded in the assault, including a large proportion of the men from the Indiana regiment. In late October the 28th was thrust again into heaving fighting west and south of Petersburg near Burgess' Mill, in the Union Army's final attempt of 1864 to turn the Confederate's flank.[51]

As the war came to a close the 28th Regiment became part of the newly organized all-black 25th Corps and experienced both the best and the worst that the Union military offered its African-American soldiers. When the Confederate capitol, Richmond, fell on the morning of April 3, 1865, the 28th and other 25th Corps regiments were among the very first troops to enter the city and help restore order. They were thus able to witness first hand the collapse of the rebel government and the end of slavery—and to join in the spontaneous celebrations among southern blacks, northern troops, and government officials (including Abraham Lincoln) that swept through Richmond in the hours and days immediately thereafter. In late May, however, the 25th Corps was restationed in Texas to serve occupation duty near the Mexican border. Thus while most white Union troops quickly returned home to family and friends, the 28th Regiment found itself in a scorchingly hot, desolate land farther from home than ever before. Adding to this indignity was a rampant outbreak of scurvy that developed during the 28th's journey to Texas and lasted through the summer. Finally, in November 1865 the 28th Regiment returned to Indianapolis and was mustered out of service.[52]

The men from Beech and Roberts settlements shared in both the misery and the glory of Indiana's black regiment. Master Sergeant Benjamin Trail, a Beech schoolteacher, was killed in action during the fighting at the Battle of the Crater, while another Beech resident, George Jones, apparently died from illness before the 28th headed into combat. Others, like Junius Roberts and Joe Winburn from Roberts Settlement, spent portions of their terms in military hospitals recovering from diseases and other noncombat maladies contracted in the field. Despite personal adversities and the horror of war surrounding them, especially during the summer and fall of 1864, none deserted the Union cause. Among the nine Beech and Roberts survivors who enlisted in the winter of 1863–1864, eight took part in the 28th Regiment's final journey to Texas; the ninth remained in service, but was too ill to make the trip. All were mustered out with their unit at the end of 1865. Most had not simply endured, but had served with distinction. Six of the nine survivors had been promoted to the rank of corporal or sergeant by the time of their discharge.[53]

The Civil War's impact on the Beech and Roberts settlements ranged far beyond the battlefield. Race relations, for one, were altered in both subtle and dramatic ways. Everyday interactions with whites grew less strained during the last months of the war and immediately thereafter, in large measure because of the exemplary service record of black troops. Equally significant, new amendments to the United States Constitution between 1865 and 1870 outlawed slavery, extended suffrage rights to blacks, and ostensibly guaranteed civil rights. Although principally passed with an eye toward freedmen, all had broad implications for northern African Americans as well. In addition, the State of Indiana during the same period enlarged the right of blacks to testify in court trials, invalidated the exclusion provisions of the Indiana Constitution of 1851, made public funds available for the first time for black schools, and granted black men the right to vote on its own accord. Many of these legal changes were introduced slowly, and some, such as public school funding, merely extended rights and privileges already granted elsewhere in the North. Nonetheless, the late 1860s were a time of considerable optimism and increased confidence, not to mention a welcome relief from the oppressive atmosphere of the previous two decades.[54]

The Civil War also brought subtle though important changes in Beech and Roberts residents' ties with their surrounding white supporters. Quakers, for one, began to redefine their relationship with the two settlements in light of developments in the South. Concerned about the plight of ex-slaves, Friends increasingly devoted their energies to raising funds and clothing for southern blacks whose lives had been dramatically altered by emancipation and the dislocations associated with the war. More than $10,000 in aid for freedmen was raised by Quakers near the Beech between 1863 and 1867, thirty times the amount collected for black educational efforts in Ripley Township over the previous four decades. With their attentions focused on the pressing needs of the South, Friends began to exhibit less concern for blacks nearby. Aid with black schooling at the Beech continued, but visits to local black families, schools, and churches apparently took a back seat to freedmen's relief drives.[55]

Finally, contact between Beech and Roberts residents and other African Americans increased dramatically because of the Civil War. Service in the military exposed many young men to a new and strikingly different slice of black America. The 28th Regiment itself brought together roughly equal numbers of Hoosiers and African Americans from Kentucky, Maryland, and Delaware, most of whom presumably were freed during the war itself. The 28th's Indiana natives, meanwhile, were as likely to come from cities and towns like Indianapolis and Evansville as from the countryside, and those from the countryside often had lived previously in much poorer rural communities near the Kentucky–Indiana border. Despite this diversity, the most lasting ties developed through the 28th Regiment were typically with others from free black backgrounds very similar to their own. At least three outsiders from the 28th married the sisters and cousins of Beech and Roberts soldiers in their units. All three men—Thomas Lawrence, Burton Stewart, and Samuel Mathews—came from light-skinned central Indiana farm families.[56]

Beech and Roberts residents also encountered greater numbers of African Americans with slave backgrounds because of a growing influx of ex-slaves to Indiana during and after the war, although again the impact of the increased contact was restricted. Overall, the state's black population more than doubled during the 1860s, reaching 25,000 by 1870. While most settled in larger towns and cities, a small number were attracted to the vicinities of Beech and Roberts settlements, the limited opportunities afforded by the neighborhoods notwithstanding. The family of Jemima Smith, a widow from Kentucky, settled in southern Ripley Township about 1865, while Nathan Rice, also from Kentucky, came to the Roberts neighborhood in 1868. Neither the Smiths nor Rice apparently had kin at their destinations. Perhaps an additional thirty ex-slave families cumulatively migrated during the late 1860s and early 1870s to the nearby Quaker villages of Carthage and Westfield, together with the market towns of Noblesville and Rushville.[57]

Beech and Roberts residents often responded to the freedmen and freedwomen settling near their communities with a complex mixture of reluctance and ambivalence. Their reluctance stemmed not from one, but several sources. Like free people of color in many other locations, they were guided in part by deeply entrenched beliefs about the distinctiveness of their free heritage, economic independence, mixed racial ancestry, and lighter skin color; in part by perceived cultural and class differences based on dialect, literacy, religion, and ideas about "respectability" and "refinement"; and in part by concern that an influx of recently freed African Americans would disrupt existing, relatively favorable race relations with surrounding whites. These beliefs and concerns, however, were partially offset by the inescapable fact that slavery's demise had greatly reduced the gulf separating free blacks and former slaves. From the Civil War onward, the fate of the two groups would be increasingly intertwined, and there was little that free people of color could do to slow this trend. Beech and Roberts residents thus knew that change was in the wind, regardless of how they responded to the newcomers.[58]

Barriers clearly existed between "old" and "new" families after 1865—indeed, as at other midwestern rural mixed race settlements, they would persist into the twentieth century—but they were never hard and fast. A small number of former slaves married long-time residents and/or settled permanently at the communities, their more limited resources notwithstanding. The children of Jemima Smith were typical of the new residents when they married into humble Beech families with backgrounds at least broadly similar to their own. Nathan Rice, on the other hand, proved the most notable exception to this pattern through his wedding to Mary Jane Roberts, the daughter of comfortably situated Wade and Mary Jane Roberts in the Roberts neighborhood. Rice ultimately became the community's largest landholder, rising to prominence through a combination of personal initiative and financial assistance from his new Roberts kin. His acceptance was facilitated in large measure by the facts that he was light skinned, an extremely able and accomplished farmer, and a Union Army veteran.[59]

≈ ≈ ≈

Amidst the turbulence of the Civil War and the expansion of the northern farm economy, the formal and informal trappings of community life at Beech and Roberts settlements evolved at a only a gradual pace. Churches and schools remained the central social focal points at both locations, much as they were in other open-country farm neighborhoods. The most significant change, perhaps, was one that is difficult to document: the further extension of what were becoming known as middle-class values. While northern rural people were not as directly affected as big city dwellers by the growing split of American society into working-class and middle-class segments—a development that became more and more apparent after the mid-nineteenth century—most nonetheless came to identify themselves with the values, beliefs, and ideals associated with the latter group. In the

Beech and Roberts neighborhoods, this more pronounced middle-class identity was expressed through residents' deepening commitment to a culture that embraced moral improvement, self-control, respectability, and refinement.

At the Beech, the Mount Pleasant A.M.E. Church continued to prosper and grow, retaining its dominant position as the community's racial, spiritual, and moral leader. As the pioneers' children set out to establish families of their own, many reaffirmed the faith of their elders through membership in the black Methodist congregation. During the 1850s and 1860s the ranks of the newly converted included those from families of all sorts, affluent and humble, old and new. While no detailed congregational records from the mid-nineteenth century are extant, it is clear that the group remained an active participant in the Indiana Conference of the African Methodist Episcopal Church, which for its part continued to emphasize the importance of racial uplift, opposition to racial injustice, temperance, and education. The Indiana Conference was especially active as a champion of education at all levels, from Sunday Schools and day schools for children through more advanced education for A.M.E. ministers. In 1856 the A.M.E. Church founded Wilberforce College (now Wilberforce University), about fifty miles east of the Beech in west central Ohio.[60]

At the same time, Mount Pleasant acted as an important link between Beech residents and other like-minded African Americans throughout Indiana. As one of the state's larger A.M.E. congregations, the church continued to exert a strong influence well beyond its boundaries. One measure of both that influence and the importance of religion at the Beech in general could be seen in the calling to the ministry felt by several young men from the neighborhood who came of age between 1850 and 1870. While most preached locally, at least four—Robinson Jeffries, Abner Roberts, William P. Q. Tootle, and Peter Davis—ministered to A.M.E. congregations throughout the Midwest. Mount Pleasant also served as a host site for the annual Indiana Conference meeting as late as 1867. It was probably events associated with the 1867 get together, in fact, that old-timers later described as the "Big [Beech] Camp Meeting," a religious revival that drew people from at least as far away as Roberts Settlement.[61]

Religious sentiment remained equally strong in the Roberts neighborhood, but was affected by the ups and downs of the Wesleyan Methodist Church. The Wesleyans' identity as a radical antislavery group encouraged vigorous growth in the 1850s, when the nation's attention was focused on the slavery controversy, but led to a period of prolonged crisis after the North's Civil War victory and the passage of the 13th Amendment. Many prominent Wesleyan leaders rejoined the Methodist Church after 1865, and Wesleyan Methodist membership declined severely. Those who remained in the Wesleyan fold were forced to rethink the denomination's distinguishing characteristics, a process that involved considerable internal controversy. Only gradually over the course of the late 1860s and 1870s did the Wesleyans successfully redefine themselves as a religious group closely associated with vehement opposition to secret societies, revivalism, and, especially, the doctrine of holiness, or a second act of sanctification. The Wesleyans continued to support many forms of middle-class reform, but now championed such causes in a much more personal and private—and less public and corporate—way.[62]

The fate of the Roberts congregation paralleled that of the larger body. The church thrived as the surrounding neighborhood expanded, replacing their log cabin meetinghouse with a frame building in 1858, apparently with a small amount of aid from local Quakers. As noted earlier, numerous revivals and quarterly meetings were hosted by the congregation throughout the decade. During the Civil War, however, serious internal divisions arose and the church disbanded. Only at the war's conclusion was the group reunited at the instigation of the Roberts kindred patriarch, Hansel Roberts. Revivals once again flourished in the neighborhood during the late 1860s and early 1870s. Many of the second generation joined their parents as members of Roberts Chapel congregation, especially in the years following the group's rebirth. Among those joining the congregation after the Civil War were three sons of pioneers—Junius, Cyrus, and Dolphin Roberts—who would later rise to prominence as Wesleyan and A.M.E. ministers.[63]

A rival religious group at Roberts Settlement, the Second Cicero Baptist Church, was also formed during the heyday of the community's growth, probably about 1860. Edmund Hurley, a Kentucky native who purchased land in the neighborhood in 1859, was the Second Baptist's pastor as well as its leading benefactor; the congregation built its meetinghouse on the northwest corner of Hurley's land, a half mile east of the Wesleyan church. Although one of eight churches in the black Indiana Baptist Association in 1864, the Second Cicero Baptist apparently never developed a large following. Hurley sold the church property in 1871 and, shortly thereafter, moved to Indianapolis; little trace can be found of the congregation's subsequent activities. The slowed migration to the Roberts neighborhood after the early 1860s and the revival of the Wesleyans perhaps dampened the Baptists' prospects and ultimately led to their decline.[64]

At both settlements a significant, new layer was also added to formal community life after 1850 through the establishment of Masonic lodges. African-American or Prince Hall Masonry had emerged in the North in the late eighteenth century, but really came into its own in the Midwest only after the mid-nineteenth century. The R. Phillips Lodge in Carthage, near the Beech, became one of the first black Masonic groups in Indiana when it was organized by local residents, mostly drawn from the Beech area, between 1850 and 1855. Another lodge was formed in the early 1860s near the Roberts neighborhood, apparently at Deming, a small village immediately to the south. Most of the members apparently were either former or current residents of Roberts Settlement.[65]

In most northern locations, Prince Hall Masons and similar fraternal groups were second only to churches and schools in terms of their overall influence within the larger black community. While limiting themselves to the "better" members of their local society, they nonetheless tried to serve the interests of the community as a whole, championing reform and voicing their protests on matters of racial injustice. In Indiana, for example, Masons would play a prominent role in the convention movement that was organized in opposition to antiblack legislation during the early 1850s. Above all else, however, Prince Hall Masons were a social group committed to cultivating refinement and respectability among African Americans both within and beyond their own ranks. Members were chosen for their honesty, sobriety, sexual fidelity, industriousness, and devotion to family. Masonic meetings and activities tried to further encourage such traits by bringing together others with shared values and beliefs in an atmosphere of wholesome association. The group's emphasis on widespread leadership opportunities for those within its ranks, meanwhile, provided enterprising African Africans with outlets for personal advancement that would otherwise have been unavailable.[66]

The limited extant information available from Beech and Roberts settlements suggests that the local Masonic lodges functioned in a similar fashion and, like the A.M.E. Church, served to encourage greater interaction with African Americans from beyond the rural neighborhoods. The R. Phillips Lodge apparently tried to cultivate an image of refinement and exclusivity by limiting its membership to the ranks of the area's most "respectable" men. The known members of the lodge tended to come from landed backgrounds—most were either farmowners, like Jonathan Roberts and James Jeffries, or the sons of such men, like Napolean Watkins, James Tootle, and Dudley Roberts. The small size of the Beech neighborhood and the modest fortunes of most residents, however, prevented the lodge from becoming too selective; several lodge members were farm tenants and laborers, albeit from kindreds with longstanding ties to Ripley Township.[67]

In the late 1860s and early 1870s the Beech and Roberts lodges were actively involved the Indiana Grand Lodge of Masons, the governing organization for the roughly fifteen or so local affiliates scattered across the state. Three of the Grand Masters during this period—John Brooks, Edward Roberts, and William Walden—were drawn from the farm neighborhoods. In addition, Masons from the Roberts vicinity apparently twice acted as hosts for groups from the Grand Lodge at picnic excursions following annual meetings. Active participation in the Masons undoubtedly brought men from the two communities into contact with other African American leaders from both cities and towns like Indianapolis and Richmond, as well as from similar rural neighborhoods. The two most dominant figures in the Indiana Grand Lodge before 1870, John G. Britton of Indianapolis and James S. Hinton of Terre Haute, were among the state's most widely regarded and influential race leaders.[68]

While the Masons were accepted with open arms by many if not most at Beech and Roberts settlements, considerable controversy nonetheless dogged the organization at the latter location. From their founding in the early 1840s the Wesleyan Methodists, like many contemporary evangelical Protestants, viewed fraternal groups such as the Masons as "secret societies" diametrically opposed to Christian moral reform. Accordingly, they forbade their members from joining. This stand against fraternal groups grew stronger after the early 1850s and came to a head during the 1860s and early 1870s, long after most Protestants had lost interest in the issue. (The A.M.E., for its part, abandoned its concern with fraternal associations after the mid-1840s.) In effect, opposition to secret societies became one of the litmus tests used to determine "true Wesleyans" from the unfaithful as the small sect redefined itself immediately after the Civil War.[69]

Roberts residents ultimately turned their backs on Masonry, but only with considerable reluctance and after prolonged debate. An obituary in a Wesleyan newspaper in 1870 noted that the initial founding of a Masonic lodge in the Roberts neighborhood about 1860 had triggered a tremendous uproar that left the local Wesleyan congregation "broken up and scattered." Even when the congregation was reunited under Wesleyan leadership in the late 1860s the matter refused to pass quietly from the scene. The Masonic lodge in nearby Deming continued to meet and its leader, Edward C. Roberts, was elected Grand Master of the Indiana Lodge in 1870. A letter submitted by a Roberts resident to a local newspaper about this time complained about the effort and money Wesleyans spent "hunting down expelled Masons," and wondered aloud if a recent donation for the relief of southern freedmen had been redirected "to buy expositions on masonry." Such grumbling notwithstanding, the Deming Masonic lodge was abandoned shortly thereafter. Wesleyanism had triumphed over Prince Hall Masonry, but only after a decade-long fight.[70]

Much less controversial were neighborhood schools. As in the frontier period, Beech and Roberts families faced an uphill struggle to provide their children with the basics of reading, writing, and arithmetic. Indiana state laws continued to bar black children from attending public schools until 1869, when revisions were made to allow the funding of separate schools for blacks. Despite such disadvantages sessions continued to be held regularly in the combination school–church meetinghouses at both settlements. In the late 1850s and 1860s Quakers reported that two or three schools were normally conducted annually throughout the Beech neighborhood, each with 20 to 30 "scholars." Most remained in session for three months, a length comparable to that of sessions attended by white children throughout Indiana. Friends continued to offer support with the tuitions of a few needy students and, less frequently, with the teaching

TABLE 14

School Attendance among Beech and Roberts Residents,
5–20 Years of Age, 1870

	Aged 5–20	In school previous year	Percentage in school
Ripley Township (Beech)	106	74	69.8%
Jackson and Adams Townships (Roberts)	96	56	58.3
Combined Beech and Roberts	202	130	64.4

Source: Census manuscripts, Rush and Hamilton counties, 1870.

chores when black instructors were unavailable; by and large, however, Beech schools were organized and operated by local residents, much as they had been in the frontier era. At Roberts Settlement, meanwhile, one or two schools were held each year, with the size and length of classes similar to those at the Beech. Quakers provided little if any assistance with schools in the Roberts area.[71]

Cyrus Roberts, who attended classes in the Roberts neighborhood during the late 1850s and early 1860s, later looked back on the schools of his youth with pride, noting that they, along with the local Wesleyan church, were the bulwarks of the Roberts community and inculcated strong moral values. Few residents of either Beech or Roberts settlements would have disagreed with these sentiments. By the end of the Civil War era attendance in local schools had become a nearly universal experience for children in both neighborhoods (see Table 14). Most came to classes for only a few years—schools beyond the elementary level remained uncommon in rural Indiana until a later date—but virtually all attended school at some point. In 1870 Beech and Roberts parents reported that two-thirds (64 percent) of their children between the ages of 5 and 20 had attended school the previous year, a proportion roughly in line with attendance rates for all children in Indiana. Two decades earlier only about two-fifths (42 percent) of the settlements' children had been in school.[72]

Adult literacy rates soared as the children and grandchildren of early pioneers finished their schooling (see Table 15). Even as late as 1850 only a quarter of the adult population at Beech and Roberts settlements—41 of 161 individuals altogether—claimed to be able to read and write, a lingering legacy of the restricted educational opportunities older settlers had faced in the South. This situation had changed dramatically by 1870, when more than three-quarters (78 percent) of all residents 21 years of age or

TABLE 15

Literacy among Beech and Roberts Residents,
21 Years of Age and Older, 1870

	Aged 21 and older	Literate	Percentage literate
Ripley Township (Beech)	116	96	82.8%
Jackson and Adams Townships (Roberts)	91	65	71.4
Combined Beech and Roberts	207	161	77.8

Source: Census manuscripts, Rush and Hamilton counties, 1870.

older were literate; a total of 161 men and women could read and write by that point, a fourfold increase in less than a generation. While literacy rates at the settlements still lagged behind those of other Hoosiers—the statewide rate stood at 92 percent in 1870—they nonetheless suggest the residents' broadening horizons.[73]

These dramatic improvements helped maintain if not actually extend the educational and literacy advantages that Beech and Roberts residents had long held relative to most other northern blacks. While educational opportunities for African-American children throughout the region began to improve after the Civil War, they did so only in a hesitant and limited fashion. Enrollments increased, especially in the late 1860s and early 1870s, but segregated, poorly funded schools remained the norm in most locations. Illiteracy, meanwhile continued to be a far greater problem in most other areas of the North. In 1870 more than two-fifths of the region's adult black population had yet to gain the fundamentals of reading and writing. At the two settlements slightly more than one-fifth shared a similar disadvantage. The overall adult illiteracy rate among Beech and Roberts adults was on par with that of black New Englanders, who had the lowest rate (22 percent) among all African Americans.[74]

⪻ ⪻ ⪻

The Civil War era (1850–1870) was an exceptionally challenging time for northern African Americans, a time of unprecedented hardship and important transitions. The 1850s stand apart from the remainder of the antebellum era because of the backlash from the crisis between the North and the South over the future of slavery. In northern cities economic opportunities for black men and women took a marked turn for the worse, with common people facing even more dire circumstances than before.

Rising racial tensions also prompted a much greater degree of activism and militancy among community leaders. The Civil War, in turn, gave way to rising expectations. The war itself was embraced by northern blacks as an opportunity to prove themselves, especially through their involvement with the Union Army. Then, in the war's immediate aftermath, there was widespread belief that America was about to cross a new threshold, with improved race relations in the years ahead.

The experiences of those in the Beech and Roberts neighborhoods both diverged from, and converged with these broader patterns. Economically, the settlements' fortunes continued to be shaped much more by the rhythms of midwestern farming than the vicissitudes of race relations. Individual families varied in their ability to adjust successfully to the new demands associated with increased access to farm markets and the maturation of the second generation, but they responded largely in ways that paralleled surrounding white families of similar statuses. This was in sharp contrast with the situation in northern cities, where free people of color faced diminished prospects relative to nearby whites. Greater economic opportunity, in turn, helped foster various forms of social "progress" involving religion, education, and fraternal associations. Land ownership also served to buffer if not isolate Beech and Roberts residents geographically from whites with the greatest propensities towards racial violence, hostility, and discrimination, much as it had during the pioneer era.

At the same time the distance separating the rural settlers from the mainstream of northern African-American society began to narrow between 1850 and 1870. The advent of railroad service near Beech and Roberts settlements encouraged greater interaction with both whites and blacks beyond the neighborhoods' proximity. The change was gradual and in many ways only beginning to gather steam as the 1860s came to a close, but it was nonetheless undeniable. The commercial transactions of large farmers, the out-migration of small farmers' sons and daughters, military service with the 28th U.S. Colored Troops, increased involvement with statewide A.M.E., Baptist, and Prince Hall Masonry groups—all were signs of a new dynamic. Beech and Roberts residents still lived largely apart from the world of most northern blacks, but the gap separating the two was narrowing as the late nineteenth century approached.

5

SETTLEMENTS IN DECLINE, 1870–1900

BORN IN 1877 in the midst of hard times, Burney Watkins had good reason to be ambivalent about his early years growing up at Beech Settlement. His memories of childhood, on the one hand, were shaped by his parents' unsuccessful struggle to make a living from their 28-acre farm. Burney's father Jack was forced to mortgage their land in order to tide the family through from one harvest to the next; a few years after Jack's death in 1884 the farm was sold at public auction, the result of a foreclosed mortgage. Burney's mother Marthaline subsequently gathered the family's possessions and resettled in nearby Carthage, five children in tow. Growing up in the countryside under such circumstances could not have been easy. Despite these experiences, however, Burney Watkins also had reasons to look back on his formative years in the countryside with satisfaction. Apparently it was at the Beech that he began to develop a strong sense of personal drive and an appreciation of the advantages associated with hard work and educational achievement. After leaving the countryside, Burney graduated from Carthage High School, attended Indiana University, and ultimately became a leading black businessmen and politician in Kansas City, Missouri. A model of black achievement in the late nineteenth and early twentieth centuries, he could undoubtedly trace at least a portion of his success back to his formative years at the Beech.[1]

Few Beech and Roberts residents in the late nineteenth century experienced the extremes of economic fortune that Burney Watkins encountered over his lifetime. Nonetheless, they, too, had reason to share whatever ambivalence he had concerning country life. After 1870 farming prospects at both Beech and Roberts settlements declined markedly. Farmers like Jack Watkins, often the descendants of prosperous pioneers, found themselves in difficult if not desperate straits, unable to provide for the well-being and future of their own children as their parents had done for them. While the black farm neighborhoods continued to offer advantages relative to other black communities in the North, the advantages were less pronounced and were available to ever fewer residents. Confronted by this new dynamic, most of the younger residents migrated to cities and towns as they came of age. A small but significant number, like Burney Watkins, built careers as professionals and business owners on the foundation of middle-class values they had acquired growing up at the Beech and Roberts communities. Others found life beyond the settlements less rewarding, largely because racial barriers limited their opportunities at seemingly every turn.

෭ ෭ ෭

After 1870 much of eastern midwestern farmers' long-standing optimism and economic self-confidence was tempered, the result of three overlapping developments. Changes in the larger American economy, first of all, gave farm families considerable reason to pause and reconsider the sources of their well-being. The nation's rapid industrialization after the Civil War was accompanied by considerable economic volatility, with periods of robust business expansion repeatedly followed by sharp, prolonged downturns. Especially devastating were the hard times following the panics of 1873 and 1893. For farmers, this turbulence was heightened by a secular decline in agricultural prices due to increased productivity both in the United States and beyond. Grain and livestock prices drifted lower from the late 1860s through the late 1890s, bottoming out only as the twentieth century approached. Corn prices, the most important benchmark of Hoosier farmers' well-being, dropped from 52 cents per bushel during the 1860s to 34 cents per bushel during the 1890s. While much if not all of this decline was offset by rising yields and lower prices for nonfarm goods, farm families generally faced far less favorable conditions than they had during the more sanguine pioneer and Civil War eras.[2]

Compounding matters further were changes in farming itself. The pace of agricultural innovation quickened after the Civil War as a steady stream of new machinery and farm techniques gained widespread acceptance. New or improved plows, corn planters, cultivators, seed drills, harrows, and reapers were introduced; drain tile and sturdier fencing and outbuildings became commonplace; and a new emphasis was given to stock breeding and seed selection. Farmers often welcomed the changes, and for obvious reasons: the changes increased productivity and, in some instances, made specific aspects of farm work less onerous. The age of "sit-down farming" had begun to arrive. At the same time, these innovations came at considerable costs, both literally and figuratively. Most required cash investments, which in turn led to increased borrowing and higher debt levels. They also encouraged a further emphasis on commercial farming, which tied farmers' fortunes more and more to outside forces. Bankers, livestock dealers, grain merchants, and railroads all loomed much larger than before in shaping farm families' destinies. Not surprisingly, midwestern farmers, like their counterparts in the South and the Plains, chafed at the increasing constraints they faced.[3]

Dwindling land supplies represented a final force adding to these growing anxieties. By 1870 most of the region's potential farmland had been placed under cultivation; relatively little uncleared acreage remained to expand farming operations. The number of prospective farmers, at the same time, was increasing dramatically as the children and grandchildren of the area's pioneers matured and established families of their own. This combination of circumstances led to difficult adjustments on the part of parents and maturing children alike. Family farms were frequently divided into smaller, less profitable holdings in order to create farming operations for younger family members. Farm tenancy rates rose as many younger farmers, unable to buy farmland of their own, chose to rent land rather than abandon farming altogether. And a large exodus of young men and women developed as the opportunities available in surrounding cities and towns grew more attractive relative to those in the country.[4]

Not everyone was affected equally by these changes. Cumulatively, the declining farm prices, increasing investments associated with commercial farming, and diminishing land supplies further extended the advantages that large-scale midwestern farmers had long enjoyed relative to their less fortunate neighbors. Families with 100 acres or more were better positioned to cope with the economic volatility of the late nineteenth century; better prepared to invest in new machinery as it was introduced; and better able to utilize innovative technology to its greatest potential. Small farmers, in contrast, had fewer resources to cushion the blows of economic downturns; were less likely to have the cash needed to improve their operations; and, given their limited acreages, were less likely to be able to take full advantage of corn planters, cultivators, and the like. Farm tenants and farm laborers confronted much greater obstacles as well. Since ever larger amounts of capital were required to establish and manage a competitive farm operation, renters' hopes of climbing up the agricultural ladder into the ranks of landowners became more and more tenuous as the twentieth century approached. The new emphasis on horse-powered machinery, meanwhile, increased owner-operators' productivity and lessened the demand for farm laborers.[5]

The late nineteenth century transformation also worked decidedly to the disadvantage of farmers in the Whitewater Valley surrounding Beech Settlement than it did to farmers in other locales. Land prices, which plummeted as the rural economy turned sour, provide one indication of the difficulties confronting the long-settled area. In the Beech neighborhood land that had traded for $50 an acre immediately after the Civil War dropped in value to $35 an acre in the mid-1870s; even at the turn of the twentieth century it commanded only $40 an acre. Similar price fluctuations were experienced throughout the Whitewater Valley as a whole. A steady out-migration from region's rural sections, meanwhile, developed as opportunities to establish new farms became more scarce. In 1900 the number of people living in the Rush County countryside, which includes the Beech, hovered at the same level (15,000) as a half century earlier. Young people coming of age, it seems, were often more enamored by the prospects beyond their immediate neighborhoods than by those closer to home.[6]

These events, in turn, profoundly reshaped Beech Settlement's prospects as a rural community. The neighborhood had always been at an economic disadvantage relative to surrounding farm communities—fewer Beech families owned land, and those that did generally owned small acreages—so the area was especially vulnerable to the late nineteenth century downturn. Opportunities to make a viable living became more limited, and many landowners were forced to sell their holdings. As older farmers retired and passed away, more and more of their children were either unable or unwilling to follow in their footsteps. Some members of the younger generations, to be sure, decided to remain in Ripley Township. But for most the rewards of urban life were simply more attractive than those found in the country. Nearby cities like Anderson, Richmond, and Indianapolis offered dynamic economies and growing black communities; the Beech, in contrast, was a neighborhood with clearly circumscribed prospects.

Even the black community's most comfortably situated farmers, those with 100 acres or more in 1870, were not entirely immune from financial difficulties. One of seven individuals in this category, William Hill, had a mortgage foreclosed in 1893, seventeen years after the loan had been established; another, James W. Watkins, apparently sold acreage in the 1890s to satisfy the demands of a mortgage obtained roughly two decades earlier. These signs of distress, however, were more the exception than the rule. Mortgage, land, and estate records indicate that most of the affluent Beech farmers remained largely unencumbered by debts and mortgage obligations throughout the late nineteenth century. They undoubtedly were hurt by slumping crop and livestock prices, but none suffered so much that they were forced to sell their entire estates. Hill and Watkins, the most strapped of the group, managed to delay meeting their creditors' demands until the early 1890s, and even then they retained ownership of portions of their holdings.[7]

If the financial downturn after 1870 did not threaten the livelihoods of the seven largest Beech farmers, old age and infirmity certainly did. Most (five of seven) were 60 years or older in 1870; all but one would pass away before the turn of the century. All of the elderly landowners devised strategies to preserve their own well-being while providing for the future of their children, although individual strategies varied widely. Two chose to manage their own farms until their final days, controlling their affairs in a seemingly independent fashion. Walker Jeffries, who owned the largest farm at the Beech, worked his 445-acre estate with the help of his youngest children, now adults, until his last illness in 1881. He died intestate and his land was passed on to his children after his estate was settled two years later. Walker's brother, Macklin Jeffries, similarly farmed his own 160-acre homestead until his death in 1891, then passed his land on to his sons and daughters in the same manner. The Jeffries brothers' ability to maintain their own farms reflected a strong measure of good fortune. Both had established a number of their older children with land in the 1850s and 60s, thus lessening any pressure they might have felt to divide their holdings for their children's benefit. Among the most prosperous farmers in Ripley Township, they apparently also were unburdened by financial debts. Then too, they were seemingly blessed with reasonably good health in their final years.[8]

Other Beech landowners, without the benefit of Walker and Macklin's good fortune, employed somewhat different strategies as they grew older. All chose to manage their own affairs but eventually passed on at least partial control over their holdings to their children. John Watkins, who earlier had provided 50 acres to his eldest son, Ellison, transferred 20 acres to his daughter, Louisa Watkins Tootle, in 1870, and 25 acres to another son, Greenberry, in 1875. John retained possession of his remaining 102 acres until his death in 1878 when, by the instructions of his will, that acreage was bequeathed to his three surviving grandchildren. Sterling Watkins, John's kinsman, similarly chose to sell part of his land, transferring 40 of his 113 acres to his daughter and son-in-law, Virginia and Newsom Archey, in 1872. Following his death a few years later, 33 acres of Sterling's land were sold to satisfy the demands of creditors, while 40 acres were passed on to his heirs. Two other large landholders, Fanny Watkins and William Hill, transferred their farms to surviving children as they grew infirm in the early 1890s, stipulating that the new owners provide for their well-being in their final years. Fanny passed on control of her 120-acre estate to two sons, Daniel and David R. (Dick) Watkins, while the Hills transferred their remaining 40 acres to a son, Charles.[9]

The array of approaches to retirement and inheritance adopted by large Beech landowners was not especially unusual or distinctive. Farmers throughout the Midwest in the late nineteenth century generally were divided in their choice of such strategies, choosing from the same types of options as Walker Jeffries and Fanny Watkins. In the end, however, the deaths of the well-to-do pioneers and the transfer of their holdings from one generation to the next had important consequences for Beech Settlement as a farm community. Through their actions most of the neighborhood's largest and most financially secure farm operations were divided and broken up. This in turn undermined the financial stability of the neighborhood, reducing the number of affluent black farmers who provided work opportunities and financial aid for kin and neighbors while increasing the number of small and marginal farms owned by Beech residents. It also fostered the further selling of Beech lands to outsiders, as many of the new owners were either unable or unwilling to work smaller, less commercially successful farm units. The fate of the estate left by Walker Jeffries, the neighborhood's largest landowner, illustrates this point. At Walker's death in 1881 his 445 acres—nearly a quarter of the black community's total—was divided among his surviving heirs, a group comprising his widow Azariah and eleven children. Four of the children, already established as landowners in Michigan, sold their combined 120-acre inheritance within months of Walker's demise. Over the next sixteen years Azariah sold her dower and each of the remaining sons and daughters disposed of their portions as they matured and moved away. By the end of 1897 all 445 acres was held by whites.[10]

Not all of the large holdings were sold to outsiders in the late nineteenth century. The heirs of Macklin Jeffries, in the most notable instance, banded together and consolidated their interests in Macklin's 160-acre estate in the hands of Thadeus, the youngest son, in 1893. The fact that most if not all of Thad's siblings had previously established themselves with farms or secure livelihoods undoubtedly facilitated the decision to keep the family homestead intact. Other Beech heirs, meanwhile, while not consolidating family holdings, nonetheless held on tenaciously to the small acreages they had purchased or inherited from their parents. At the turn of the century Newsom and Virginia Archey, Charles Hill, David and Richard Watkins, and the heirs of John and Sterling Watkins all continued to work at least a portion of the lands they had acquired through inheritance or the assistance of their parents. Most owned farms with 40 acres or less.[11]

Small landholders at the Beech generally enjoyed less stability than those with larger acreages. More than three-quarters of the 30 black farmowners with less than 100 acres in 1870 failed either to hold onto their land through the turn of the century or to pass it on through inheritance to their heirs. One by one the neighborhood's small farmers—by far the largest group of landowners at the Beech—sold their acreages and, for the most part, moved away. Those with marginal holdings of 20 acres or less were particularly likely to sell out; most of the surviving heirs of onceprominent farmers Turner Newsom and Daniel Watkins, for example, sold their holdings during the hard-luck years of the 1870s and 1880s. At least one of Daniel Watkins' heirs, John D. Watkins, fell victim to a mortgage foreclosure in the 1880s; others may well have sold their holdings before realizing similar setbacks. The handful who survived or passed on their land to their children, meanwhile, undoubtedly benefited from close ties to the area's more prominent farmers. Wright Jeffries and Ellison Watkins, both members of the neighborhood's most comfortably situated kindreds, actually increased the size of their holdings modestly during the late nineteenth century; their fates, however, were much more the exception than the rule.[12]

TABLE 16

Rural Black Population of Ripley Township (Beech)
and Jackson and Adams Townships (Roberts), 1870–1900

	1870	1880	1900
Ripley Township (Beech)			
Number of households	51	44	23
Total population*	280	245	98
Jackson and Adams Townships (Roberts)			
No. of households	35	51	33
Total population**	206	266	154

Source: Census manuscripts, Rush and Hamilton counties, 1870–1900.

*Includes the following number of individuals living in households headed by whites: 12 in 1870; 7 in 1880; and 0 in 1900.

**Includes the following number of individuals living in households headed by whites: 1 in 1870; 1 in 1880; and 3 in 1900.

Much of the land sold by small Beech farmers belonged to early pioneers. Two of the neighborhood's oldest and most respected farmers, Goodwin Hunt and Allen Brown, apparently sold their holdings upon retiring from active farming in the late 1860s. A third, Anthony Roberts, divided his 80-acre farm for the benefit of three grown children shortly before his death in the mid-1880s; the children, in turn, sold their inheritances shortly thereafter. The lands of other, long established pioneers, meanwhile, were sold shortly after their owners' death in order to settle outstanding debts. Farms once held by Eaton McDuffey, Martha Newsom, and David Winslow were conveyed by estate administrators to outsiders in the 1870s and 1880s in order to meet creditors' demands. Slowly but steadily, small farms held by blacks in the 1830s and 1840s made their way into the hands of whites from the surrounding area. With their children scattered and mostly far away, little remained but memories of the modest free black pioneers who had carved out independent lives as farmowners a generation earlier.[13]

Beech Settlement's predicament in the late nineteenth century was aggravated by the fact that few black newcomers migrated to rural Ripley Township. A small number arrived from the border and Upper South states in the years immediately following the Civil War, as noted in chapter Four, but none had the resources to buy substantial acreages. Most African Americans, whether of free or slave heritage, were simply too poor

TABLE 17

Black Landownership in Ripley Township (Beech)
and Jackson and Adams Townships (Roberts), 1870–1900

	1870	1880	1890	1900
Ripley Township (Beech)				
No. of black landowners	34	25	21	18
Total acreage held	2,496	2,013	1,300	866
Jackson and Adams Townships (Roberts)				
No. of black landowners	25	24	29	26
Total acreage held	1,738	1,449	1,459	1,339

Source: Rush County land deeds.

Note: Holdings totaling less than 10 acres are not included.

in the late nineteenth century to purchase land in a neighborhood such as the Beech, where 40-acre farms sold for $1,200 or more even during the most difficult of times. And certainly there were more attractive destinations for those who had such funds and were willing to migrate to the Old Northwest. Black farm communities farther north and west, like Roberts Settlement, offered better lands, lower prices, and more dynamic social settings. Without newcomers the deterioration of the Beech became even more difficult to stop as younger residents, discouraged by the neighborhood's social and economic malaise, felt less and less inclination to remain.[14]

Both the population and size of the Beech community grew progressively smaller after 1870. While 40 or so African-American families were scattered across the Ripley Township countryside at the end of the Civil War, only 20 remained by the turn of the twentieth century (see Table 16). In a general sense, the decline was reflective of a broad trend throughout the Midwest in the late nineteenth century; in many, if not most, regions, rural populations were thinned by the exodus of families to surrounding villages, towns, and cities. At the Beech the process was simply sped up by the sale of farmland to surrounding whites. The amount of acreage held by black farmers, meanwhile, declined by almost two-thirds between 1870 to 1900. As Table 17 indicates, in 1870 more than twenty blacks owned farms totaling approximately 2,300 acres. By 1900 only 18 landholders remained; together, they held less than 900 acres.[15]

Beech Settlement did not fade away in the late nineteenth century.

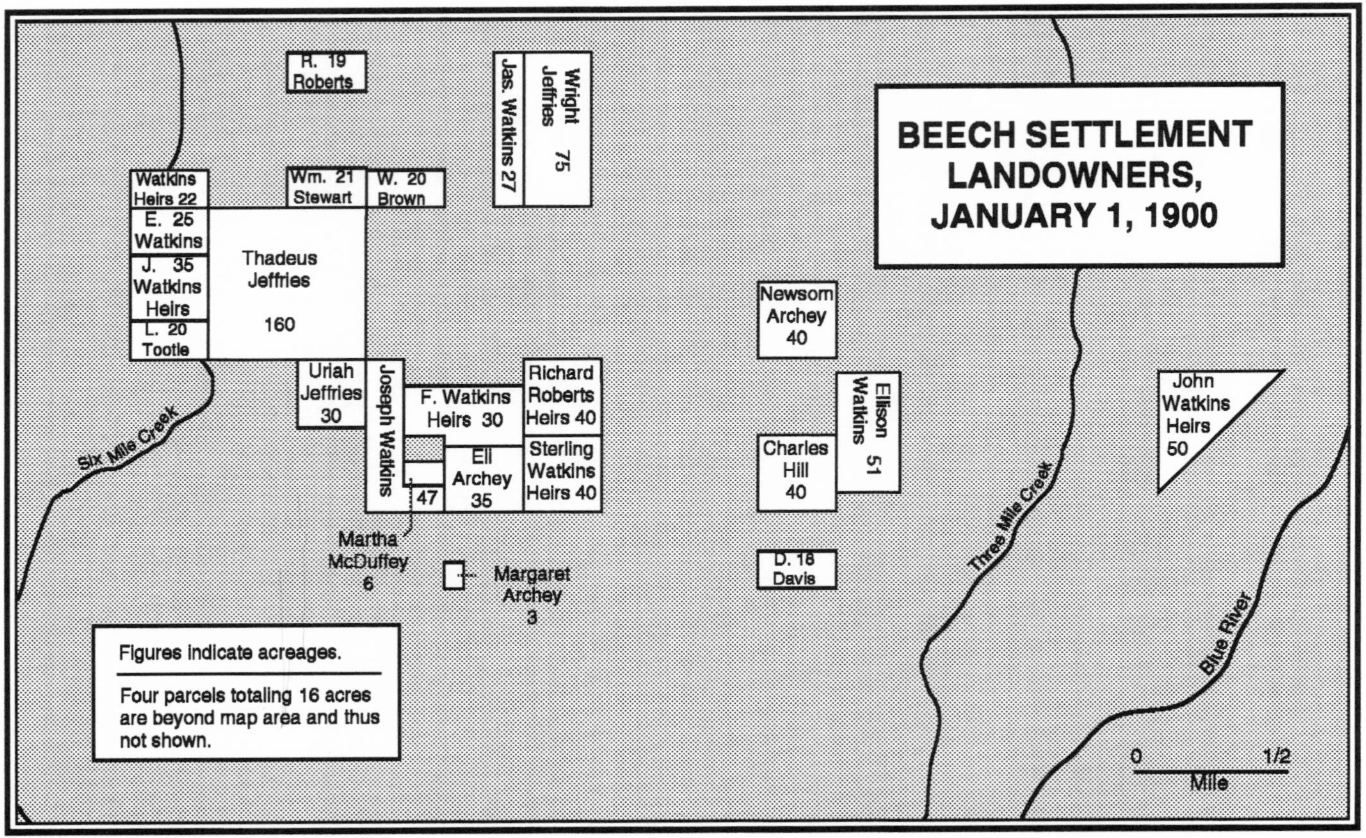

BEECH SETTLEMENT
LANDOWNERS,
JANUARY 1, 1900

John
Watkins
Heirs
50

Blue River

Three Mile Creek

Ellison
Watkins 51

Newsom
Archey
40

Charles
Hill
40

D. 18
Davis

0   1/2
Mile

Wright
Jeffries 75

Jas. Watkins 27

Richard
Roberts
Heirs 40

Sterling
Watkins
Heirs 40

F. Watkins
Heirs 30

Ell
Archey
35

47

Margaret
Archey
3

Joseph Watkins

Martha
McDuffey
6

R. 19
Roberts

Wm. 21
Stewart

W. 20
Brown

Thadeus
Jeffries
160

Uriah
Jeffries
30

Watkins
Heirs 22

E. 25
Watkins

J. 35
Watkins
Heirs

L. 20
Tootle

Six Mile Creek

Figures indicate acreages.

Four parcels totaling 16 acres
are beyond map area and thus
not shown.

Map 10

Many of the area's black landowners continued to work their holdings until they reached an advanced age, and, in several instances, members of the younger generations acquired farms of their own. Yet signs of community decay and deterioration were not hard to find. Spatially, the Beech became a more fragmented neighborhood. By 1900, as Map 10 illustrates, much of the land near the center of the black settlement had been sold to surrounding whites. The geographic cohesiveness of the Beech neighborhood had become a thing of the past. An even more ominous sign could be seen in the shrinking number of viable, black-owned farms. In 1870 seventeen Beech residents owned farms of 40 acres or more, thus providing themselves and their families with the means for a modest if not comfortable living. Over the following thirty years the number of such farmers declined by two-thirds; by the turn of the twentieth century, only six Beech residents held farms of at least 40 acres. A large majority of area residents farmed marginal acreages of their own and/or rented land from surrounding landholders. Theirs was a future with a clearly limited horizon.[16]

⤙ ⤙ ⤙

Conditions at Roberts Settlement were markedly different. For one thing, land prices did not suffer the dramatic decline evident in the Whitewater Valley, where population pressures had driven up values to extremely high levels earlier. In central Indiana land prices dropped after 1873 but recovered within a decade, then climbed to new peaks in the 1880s and 1890s. Farms that were valued at $40 an acre in 1870 were reassessed at $45 to $50 an acre at the turn of the century. Relatively more land remained to be cleared as well. A larger proportion of sons and daughters of the region's pioneers were able to acquire farms of their own as the late nineteenth century wore on. Families at Roberts Settlement also tended to be financially more secure than their counterparts at the Beech. Fewer families at Roberts were either landless or marginal farmers in the early 1870s. As a consequence, the neighborhood as a whole survived the late nineteenth century in much better shape. Roberts Settlement remained a stable, if not prosperous, farm community (see Map 11).[17]

Many farmers at Roberts, to be sure, faced their share of problems. Nearly a dozen marginal landholders sold out, apparently unable to make ends meet on limited acreages. John Sweat, for example, purchased a 21-acre farm in the winter of 1871–72. After struggling to meet the demands of mortgagors over a five-year period, he sold the parcel and became a farm tenant. Others, like Flavius Roberts and William Winburn, disposed of small acreages and migrated to urban settings, abandoning farm life altogether. Several of the community's pioneer landowners, meanwhile, failed to pass on their holdings to heirs. Included in this last group were seven farmers, each of whom had purchased between 20 and 100 acres before 1860. The situation varied from case to case. In some instances, farms were sold by estate administrators to satisfy creditors' demands; in

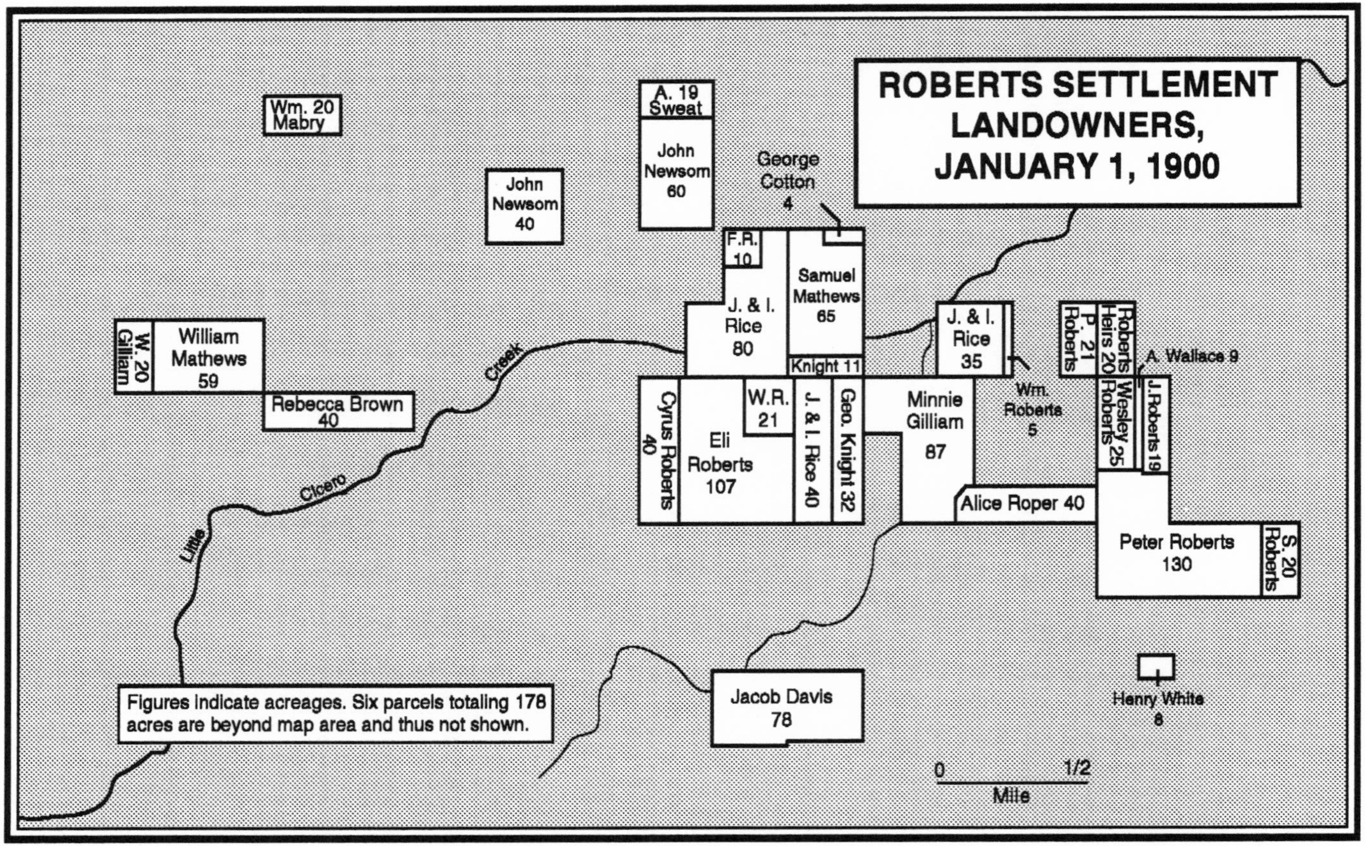

ROBERTS SETTLEMENT
LANDOWNERS,
JANUARY 1, 1900

S. 20
Roberts

A. Wallace 9

J. Roberts 19

Roberts
Heirs 20

Wesley
Roberts 25

P. 21
Roberts

Peter Roberts
130

Henry White
8

Wm.
Roberts
5

Alice Roper 40

J. & I.
Rice
35

Minnie
Gilliam
87

0   1/2

Mile

George
Cotton
4

Samuel
Mathews
65

Knight 11

Geo. Knight 32

J. & I. Rice 40

Jacob Davis
78

F.R.
10

J. & I.
Rice
80

W.R.
21

A. 19
Sweat

John Newsom
60

Eli
Roberts
107

Cyrus Roberts
40

John
Newsom
40

Creek

Wm. 20
Mabry

Rebecca Brown
40

Cicero

William
Mathews
59

Little

W. 20
Gilliam

Figures indicate acreages. Six parcels totaling 178
acres are beyond map area and thus not shown.

Map 11

others, farms were divided for sons, daughters, and other heirs, then quickly sold by the new owners.[18]

Not all farmers in the Roberts neighborhood, however, found themselves in such difficult straits in the late nineteenth century. More than at the Beech, families managed to keep their holdings together. Roughly a quarter of the community's farmowners in 1870 either continued to farm their own land through the turn of the century, or successfully passed on their holdings to surviving heirs. Included in this group were landowners both small and large. As a result of this continuity roughly half of the land comprising Roberts Settlement remained in the hands of the same owners or family groups over the course of the late nineteenth century. Most of the acreage in these farms, moreover, remained in viable small farm units of 40 acres or more.[19]

A small but significant number of Roberts farmers, meanwhile, increased their landholdings after 1870, adding to their financial prosperity despite the troubled nature of midwestern farming. The most successful, Nathan Rice, was an ex-slave who had arrived with limited resources immediately after the Civil War. Marrying the granddaughter of neighborhood patriarch Hansel Roberts, he combined hard work, farming skills, and family connections to build up a comfortable estate totaling 242 acres by the early 1890s. Others added to their acreages in more modest ways. Jesse Newsom, for example, increased the size of his holdings from 60 to 100 acres in the early 1870s by acquiring additional lands in a piecemeal fashion. His estate was transferred intact to five heirs following his death in 1879. Jesse's son John, in turn, managed to carve out a successful niche as a farmer as well. Beginning with a 20-acre inheritance, he built up holdings totaling 100 acres in the late nineteenth century following the same pattern of incremental purchases. Acquisitions by farmers like John Newsom and Nathan Rice partially offset the selling of land by other Roberts residents. Much of the land bought and sold by neighborhood members, in fact, involved direct transfers of title from one black family to another. Kindreds like the Gilliams, Newsoms, and Rices became owners of holdings once held by the Hurleys, Winburns, and Roadses.[20]

Roberts Settlement also benefited from a small influx of newcomers who purchased land in the neighborhood after 1870. A half dozen or more black farmers, either individually or with their families, migrated to Roberts Settlement between 1870 and 1900, acquiring farms shortly after their arrivals. Most if not all were either free-born natives of the Old Northwest or ex-slaves from Kentucky and North Carolina who had settled previously north of the Ohio River. William, Jacob, and Samuel Mathews, for example, were eastern Indiana natives who had lived previously in other midwestern rural settings; George Knight was a native of Cincinnati; and Jacob Davis was an ex-slave from Kentucky who had owned a homestead in southern Indiana before settling permanently at Roberts. While a few may have benefited from marriages to established Roberts residents, most apparently arrived with financial resources of their own. Jacob Davis, the most successful of the newcomers, purchased 130 acres south of the neighborhood's center by 1900. Six others, settling in locations scattered throughout Jackson and Adams townships, owned farms ranging in size from 20 to 79 acres.[21]

Overall, the late nineteenth century brought mixed farm prospects to Roberts Settlement. The number of black families living in rural Jackson and Adams townships actually increased during the 1870s, as newcomers continued to trickle into the neighborhood and several sons and daughters of early pioneers were able to set up households of their own and make a living as either farmers or farm laborers (see Table 16). By 1880 more than 50 black households comprising over 250 people dotted the Jackson-Adams area, with most located in the immediate vicinity of Roberts Settlement proper. Thereafter the area's black population began to decline, although at a less precipitous pace than at the Beech. At the turn of the twentieth century roughly 30 black families totaling 150 residents remained.[22]

The total size of African-American landholdings in the Roberts neighborhood shrank as well, largely due to the disposal of small farms by the settlement's founders and their heirs. As Table 17 indicates, the combined holdings of black families in the Jackson-Adams area dropped by approximately one-sixth during the 1870s, remained steady through the 1880s, then declined by one-tenth in the 1890s. Altogether, the holdings of local black farmers dropped by 400 acres during the period, from roughly 1,700 acres in 1870 to about 1,300 acres at the turn of the twentieth century. The gradual erosion of Roberts Settlement holdings undoubtedly left the neighborhood in a more vulnerable economic position. With fewer acres in the hands of black landowners, area residents were forced to turn to outsiders either to rent land or to find work as laborers. The decline of Roberts Settlement as a self-supporting farm neighborhood, however, was far from complete in 1900. Despite the fact that the majority of its landowning members were small farmers—those hardest hit by the late nineteenth century downturn—the community remained essentially intact.[23]

≈ ≈ ≈

Beech and Roberts families grappled with shifting race relations as well as mixed farming prospects in the decades after 1870. In Indiana, as throughout the North, existing patterns of white-black interactions were brought into question by events associated with the Civil War and Reconstruction. African Americans continued to face pervasive racial discrimination but achieved new civil rights during the late 1860s and 1870s. Public schooling was opened to black as well as white children; black men were extended suffrage rights; and many legal disabilities confronting black Hoosiers were eliminated. A new day seemed to be dawning. Yet in many respects the changes were more illusory than real. New federal and state civil rights statutes, for example, formally guaranteed equal access to public accommodations, but in practice did little to end practices of segregation in hotels, restaurants, and theaters. Moreover, race relations in Indiana, as elsewhere, took a serious turn for the worse after the mid-1880s. Racial tensions mounted and discrimination concerning matters like housing and employment became more, not less, pronounced. African Americans were repeatedly targets of rural vigilante groups and lynch mobs, especially in southern Indiana, with more than a dozen blacks killed by white "regulators." The informal "color line" separating blacks and whites grew more, not less, pernicious as the turn of the century approached.[24]

More than in previous periods, residents of Beech and Roberts settlements found themselves directly affected by the shifting tides of race relations. The danger inherent in these treacherous undercurrents became apparent in the brutal lynching of William Keemer, a Beech native, in the summer of 1875. The incident began on a hot summer day when the twenty-six-year-old Keemer stopped to ask for a drink of water at the home of Lucetta Vaughn, a local farmwife who lived a few miles from the Beech. What happened subsequently is open to question. According to Vaughn, Keemer used the request as a pretext to gain entry into her household; then, she told authorities, the young black attacked and raped her. Beech residents and Keemer himself offered a different explanation. In the eyes of local blacks, Billy Keemer's "crime" was no crime at all. The young man had simply stopped to ask for a drink of water; Vaughn, ill at ease in the presence of a dark-skinned man, misjudged his intentions and became hysterical at the thought of what he might do to her.[25]

Despite conflicting accounts, the results of the encounter are unquestionable. Keemer quickly fled when Vaughn panicked, well aware that whites might respond violently to the situation that had unfolded. Apprehended by local authorities in Carthage, he was brought first to the Rush County jail in nearby Rushville, then transferred to a supposedly more secure jail in Greenfield, the seat of adjacent Hancock County. Keemer's stay in Greenfield was brief. The night of his arrival a crowd of more than 150 whites gathered at the holding area and demanded that "justice" immediately be served. Forcibly removing Keemer from his cell, they proceeded to the edge of town and lynched him. Less than forty-eight hours after he stopped to request a drink of water, Billy Keemer's life came to an abrupt end.[26]

Keemer's execution at the hands of an outraged white community was ostensibly an isolated, exceptional incident. It marked the only occasion at either Beech or Roberts settlements when a community member was attacked by a white mob, when the normal, peaceful race relations of the countryside were shattered by an act of wanton, race-related violence. Yet Billy Keemer's murder was clearly a reflection of troubled times. Late nineteenth century lynchings were symptomatic of the uneasy tensions that existed between whites and blacks in the aftermath of the Civil War as greater freedoms were extended to all African Americans, both in the South and in the North. Vigilantism represented an increasingly acceptable way of discouraging blacks from becoming too assertive in a white-dominated society. As Keemer himself undoubtedly knew, the details of his encounter with Lucetta Vaughn were irrelevant to many of the respected citizens who gathered at the Greenfield jail demanding his execution; Billy Keemer's "crime" was not rape per se, but being caught in a situation where the possibility of a rape involving a black man and a white woman existed and, in the eyes of worried whites, may have transpired. Keemer's death was a strong warning to all blacks to remain in their "place" or risk the consequences.[27]

Roberts and Beech families were increasingly exposed to such realities as the isolation of the farm neighborhoods continued to erode during the late nineteenth century. New gravel roads and country turnpikes made the two settlements less remote and made traveling from the countryside to surrounding villages like Carthage, Knightstown, and Arcadia easier than before; improved railroad connections, meanwhile, brought better access to larger Indiana towns and cities such as Kokomo, Richmond, and Indianapolis. More and more frequently Beech and Roberts residents took advantage of the new opportunities brought by the closing of the gap between town and country. Regular trips were made to sell farm commodities, to buy farm and domestic supplies, to take care of legal and political matters, and to visit friends and kin who now worked and lived in towns and villages. Even the desire for advanced educational opportunities encouraged greater contact with the outside world, since high schools and academies were located only in larger villages and towns.[28]

Relations between local whites and Beech and Roberts residents varied from one urban setting to the next. In most of the surrounding villages blacks were grudgingly tolerated as long as they followed existing racial norms and maintained an air of deference in the company of whites. Arcadia, which became the principal market destination for Roberts Settlement farmers after the Civil War, was perhaps typical of such communities. Roberts children were allowed to attend Arcadia High School following its opening in 1883, thus gaining access to secondary schooling on an equal footing with white children from surrounding neighborhoods. White townspeople also were willing to accept the business of Roberts families for both farm and domestic goods. At the same time, however, Arcadians were more than a bit hesitant to accept African Americans as neighbors and discouraged Roberts residents from establishing any sort of permanent ties in the community. Roberts farmer Nathan Rice, one of the most prominent landowners in Jackson Township, was rebuffed by local whites when he attempted to buy a home in the town; even prosperous blacks, it seems, had no place in late nineteenth century Arcadia. Despite its proximity to Roberts Settlement, only 4 of the town's 1,400 residents in 1900 were African Americans.[29]

Ties between whites and blacks were somewhat more cordial at the "Quaker towns" near the two settlements—Westfield, ten miles south of Roberts Settlement, and Carthage, a mile or so from the Beech. As in earlier periods, local whites welcomed blacks at the Friends' schools, public and private; openly accepted the business of nearby farmers; and did little to dissuade African Americans from settling within their bounds. Both towns had sizable black populations in the late nineteenth century, in part because of their hospitable reputations. Yet for all of their openness Westfield and Carthage nonetheless were towns sharply divided along racial lines. Increasingly black residents lived in the same neighborhoods, found work only in unskilled occupations, and, at least in Carthage, remained excluded from the town's most prominent voluntary associations. (By the first decade of the twentieth century civic leaders in Carthage would reestablish segregated common schools for the town, a move intended "to give the colored children better [educational] opportunities."[30])

As events in Carthage suggest, the special bond shared by Beech and Roberts families and their surrounding white neighbors was loosened if not altogether undone in the late nineteenth century. Former abolitionists throughout the North generally lessened their commitment to fighting for racial equality after the Civil War, believing that conditions had significantly improved for African Americans. Slavery's demise and the passage of civil rights legislation had provided blacks with a roughly equal footing in American society, most felt; it was now up to blacks to make their own way in the world, without further assistance from whites. This line of thought, which implicitly ignored the persistence of racism and racial discrimination in America, influenced the beliefs and attitudes of Quakers and Wesleyans near the Beech and Roberts communities. Relations between black and white neighbors remained cordial if not friendly, but lost at least a portion of the exceptional closeness fostered by earlier fights for abolition and civil rights.[31]

For Quakers, the process of declension centered around the abandonment of the local vigilance committees that for thirty years had monitored the civil rights and educational progress of Beech and Roberts families. Shortly after the Indiana Assembly passed legislation guaranteeing blacks public school funding and civil rights protections, these Committees on the Concerns of People of Color began to reconsider their involvement with their black neighbors. In the late 1860s Friends watched approvingly as Beech and Roberts schools received state funding, thus eliminating the need for their assistance in helping to pay the tuition of the communities' poorer children. A few years later, satisfied that the schools had become self-sustaining and that the basic civil rights of Beech and Roberts residents were no longer threatened, the committees were formally disbanded. Individual Quakers continued to befriend their black neighbors on occasion, but little additional, direct contact came between the Friends as a religious group and the two settlements.[32]

The Wesleyans' retreat from active involvement on racial issues occurred more gradually and over a longer period of time. The Wesleyans originally had separated from the Methodist Episcopal Church because of their antislavery beliefs; after the Civil War the sect continued to stress its radical beliefs in racial equality as part of its effort to maintain an identity separate from the Methodists following slavery's destruction. Throughout the late 1860s and 1870s Wesleyans continued to stress the need for a vigilant defense of blacks' civil liberties in both the North and the South; they were also quick to point to the discriminations still facing black Americans, especially within the Methodist Church. Nonetheless by the end of the 1870s the Wesleyans began to shrink from their advocacy of black rights. Increasingly the religious doctrine of holiness became the group's most distinguishing characteristic, while improved race relations became merely one of several reforms it championed.[33]

Wesleyanism's transformation undoubtedly affected the way whites and blacks worshipped together. Cyrus W. Roberts, a member of the Roberts community who was ordained as a Wesleyan minister in the mid-1870s, became increasingly disgruntled with the sect because of racial slights he encountered while serving Wesleyan congregations throughout Indiana and Ohio. In 1880 Roberts complained to the group's national newspaper, the *American Wesleyan*, that white congregations were reluctant to provide him with financial support because of the color of his skin. "Colored people," he noted, "have poor encouragement to be Wesleyans, not withstanding the foundations of the Wesleyan Church. . . . I like the Wesleyan Church, her rules of government, her reformatory principles, but not her practice." Wesleyan "practice" apparently grew more discriminatory in the 1880s, with black congregations increasingly served by black ministers and white congregations served by whites. The Reverend Roberts watched with frustration as his own opportunities to minister to Wesleyan congregations dwindled with emergence of this new color line. In 1889 he felt compelled to switch his religious affiliations and become a minister in the African Methodist Episcopal Church, "there being so few colored Wesleyans in the North to preach to."[34]

Whether members of the Roberts Wesleyan congregation became as disenchanted with the sect as Cyrus Roberts is a matter open to question. On the surface, at least, relations between the Roberts congregation, nearby white Wesleyans, and white Wesleyan ministers remained warm and strong. Interracial revivals and "protracted meetings" were held at Roberts Chapel on a number of occasions after 1870; the congregation continued to share the services of local white circuit ministers; white ministers from surrounding communities often presided at the funeral services of Roberts residents; and prominent local Wesleyan families such as the Teters, who lived immediately to the west in Boxley, continued to maintain close ties to the community well into the twentieth century. If the Wesleyan's declining commitment to racial equality changed the way white and black co-religionists viewed one another, it did not lead to a dramatic change in the patterns of religious interaction at Roberts Settlement. Some members of the community, like Cyrus Roberts, may have become disenchanted with the Wesleyans, but the congregation as a whole remained steadfastly loyal to the sect, accommodating themselves to an evolving Wesleyan religion rather than abandoning it for the A.M.E. or another African-American denomination.[35]

This sense of accommodation was less a sign of resignation than one of pragmatic compromise. Members of the Roberts Wesleyan congregation realized that they were still accepted on broadly equal terms by surrounding white co-religionists. Despite a declining commitment on racial matters, Wesleyans' views of African Americans generally were more positive than those held by other whites. Relations between Roberts residents and nearby white Wesleyans, moreover, had been forged by common experiences over successive generations. Whites and blacks in the Roberts neighborhood knew and respected one another because of their deep roots in the area, their shared history of abolitionist struggle, and their long-standing commitment to the Wesleyan Church. The Roberts congregation may have been disappointed with the direction of the Wesleyans on racial matters, but withdrawing from the sect altogether would hardly have made matters any better.

This sense of pragmatism was not limited to the Roberts Wesleyan congregation. Beech and Roberts families in general may have decried the changes in the larger world around them, but were nonetheless aware that conditions in their immediate neighborhoods were more hospitable than those in the towns and cities beyond. Signs of racial harmony and goodwill were readily apparent, the erosion of the special bonds with Friends and Wesleyans notwithstanding. Men and women who grew up at Roberts Settlement in the late nineteenth and early twentieth century, for example, later recalled the warmth of their families' ties with surrounding whites during their formative years. White children occasionally attended the Roberts common school, despite the fact that the teachers, along with the majority of students, were African Americans; personal respect for the residents of Roberts Settlement overcame white parents' racial qualms, at least when the alternative was to send their children a mile or so farther down the road. A similar sense of racial cooperation and mutual respect was evident near Beech Settlement when an integrated secondary school was established at Carthage in 1879. At a time when most Indiana whites sought ways to establish or maintain segregated school systems, local residents in Carthage broke down the color barrier by combining village schools that had previously been divided along racial lines.[36]

Another revealing aspect of this decidedly mixed racial dynamic came in the realm of politics. When suffrage rights were extended to black men in the spring of 1870, Beech and Roberts residents quickly joined ranks with the Republicans, the party most closely associated with prosecuting the Civil War, ending slavery, and championing civil rights legislation. "The party that reformed us into citizens will do for us," one Roberts correspondent noted in a letter to a Hamilton County newspaper during the inaugural election campaign. Through the end of the nineteenth century each neighborhood's voters formed a dependable Republican voting block. Beech and Roberts men immersed themselves into the party's internal affairs, actively working to bring out the African-American vote both within their own neighborhoods and in surrounding towns and villages such as Carthage, Knightstown, and Noblesville. Local Republican officials, in turn, regularly selected a number of men from each neighborhood, roughly proportionate to the communities' voting strength, to participate in the party's county and state conventions.[37]

Beech and Roberts farmers' involvement in the electoral process quickly paved the way for tangible political rewards. Four men from the settlements—William Roberts and Elijah Gilliam from the Roberts area, along with William Walden and John Pettiford from the Beech—were elected as constables of their surrounding townships before 1900. A fifth, Beech native John J. Roberts, was chosen by voters to be a justice of the peace for Ripley Township. The significance associated with these victories varied according to one's perspective. From one vantage point they bore testimony to local whites' willingness to vote for black candidates, and to the respect accorded the Beech and Roberts communities. Very few African Americans were elected as constables in the Midwest during the late nineteenth century, and black justices of the peace were even more exceptional. (John J. Roberts, in fact, was reportedly the first black to be elected as a justice of the peace in Indiana.) From another vantage point, however, the amount of power wielded by the successful black candidates was exceedingly small. Constables and justices of the peace presided over law enforcement and judicial matters, but only for minor concerns and only at the village and township levels. At bottom they exerted little influence beyond their own immediate neighborhoods.[38]

When men from Roberts Settlements did try to pursue greater political rewards—when they ran for countywide rather than township-level offices—they quickly found themselves dismissed if not disabused by a large proportion of their fellow Republicans because of their African-American heritage. William P. Roberts addressed this issue in a letter to the editor of the Noblesville *Ledger* in April 1880. Drawing attention to the fact that the area's Republicans had rejected two well-qualified black candidates from Hamilton County in previous primaries, he urged his fellow party members to put aside their prejudices and judge candidates based on their merits rather than their skin color:

> . . . we know of no good reason why colored men who are so competent
> and as worthy as their white neighbors, should not hold office in this

county. We . . . press ourselves upon you: we have supported the Republican party ever since we have had the privilege to do so; we pay taxes just the same as our white neighbors do, and we were compelled to do this even when we had not the right to vote. . . . We helped prosecute the war that saved the government from ruin and disgrace, and that freed our own race from the vile system of slavery, therefore we claim that we have just as good a right to ask for an office, as any other people in America.

We claim that we have as good a right to ask the white man to vote for us as he has to ask us to vote for him. We believe that there are colored men in this county that are capable of filling any office in the county. We have been told by some Republicans in the past that the colored man's time had not yet come that they should ask for office; that we had better hold on for a while. . . . We believe that any man who would object to a man of color holding office, simply because he is colored, is not worthy to be called a Republican.

In his conclusion William Roberts urged voters to give Eli N. Roberts, a well respected Roberts farmer, a fair hearing in his bid to become the party's nominee for the office of Hamilton County recorder of deeds. Only through the latter's nomination, he asserted, would local Republicans "put to silence the charge of the Democrats, who charge upon you the infamous crime of using the colored men as tools to keep you in office and your party in power." The editor of the *Ledger* concurred, noting that Roberts' letter contained "wholesome truths, told in plain and unmistakable language."[39]

William Roberts' observations and counsel hit their mark but had little impact on Hamilton County Republicans as a whole. Instead of rallying behind Eli Roberts, the party's leaders apparently continued to take advantage of their black constituents at every possible turn. A subsequent article in the *Indianapolis World*, a black Republican newspaper, alleged that between 1878 and 1886 Roberts area politicians had fallen victim at whites' hands to primary election chicanery on three separate occasions. In each instance black leaders had agreed to support combined slates of candidates for several county offices in exchange for quid pro quo support for a Roberts-linked candidate for the county recorder's office. In each case Roberts voters fulfilled their part of the bargain, only to have a decisive number of whites withhold their votes for the black candidate. While the *World's* allegations cannot be corroborated fully, they do comport well with published election results. In the closest race involving a Roberts candidate, Eli N. Roberts garnered a majority of the vote in the townships immediately surrounding the farm neighborhood, but lost his supposed political partners' districts by significant margins.[40]

Roberts' seeming betrayal was also in keeping with the broader pattern of black political participation in the North during the late nineteenth century. African Americans were generally welcomed by Republicans with open arms and became an important element in the party's electoral coalition, especially in states like Ohio, where the voting popula-

tion was evenly split between Republicans and Democrats. Political offices
were another matter entirely. Party leaders routinely neglected their black
followers, seldom nominating African Americans for offices more prestigious than constables and providing very few patronage positions. Black
politicians and voters chafed at this mistreatment, much as William Roberts did, but had little recourse other than to abandon the party in favor
of the Democrats. The Republicans' archrivals, for their part, were even
more disdainful towards African Americans and less inclined towards racial amelioration.[41]

In the last analysis, race relations between residents of the two farm
communities and surrounding white neighbors were not entirely of one
cloth after the Civil War. In very important ways Beech and Roberts families were drawn more and more into the affairs of the surrounding world
and forced to accept harsh new realities. Billy Keemer's lynching was a
loathsome incident with a clear message: blacks were not to threaten white
supremacy. It was a message not to be forgotten when visiting friends
or shopping in towns and villages, whether in Arcadia, Knightstown, or
even Carthage. The willingness of Quakers, Wesleyans, and others with
abolitionist leanings to abandon civil rights and to go their own separate
ways also had significant implications. No longer were the ties between
whites and blacks as close as they once had been. Beech and Roberts voters, meanwhile, learned all too well that they had limited political power
beyond their immediate neighborhoods. Yet all of this notwithstanding,
race relations at and near the two farm communities remained less con-
frontational than those throughout the Midwest as a whole. Families at
Roberts Settlement still worshipped in harmony with surrounding white
co-religionists; black and white children attended integrated schools at
and near both settlements; and men from both settlements were repeatedly elected to township-level political offices. African Americans in cities
such as Indianapolis and Chicago were less likely to be accorded even these
limited degrees of respect and equality. The gulf between the relatively
favorable relations experienced at Beech and Roberts settlements, on the
one hand, and midwestern urban settings, on the other, undoubtedly was
closing in the late nineteenth century. Nonetheless the gap still remained,
and families at the farm communities were aware of the resulting advantages afforded by the countryside.

≈ ≈ ≈

In the 1820s and 1830s prospective Beech and Roberts pioneers had faced
a difficult choice: to remain in the Old South, in a familiar but troublesome setting, or to move to the frontier, a land rich with potential but
filled with uncertainty. Two generations later the grandchildren of the
early pioneers confronted a new dilemma, centering once again around
whether to stay or move away. The alternatives were not entirely similar—
nearby cities and towns in the 1880s and 1890s represented a "frontier"

quite unlike that of the antebellum Old Northwest, and deteriorating race relations were a less significant factor in determining individual decisions in the late nineteenth century—but the process was nonetheless extremely difficult and heartrending, much as it had been fifty years or so before. Community elders, especially in the last years of the century, worried that their neighborhoods were coming apart and that none of their children would remain behind to maintain their family farms. Some, like Nathan Rice and Peter Roberts at Roberts Settlement, tried to increase their children's awareness of their distinctive heritage as a means of encouraging them to stay in their native communities. Members of the younger generations weighed their options, meanwhile, considering the pros and cons of remaining or moving on.[42]

Economic considerations, as suggested earlier, undoubtedly played the largest role in determining the decisions of individual community members. Those with limited or no opportunity to acquire farmland tended to leave the settlements, while those with viable holdings almost invariably remained in the countryside and pursued careers as farmers, much as their parents and grandparents had before them. For families in the latter category, the late nineteenth century was often marked by economic stability and gradually improving circumstances. Farmers like Peter Roberts and Nathan Rice in the Roberts neighborhood and James Jeffries at the Beech were able to maintain profitable farm operations throughout the troubled decades that ended the century, acquiring new farm machinery and making improvements through the addition of drainage tile, more secure fencing, and new out-buildings, much in the same fashion as other northern farmers of similar status. The wives and children of such leading farmers grew accustomed to higher standards of living as well. Drafty and cramped log cabins from the pioneer period were replaced by larger, more comfortable frame houses; foot-powered sewing machines, a post–Civil War "luxury," became an essential household machine for many families; and weekly trips to market were now made in fashionable buggies rather than the rough-and-tumble farm wagons of an earlier era. For families like those headed by Peter and Celia Roberts and James and Henrietta Jeffries there was little reason to think of moving to surrounding villages or towns.[43]

Families with marginal prospects, those with farms of 15 to 40 acres, faced a more difficult set of decisions. As small farmholders they could carve out careers in the countryside, but only with considerable effort. The efforts of all family members—fathers, mothers, and children alike—were geared less toward acquiring consumer goods and other middle-class comforts and more toward maintaining a strong degree of self-sufficiency. For male household heads, providing for the family's welfare often meant obtaining a supplementary income, either through renting additional land, working part-time as a farm laborer, or pursuing some other secondary form of employment. John Roberts of the Roberts neighborhood, for example, found it all but impossible to support his family on the 17 acres of land he inherited in the early 1870s. To make ends meet he devoted his spare time to carpentry work, making furniture for surrounding farm families. He was far from alone in dividing his time between two callings. Lon Gilliam from Roberts Settlement split his time focusing on careers as a farmer, an attorney, and a minister; William P. Roberts and other descendants of Hansel Roberts rented out portions of the latter's estate following his death in 1871; and John Tootle of Beech Settlement worked part-time as a barber in nearby Carthage. All were small landholders who, working together with their wives and children, devised successful strategies to enhance their incomes and continue living in the countryside.[44]

Decisions to remain at Beech and Roberts settlements were not determined by economic calculation alone. If they had been, many more of the marginal farmers who clung to their holdings presumably would have sold their acreages and moved on. Yet many hesitated to leave, even when common sense seemed to suggest otherwise. Why did they remain? Little direct evidence exists to explain the motives of the small and landless farmers who stayed at the settlements in the late nineteenth century, but a number of reasons may be suggested. One factor may have been satisfaction with farming as a way of life and/or a reluctance to adapt to the markedly different demands of living and working in cities and towns. Moving to an urban setting would have meant abandoning a distinctive way of life that had been passed down from generation to generation, one that involved working together with family and neighbors to provide much if not most of the goods needed for survival. At once familial, communal, and self-reliant, it was a lifestyle that had little counterpart in cities and towns, where men typically worked for wages and families were more dependent on outside forces. In the late nineteenth century many marginal farmers in the Midwest, white and black alike, apparently resisted making the transition from country to town because of the changes that were involved.[45]

Members of the Beech and Roberts communities may well have valued country living even more than their white neighbors. As farmers they were dependent largely on family and black neighbors for their well-being and encountered only limited economic discrimination because of their race. Collectively the black families in each neighborhood were able to succeed or fail according to their own merits, with little outside interference from whites. If they moved to cities and towns, however, they would confront very different circumstances. Living in urban centers normally meant working for other people, often whites. And it meant having to cope with racial discrimination in the workplace. In the late nineteenth century Midwest, African Americans were shut out of most skilled and professional positions, and the wages paid to blacks were typically lower than those paid to whites for comparable work. Under such circumstances the greater economic independence afforded by farming and rural life may have made them more appealing than they might otherwise have been.[46]

Many Beech and Roberts residents also preferred to remain in the countryside because of the community life in their rural neighborhoods. At the settlements, after all, strong bonds of kinship and common heritage tied residents together. Neighboring families had known one another for decades, if not generations, and routinely relied upon each other for mutual support. Moreover, most members of the Beech and Roberts communities shared a similar cultural background: mixed racial ancestry, a distinctive free black heritage, long-standing ties to the midwestern countryside, strong affiliations with the A.M.E. and Wesleyan churches, and a decidedly middle-class orientation. African Americans in towns and cities like Indianapolis and Richmond, in contrast, often came from quite different backgrounds. Most were southern-born ex-slaves or their children, people from less advantaged backgrounds who had a limited familiarity with northern culture and customs.[47]

Beech and Roberts settlements were also special, at least in the eyes of some residents, because of the strength of the neighborhoods' social institutions and organized social activities. The economic and demographic "decline" of the neighborhoods notwithstanding, area churches and schools continued to receive strong support through the late nineteenth century. Scattered bits of evidence also indicate that Beech and Roberts residents gathered on church lawns and in meetinghouses and classrooms for many of the social activities common to most midwestern rural neighborhoods: religious revivals and protracted meetings, temperance rallies, school programs and recitals, performances by neighborhood singing quartets, and the like. These special get-togethers served to reinforce a shared set of social and moral values, and to instill a sense that each settlement was distinctive if not unique.[48]

One of the most important sources of community pride in the late nineteenth century came through the educational opportunities and achievements of Beech and Roberts residents. Public funding for the schooling of black children after the mid-1860s made it possible to place schools at both locations on a more secure footing, ending the need for outside assistance from surrounding whites and opening up access to children whose parents might otherwise have been unable to pay private tuition fees. Control of the neighborhood schools remained firmly in the hands of local parents, as was true in all rural school districts, and Beech and Roberts residents apparently used that power judiciously. Teachers at the schools continued to come largely from the ranks of community members, as in the antebellum era, but the quality of the teachers' formal training improved, in keeping with state-mandated reforms. The length of the school year, meanwhile, was more than doubled at both locations, from two to three months in 1860 to six to eight months by the end of the century.[49]

Beech and Roberts parents could justifiably point out that the educational opportunities available to their children were as good as, if not better than, those afforded in other black communities throughout the

Midwest. Several of the settlements' teachers were extremely able educators, individuals whose abilities were recognized far beyond their native communities. Three of the most popular instructors—Robert A. Roberts (Beech), Louise Watkins Holbert (Beech), and Adora Knight (Roberts)—eventually left the settlements to pursue successful teaching careers at all-black schools in various Midwestern cities and towns. Other instructors were men and women of exceptional abilities who would later gain prominence as professionals in fields aside from education—men like Ira Roberts (Beech) and Lon Gilliam (Roberts), who became lawyers, and women like Martha Harris McCurdy (Beech), a southern missionary and temperance advocate.[50]

Armed with a solid common school education, a significant number of Beech and Roberts students went on to complete course work at the high school and college levels. Local histories indicate that no fewer than a dozen men and women from the two settlements graduated from surrounding high schools in the late nineteenth century, an accomplishment of considerable distinction at a time when only a small proportion of prospective students, black or white, attended any school beyond the elementary level. Even more impressive were the ranks of those who attended—and graduated from—colleges and professional schools throughout the Midwest. Roberts Settlement families could point to at least six local residents who completed post-secondary degrees between 1870 and 1900, including Marcus Gilliam, an early graduate from Valparaiso College; Adora Knight (Indiana Normal College); Ezra Roberts (Butler College); Dolphin Roberts (National Medical College); and Almary Wallace (Wilberforce College). Less is known about Beech residents coming of age in the late nineteenth century, although at least one, Theron Watkins, attended Indiana University.[51]

≈ ≈ ≈

Unquestionably, life at Beech and Roberts settlements had its advantages in the late nineteenth century. Residents found a special sense of place and identity in their country neighborhoods: they knew each other and each other's families intimately, continued to get along peacefully with surrounding white neighbors, and took exceptional pride in their schools and churches. Some, like the Nathan Rice family in the Roberts area, even prospered financially. For most of those coming of age in the late nineteenth century, however, these advantages were more than offset by other, more pressing concerns. Close personal ties, after all, could not put food on the table or provide a secure future for their children. With little opportunity to acquire farmland of their own, and with the demand for farm laborers in their own immediate neighborhoods on the wane, many felt that they had little choice but to leave their homes and seek their fortunes elsewhere. The countryside could simply not support all who wished to remain.

While farming was becoming a more difficult calling in the late nine-teenth century, opportunities to find work in nearby villages and towns were generally expanding. The discovery of a large natural gas field under much of central Indiana in the mid-1880s triggered a period of rapid ur-ban growth and industrialization that would last well into the next cen-tury. Glass, tinplating, and strawboard factories sprang up seemingly over-night in communities of all sizes, creating bustling urban centers out of market towns like Anderson, Kokomo, and Marion while bringing in-stant prosperity to smaller villages such as Cicero, Fairmount, and Elwood. Many of the most dynamic communities were located within short dis-tances of Beech and Roberts settlements. Kokomo, for example, could be reached within a few hours from the Roberts neighborhood, while Ander-son, Muncie, and a host of other cities were readily accessible by train from the Beech. Additional work opportunities, meanwhile, were avail-able in nearby towns and villages that were expanding to meet an increased demand for the farm marketing facilities, consumer goods, and other ser-vices they provided. Carthage, Westfield, Noblesville and other market-ing towns did not grow as rapidly as their gas boom neighbors but ex-panded nonetheless, offering employment for hundreds of new residents each year.[52]

Beech and Roberts residents, especially those who were young and con-fronted with limited prospects in the countryside, undoubtedly watched the rise of new businesses, factories, and homes in surrounding urban cen-ters with mixed feelings. On the one hand, as noted earlier, they had con-siderable reason to be skeptical about the extent to which they would ben-efit by moving to a nearby town or village. The color line was sharply drawn in Indiana during the late nineteenth century, and there was good reason to wonder how they would fare in a small town like Noblesville or a larger one like Anderson. They knew, for example, that there was little hope of landing work as a skilled worker in one of the new glass or straw-board factories; those positions were for whites only. Nor, for that matter, was there any realistic hope of finding work in a variety of other areas from which blacks were either barred or strongly discouraged. Nonetheless work was plentiful and, racial animosities notwithstanding, it was not difficult to find unskilled work as a teamster, domestic, or laborer. For those unable or unwilling to make a go of life in the countryside, there was at least the possibility of a more secure future.

The rapid growth of towns and cities throughout central Indiana also brought with it the rise of larger black urban communities, another fac-tor that increased the attractiveness of such locations. As places like Mun-cie and Kokomo doubled and trebled in size during the final decades of the nineteenth century, the numbers of African Americans living within their boundaries increased at a pace often equaling or exceeding that of the population overall. Such growth meant that towns which formerly had only a handful of black families now had dozens, if not hundreds of families, thus providing the basis for a much more expansive and dynamic community life. Towns like Marion, Kokomo, and Anderson offered their black residents the opportunity to pick and choose among competing churches, fraternal lodges, baseball teams, and other social groups in determining how to spend their leisure time. The lure of such communities must have grown especially appealing to Beech and Roberts residents as the turn of the century approached. While the social opportunities in their immediate neighborhoods diminished with the out-migration of local residents, those in surrounding urban centers only seemed to expand and become more diverse.[53]

Even concerns about the cultural and social differences between Beech and Roberts members, on the one hand, and other African Americans in nearby cities and towns, on the other, could not dampen the appeal of black urban community life. Whatever hesitancy the settlements' residents had about living in other black communities, in fact, seems to have subsided over time. In part concerns and doubts may have subsided because of the increasing influx of blacks from the Beech, Roberts and other rural areas of Indiana into towns like Kokomo and Anderson. As the number of newcomers from the countryside grew, it was possible to find others who shared a common background and outlook. By the end of the nineteenth century younger immigrants from the settlements, at the same time, harbored fewer reservations about moving to cities and becoming a part of communities with people from diverse settings. Having grown up in the countryside during hard times, they were less enamored with rural life and more willing to accept that their fate and those of southern-born blacks were intertwined.[54]

With both the drawbacks of country living and the attractions of urban living mounting, the process of out-migration from Beech and Roberts settlements accelerated over the course of the late nineteenth century. Watching their neighbors move on, certainly, was not a new phenomenon to residents of either community. From the very first days each area had had its share of transient and mobile families. Before the Civil War, however, out-migration had been more limited and selective, especially in the Roberts neighborhood. Those who had left had generally been either landless people without deep ties to the settlements or younger families seeking better farm lands at lower prices. Now the exodus became widespread, included the vast majority of both settlements' residents, and was more urban in direction. Moreover, as the tempo of out-migration picked up after the 1870s it seems to have encouraged even those with viable futures in the country to consider the prospects of moving away.[55]

Tracing the fate of Beech and Roberts settlement residents once they left their countryside homes is a difficult task. Out-migrants chose new homes in literally dozens of locations, often nearby but occasionally in such faraway places as California, New York, Florida, and Canada. Many settled in more than one new setting, staying briefly at one community

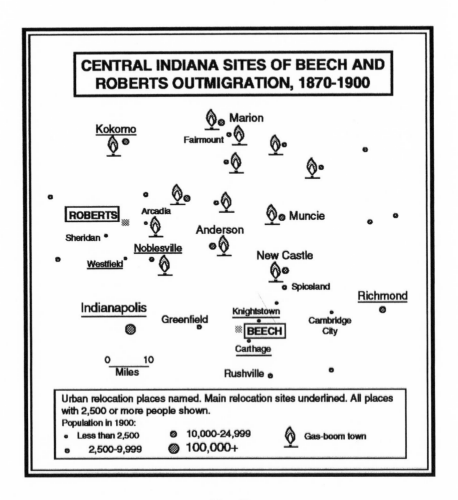

CENTRAL INDIANA SITES OF BEECH AND ROBERTS OUTMIGRATION, 1870-1900

Marion

Kokomo

Fairmount

ROBERTS

Arcadia

Sheridan

Anderson

Muncie

Noblesville

Westfield

New Castle

Spiceland

Indianapolis

Richmond

Greenfield

Knightstown

Cambridge City

BEECH

Carthage

0   10
Miles

Rushville

Urban relocation places named. Main relocation sites underlined. All places with 2,500 or more people shown.
Population in 1900:
- Less than 2,500
- 2,500-9,999
⊘ 10,000-24,999
◉ 100,000+
🔥 Gas-boom town

Map 12

before moving to one or more additional locations. This "scattering of the tribes" makes it virtually impossible to follow and assess the circumstances of all or even most former residents as they made their ways in the world beyond. Significant lapses in census manuscripts during the late nineteenth century compound the problem even further. Nonetheless, genealogies, local histories, and available census records provide glimpses into the lives of almost two hundred residents who left the black neighborhoods between 1870 and 1900. Information on this sizable minority, perhaps totaling one-third to one-half of those who departed, sheds considerable light onto the out-migration process and its consequences.[56]

Most of the traceable group migrated only a short distance from their former homes, thus avoiding the prospect of completely severing ties with longtime friends and relatives (see Map 12). Fully one-half resettled at least initially within ten miles or so from their old neighborhoods. Ex-Beech residents often relocated in Carthage and Knightstown, both within five miles of the Beech neighborhood, while ex-Roberts residents frequently resettled in Noblesville and Westfield, both within ten miles of the Roberts vicinity. Many others moved farther away, either to bustling gas boom towns or to other emerging cities throughout central Indiana, but they, too, tended to be attracted to locations that were easily accessible from the settlements. A large number of Roberts natives migrated to Kokomo and Indianapolis, both of which were located on a major north-south thoroughfare which cut through settlement lands. Several members of the Beech community chose to move to Indianapolis, Richmond, and other points along the National Road, located a few miles to the north. Continuously upgraded and expanded railroad service made all of these cities, along with Muncie, Anderson, and others in the area, seem even closer—and more attractive as destinations—as the century came to an end.[57]

In a variety of ways migrating to nearby cities and towns allowed former settlement members to adjust more gradually to life beyond the countryside than might otherwise have been possible. Out-migrants were able to remain in touch with family and friends back in their former neighborhoods. Beech natives in Knightstown and Carthage, for example, could conveniently return to visit with those left behind or, conversely, invite old friends and relatives to join them for brief stays in their new homes. Such visiting patterns, common to the rural Midwest in the late nineteenth century, could last for several days or even weeks at a stretch. Ex-settlement members also benefited from the focused nature of much of their out-migration. Because they resettled in a few select locations, many if not most continued to reside near kin or neighbors from their former communities. Members of the Roberts, Winburn, White, and Sweat families, for example, often migrated from the Roberts neighborhood to Noblesville, where they lived in one of the town's two "colored sections"—Federal Hill, on the northwestern outskirts, or the south side. While joining in a new community life that included African Americans from diverse backgrounds, they nonetheless participated in social activities with many people from the Roberts area, attending the same churches, joining the same fraternal lodges, and sending their children to the same schools. Similar patterns undoubtedly could be found among ex-Beech and Roberts residents in towns and villages such as Kokomo, Westfield, Carthage, and Knightstown. Former residents left the countryside but did not abandon the personal lives they had developed there.[58]

A small number of former settlement members maintained ties with the past in another way. Through various means they found work as farmers, either as farm laborers, farm tenants, or farm owners. A few actually went further west or north in search of opportunities to acquire less expensive lands. Bradford Jeffries of the Beech, for example, moved to Cass

County, Michigan during the 1870s to take up farming with older siblings who had migrated to the area a decade or so earlier. More common, however, were landless farmers who sought work as tenants or laborers in surrounding farm regions. Some were members of long established families who were reluctant to abandon farm work, even after the prospects in their immediate neighborhood had turned sour. John and Olive Sweat, for instance, had raised a large family at Roberts before losing their small homestead in the 1870s; a short time later they moved several miles south and began renting a farm in adjoining Washington Township, apparently hoping to gain a fresh start in a new location. Others, typically younger residents who were either single or recently married, pursued brief careers as farmhands or tenants before settling into more permanent, urban occupations. Many found farm laboring positions on the fringes of small towns such as Carthage, Knightstown, and Noblesville, apparently supplementing farm work with casual jobs as laborers during slack times.[59]

Increasingly, however, those trying to make a living off the countryside proved to be the exceptions rather than the rule. The future lay in the towns and cities surrounding Beech and Roberts settlements, and most of those coming of age in the late nineteenth century were compelled to find urban callings. The fate of ex-residents in adjusting to the demands of work beyond their rural neighborhoods varied tremendously. A large and impressive number made the transition with more than a small measure of success. Several men and women from the settlements carved out enviable careers as African-American professional and business leaders in cities and towns throughout the Midwest, capitalizing on the steady growth of the black urban population throughout the region; a small number rose to regional and/or national prominence. Many more, at the same time, experienced considerable difficulty in finding anything other than unskilled work.

Dolphin P. Roberts of the Roberts neighborhood exemplified the good fortune that came to many Beech and Roberts natives in the post–Civil War era. The son of pioneer landowners Elias and Mariah Roberts, Dolphin first attended Westfield High School and Spiceland Academy, schools taught by Quakers and Wesleyans, respectively, in the 1870s. Following his graduation he pursued a career as a minister, first joining the ranks of the Wesleyan clergy in 1876, then switching his affiliation to the A.M.E. denomination a few years later. His decision to join the A.M.E. proved extremely fortunate, for the influence and prestige of the denomination steadily increased as the Midwest's black population expanded over the course of the late nineteenth and twentieth centuries. Articulate, handsome, and well versed in the middle-class culture of his native region, Roberts soon gained a reputation as a popular, no-nonsense minister. Assigned to prominent churches in Chicago, Indianapolis, and other midwestern cities, he repeatedly proved his abilities to manage all aspects of his congregations' needs; under his guidance nearly a thousand individuals were baptized, several church mortgages were canceled, and the civil rights of black people were consistently championed. Like many other black ministers Roberts became a political as well as a spiritual leader. During the presidential administration of Benjamin Harrison he served as Recorder of the General Land Office of the United States, reportedly the highest patronage position held by an African American at the time.[60]

As Table 18 indicates, Dolphin Roberts' career was distinctive but not altogether exceptional when compared with the careers of other Beech and Roberts residents. Nearly two dozen men and women—roughly a tenth of the entire group who came of age at the settlements between 1870 and 1900—rose to prominence as successful professionals and entrepreneurs. A small number gained regional if not national recognition. Cyrus W. and Junius B. Roberts, perhaps most notably, established careers as nationally known A.M.E. ministers, much in the same fashion as Dolphin. Others gained prominence in African-American communities closer to home, serving as ministers, teachers, and business leaders in cities and towns such as Terre Haute and Indianapolis. The success of so many Beech and Roberts natives is especially striking when compared to the fate of black workers generally during the late nineteenth century. In cities such as Boston, Cincinnati, and Evansville, professionals and entrepreneurs represented only a small fragment of the black work force, typically 2 to 3 percent of all men and women who were gainfully employed.[61]

Beech and Roberts natives apparently were better able to make the transition to urban careers because of advantages they had acquired before leaving the countryside. Virtually all had grown up in stable, if not prosperous, families and had been imbued with strong middle-class values. Working day in and day out with their parents and kin on family holdings, and worshipping alongside family members at church meetings, they adhered strongly to the beliefs associated with the Protestant ethic, the values of self-help, hard work, thrift, diligence, and perseverance. Many if not most also had benefited from educational opportunities that were relatively advanced by the standards of the day. As noted earlier, several individuals from each of the settlements had attended local high schools, colleges, and professional schools. Thus, like Dolphin Roberts, many Beech and Roberts residents set out in the world with the values, skills, and background that would enable them to get ahead economically and socially in urban settings.[62]

With or without these advantages, the opportunities available to former settlement residents were shaped and frequently constrained by their status as African Americans. Because they were black, the doors of many professions and skilled occupations were either closed entirely or, at best, opened only part way. Whites were unwilling to countenance or support blacks in high status positions where blacks, not whites, would be in a position of unchallenged authority. Thus Roberts and Beech natives had little hope of establishing careers as bankers, lawyers, or doctors unless

TABLE 18

Prominent Individuals Raised at Beech
and Roberts Settlements in the Late Nineteenth Century

Name	Birth-date	Birth-place	Principal occupation(s)	Parent's status
Alonzo Gilliam	1872	RS	lawyer; minister	small landowners
John Gilliam	1857	RS	teacher	small landowners
Marcus Gilliam	1867	RS	teacher; principal	small landowners
Louise Watkins Holbert	1869	BS	teacher	small landowners
Raymond McDuffey	1873	BS	minister	small landowners
Cyrus Roberts	1848	RS	minister	small landowners
Daniel Roberts	1866	BS	physician	small landowners
Dolphin Roberts	1856	RS	minister	large landowners
Frank Roberts	1863	RS	minister	small landowners
Ira Roberts	1854	RS	teacher; lawyer	large landowners
Junius Roberts	1840	RS	minister	small landowners
Robert Roberts	1862	BS	teacher; principal	small landowners
Stephen Roberts	1848	RS	livestock dealer	small landowners
William Tootle	1840	BS	minister	small landowners
John Watkins	1873	BS	mortician	small landowners
Joseph Watkins	1856	BS	mortician	small landowners
Theron Watkins	1877	BS	mortician	small landowners
George Winburn	1851	BS	teacher	small landowners

Sources: Census manuscripts; Lawrence Carter; Edgar Conkling; obituaries; estate records.

Note: Included are only those who were born and raised at Beech and/or Roberts settlements during the late nineteenth century. Excluded are those who were born at other locations, those who were born at the settlements before 1840 or after 1880, and those who were born at the settlements but raised primarily in other locations.

Several former residents rose to prominence but do not meet the above criteria. Included in this group are Ezra Roberts, head of the Education Department at Tuskegee Institute; Edgar Keemer, a pharmacist and faculty member at Howard University; and Adora Knight, principal of a Terre Haute school.

their customers, clients, and patrons were largely, if not exclusively, African Americans. Those few former residents who challenged the color line on such matters faced considerable difficulties. Lon Gilliam from Roberts Settlement, for example, established an interracial law practice in nearby Arcadia, but failed to achieve the strong base of support that he might have achieved had he been white; eventually he abandoned law and became a Wesleyan minister, serving as a missionary to black Wesleyans in Alabama and Tennessee. Even greater obstacles were placed in the path of Roberts natives Benjamin and Amy (Roberts) Sweat. After opening a boarding house in Fairmount, a gas boom town near Marion, they became victims of arsonists who burned their building in an attempt to drive them away.[63]

Faced with such barriers most of the advantaged ex-residents chose to pursue professional or business careers that did not violate the norms of racial etiquette. The few who did business directly with whites did so in an accommodating fashion. Stephen Roberts of Roberts Settlement, for example, became one of Hamilton County's most respected and widely known livestock dealers, but he also operated his business in partnership with Sam Craig, Marion Aldred, and other whites, a fact that apparently minimized his exposure to any sort of white backlash. Others established businesses that were acceptable to whites, such as barber shops, or concentrated their efforts in business ventures within black neighborhoods. Among the most successful former Beech residents in the late nineteenth century were Theron, Joseph, and Burney Watkins, three brothers who operated a thriving undertaking establishment in Kansas City, Missouri; their patrons came largely, if not exclusively, from the surrounding black community.[64]

Most of the prominent Beech and Roberts natives chose to pursue careers as teachers and ministers. The decision to enter these fields was an easy and obvious one for many former residents. For generations their elders and ancestors had placed a high value on religion and education; piety and a thirst for learning had been inculcated from an early age, providing many with both the inclination and the ability to pursue such vocations. Other, more practical concerns also made professional careers in education and religion attractive. Ministers and teachers formed the bulk of the black professional class in the late nineteenth century and were among the most highly regarded members of African-American communities. Moreover, opportunities in both areas were steadily expanding as the size of the Midwest's black population increased over time. Well qualified and inclined toward careers in religion and education, ex-residents often found the move from farms to pulpits and schoolrooms an extremely appealing option.[65]

Despite the success of so many Beech and Roberts natives in the late nineteenth century, their fates were by no means typical of all, or even most, of those who departed the settlements for cities and towns. A large majority did not join the ranks of business people and professionals, but instead found themselves shunted into jobs involving limited skills, low pay, and little chance for advancement. The common experiences of most Beech and Roberts natives—perhaps two-thirds or more of all who migrated to urban settings—are suggested by the fates of Peterson Hunt, Thornton Parker, and Phariba Page. Hunt, the son of Beech pioneer Goodwin Hunt, pursued several callings in the late nineteenth century, working as a Ripley Township farm tenant and farm laborer before finally resettling in Carthage, where he became a teamster, apparently hauling goods for local merchants. Parker, who married Flavella Roberts, the daughter of a landless Roberts farmer in the late 1860s, worked for a brief time as a farm laborer in the Roberts area before migrating with his family to Kokomo between 1870 and 1880; leaving farm work behind, he accepted work as a church janitor. Page, the wife of Beech farm renter George Page in 1880, migrated to Noblesville and took up washing and ironing work after she and her husband separated. In 1900, census records indicate, she also supplemented her meager income by taking in other African Americans as boarders.[66]

As the lives of these three individuals suggest, those who were forced into menial work often came from humble if not impoverished backgrounds. Some, like Peterson Hunt, were the sons and daughters of farmers with holdings of 40 acres or less; others, like Thornton Parker and Phariba Page, came from landless farm families. With fewer material, educational, and cultural advantages than their more prosperous Beech and Roberts neighbors, they were much less likely to be able to move into the ranks of the small class of black professionals and business owners. And, because of their limited advantages, they were much more likely to face the pervasive occupational discrimination that confronted African Americans in the North during the late nineteenth century. Denied the opportunity to work at many callings—government patronage positions, retail sales, the construction trades, skilled factory work, and other jobs were often if not always off limits to blacks—most could find work only in positions involving unskilled labor and/or personal or domestic service. Whether in nearby Carthage and Westfield or in faraway Terre Haute and South Bend, ex-residents were forced to take jobs as day laborers, teamsters, whitewashers, hod carriers, janitors, household servants, and washerwomen.[67]

While the lives of ex-residents were shaped adversely by exclusionary employment opportunities, the impact of the disadvantages on particular individuals and families varied significantly. Some with menial jobs struggled merely to make ends meet. Like much of the black working class in midwestern cities and towns, they found it difficult if not impossible to acquire the basic comforts and security shared by middle-class Americans. While they might aspire to decent wages that would allow their families to get by on a single income and to purchase their own homes, the reality of their existence was something quite different. Everyday life required an unusual degree of resourcefulness and frequently an extra income or two. Some resorted to taking in boarders to stretch their wages; the case of Phariba Page, noted earlier, was hardly exceptional. In other households both husband and wife had to work. Roberts natives Albert and Lucy Gilliam, for example, combined his income as a hod carrier with hers as washerwoman when they moved to Noblesville. Still other families apparently depended upon the paychecks of teenage or young adult children who still resided at home and worked part- or full-time as servants or laborers.[68]

Not all families headed by ex-Beech and Roberts residents faced such difficult straits. A significant number, including many of those confined to low-paying jobs, succeeded in achieving varying degrees of financial comfort and security. Most of those who resettled in the small villages and towns of Hamilton and Rush counties, for one thing, managed to meet their families' needs on one income alone; in 1900 roughly four-fifths of the ex-Beech and Roberts householders reported to census enumerators that their households included only a single wage earner. Thus, in most instances, families were able to get by on the pay brought home by the family head alone. Perhaps even more tellingly, half of the householders also reported owning their own homes, an impressive achievement when compared to the ownership rates of all Indiana householders (45 percent) and all Indiana black householders (28 percent). Whether this success in obtaining homes reflects the low costs of housing in small towns, the work ethic and middle-class values of former residents, or favorable work prospects for blacks in central Indiana towns is uncertain; all three factors together may well offer the best explanation. What *is* clear is that economic exclusion and discrimination did not deter all, or even most, Beech and Roberts natives from making some tangible headway in the world beyond their native settlements.[69]

Nor were the limited opportunities associated with domestic and unskilled work necessarily passed on from one generation to the next. Many members of the second generation enjoyed some measure of upward occupational mobility, either joining the ranks of the black professional class or moving into more promising positions as postal workers, business clerks, and the like. Although they were the sons and daughters of domestics and day laborers, a significant number were given the opportunity to pursue an advanced education and, occasionally, professional training. Benefiting from their parents' sacrifices and their own sense of determination, several went on to establish outstanding careers of their own. Edgar Keemer, for example, the son of a Carthage laborer, became head of the pharmacy department at Howard University; Ezra Roberts, the son of a Kokomo carpenter, served as head of the education department at Tuskegee Institute; Irvin Armstrong, son of a Westfield laborer, became a prominent Indianapolis schoolteacher; and Martha McCurdy, daughter of a Carthage blacksmith, worked as a southern missionary and temperance advocate. For some, at least, the values passed down from one generation to the next, from the countryside to the cities and towns of the Midwest, acted as a stimulus that even the color line could not deter.[70]

≈ ≈ ≈

A final, elusive aspect of the two neighborhoods' late nineteenth century evolution involved light-skinned residents "passing" into the ranks of whites. Passing was far from new at the time. Throughout America's long and troubled history of race relations the greater opportunities, rights, and privileges associated with "whiteness" had always served as a lure for those with fair skins and Caucasian features to present themselves as white. At times individuals passed on a selective or intermittent basis in order to gain a specific advantage or access that otherwise would have been denied them. A person like Macklin Jeffries, for example, might "go for white" when traveling to towns and cities beyond the immediate Beech vicinity as a means of gaining access to meals, a place to stay, or travel accommodations that would otherwise have been prohibited. Others chose to pass permanently, in effect abandoning their non-white ancestry completely in an attempt to gain the full advantages accorded to whites. Decisions to take on a white identity full time were not taken lightly, as they usually involved severing ties with family and friends and moving away.[71]

In the late nineteenth century the temptations of passing permanently grew considerably stronger than ever before. The higher status traditionally accorded to mulattoes relative to dark-skinned African Americans eroded, as whites increasingly came to view all blacks as part of a single group; and the social and economic racial barriers confronting all African Americans became much stronger and more rigid as the color line was extended in a number of new directions. Faced with such deteriorating circumstances, the numbers who chose to pass as whites apparently reached their highest proportions between roughly 1880 and 1925. Civil rights leader Walter White later estimated that 12,000 individuals quietly assumed white identities each year. Those attempting to pass came from both the North and the South, rural as well as urban settings, and from all classes of black society. A significant number came from families that had once been prominent leaders in their African-American communities.[72]

Notwithstanding a discreet, secretive nature that makes it difficult to trace, passing appears to have followed a similar course in the Beech and Roberts neighborhoods. Efforts to take on white identities both intermittently and permanently seemingly became more common as the future of farming became more circumscribed, the relatively favorable position of mixed-race people declined, and the opportunities afforded to African Americans in northern cities grew more restrictive. At least a small number of residents seized on the chance afforded by their lighter skin color to attend colleges and professional training schools that would otherwise have been off-limits. Others discreetly chose to keep their mixed racial heritage "under their hats" in order to pursue career paths and professional appointments that were ostensibly available to whites alone.[73]

Many if not most of those choosing to pass permanently came from the ranks of Beech and Roberts settlements' most prominent families. Two of Macklin and Mary Jeffries' children at the Beech, for example, chose white marriage partners from areas well beyond the Beech, in neighboring Hancock County. After their marriages they relocated in those vicinities, apparently limiting their ties to their native community. Similarly, several of Walker and Azariah Jeffries' children reportedly "went away and became white." In the Roberts neighborhood, the son of Elias and Mariah Roberts emigrated to Iowa, passed as white, and became a successful judge. All had grown up in farm families with holdings in excess of 200 acres during their youth.[74]

In order to place the matter of passing among Beech and Roberts residents in a balanced perspective, two points deserve emphasis. One is to note again that passing was at its height in the late nineteenth and early twentieth centuries and that the two farm settlements' experience was far from exceptional. W. E. B. DuBois commented on a similar pattern at a mixed-race community in Darke County, Ohio that he visited in the early twentieth century. According to DuBois, fifteen men from the area had married local white women and gone away to establish new identities. Historian James DeVries has also noted that passing was common in a small Michigan town at this same time. Second, passing ultimately was a restricted phenomenon affecting settlements' overall development in only limited ways. Passing was but one option among several that were available to light-skinned Beech and Roberts residents in the late nineteenth century. While many chose to pass, far more cast their lot with those identified as African American. The most common paths to success, in fact, involved serving the larger black community as ministers and educators.[75]

DuBois admiringly noted the collective consciousness among those he met at Darke:

> Fully half of them tomorrow could lose themselves among their white neighbors and never be suspected of black blood. Yet they keep themselves aloof, quiet and loyal, refusing to associate with anyone who cannot associate with their friends and relatives. Beneath the placid beauty of their fields run the waters of bitterness, but it cannot spoil their cherished past.[76]

Much the same can be said of those at Beech and Roberts settlements.

᠗ ᠗ ᠗

Northern African Americans faced an increasingly hostile world as the nineteenth century came to a close. Lynchings and racial violence, segregation in schools and other public settings, and exclusionary job practices all became more commonplace in the 1880s and 1890s. In many respects the doors of opportunity were closing, not opening for blacks in the region. Unfortunately for Beech and Roberts residents, these changes for the worse occurred as their destinies were becoming more closely associated with those of other northern African Americans. The neighborhoods had long benefited from their "specialness," an amalgam of the social and economic independence derived from land ownership, positive relations with nearby whites, and the greater isolation of rural life. As the twentieth century approached that specialness remained, but in an attenuated form. Farm prospects were eroding, ties with local whites were becoming less exceptional, and the gulf between town and country was narrowing.

The relative advantages afforded by Beech and Roberts settlements nonetheless persisted. A small if diminished number of families remained in the countryside and operated their own farms largely free from outside interference. Couples like Nathan and Mary Rice remained largely self-reliant, enjoyed good relations with neighboring white families, and provided their children with the type of educational and religious background they desired. Theirs was a world which, while not free of racial barriers, was certainly less troubled than that of most black Americans. Perhaps even more significantly, Beech and Roberts settlements provided those who did emigrate with an upbringing that enhanced their chances of success in the world beyond their rural neighborhoods. Former residents in disproportionate numbers were able to move into the ranks of the black middle class, usually as teachers and ministers. Others were forced to accept menial jobs but managed to acquire their own homes and help their children move ahead. Long after their residents departed the countryside, the advantages of having been raised at Beech and Roberts settlements remained.

Conclusion

Growing up at Roberts Settlement at the turn of the twentieth century, Carl G. Roberts had little desire to remain in the countryside. His parents, John and Nancy Roberts, owned a modest, 25-acre farm and constantly struggled to make ends meet. Carl himself, born in 1886 in the midst of depression, set his sights early on leaving the settlement to pursue a career as a doctor. His father tried to convince him otherwise, hoping that his youngest son would remain and take over the reins of the family claim. Neither John's pleadings nor improved farm conditions beginning in the late 1890s, however, could deter Carl from his goals. Running away to his sister's home in Fairmount, Indiana at the age of thirteen, he escaped the difficulties of a small farmer's life and pursued his own seemingly more modern ambitions. Ultimately he became a prominent Chicago gynecologist, one of the first blacks elected to the American College of Surgeons, and a president of the black National Medical Association.[1]

Scores of Beech and Roberts residents maturing after 1900 shared Carl Roberts' belief that their fortunes lay beyond the countryside. Outmigration from both settlements continued, even though the economic doldrums of the late nineteenth century gave way to a period of improving agricultural opportunities through World War I. At the Beech settlement less than a half dozen families remained by the mid-1920s. None had the resources needed to remain competitive as the scale and costs associated with commercial agriculture continued to expand. The last remaining African American farming in Ripley Township, Sanford Hill, passed away in 1955. Conditions were somewhat more promising in the Roberts neighborhood, where several hundred acres of land remained in the hands of mixed-race families through the end of the twentieth century. The number of owners actively working their own land, however, dwindled to less than a dozen by the early 1930s, remained more or less stable for a generation, then declined still further in the 1960s. Only a handful held farms with 80 acres or more at any time after 1920.[2]

The ongoing exodus, in turn, served to undermine the rural neighborhoods' schools and churches, the long-standing social institutions that had long been responsible for so much of Beech and Roberts' pride and identity. Change came first and most abruptly at the Beech. Both the neighborhood's school, known in later years as Ripley Township School #3, and its original church, Mount Pleasant A.M.E., apparently closed their doors between 1900 and 1910. The Beech's proximity to Carthage, which was home to two black churches and a larger elementary school that welcomed black students, may have hastened their demise. Regardless, without the centers of its community life, the Beech neighborhood became a mere shadow of its former self.[3]

Roberts Settlement experienced a more gradual decline. The Roberts school, Jackson Township School #5, fell victim to declining enrollments and the rural school consolidation movement in 1915. Local students attended schools two miles from the neighborhood center during the following decade, then were bused even further during the period thereafter. The Roberts church, meanwhile, experienced a prolonged decline in membership that made it ever more difficult to meet the financial obligations associated with inclusion in the Wesleyan Methodist Church. In the late 1930s the congregation withdrew from its local Wesleyan circuit; an almost 100-year tradition of sharing quarterly meetings with surrounding white Wesleyan congregations came to an end. The Roberts Church continued to meet, but was forced to scramble to find ministerial guidance. Over the next fifty years the community would draw its spiritual leaders from its own lay members, various Wesleyan and A.M.E. ministers, and divinity students from Anderson College, an institution associated with the Church of God.[4]

As the communities' dissolution continued, current and former residents continued to maintain close ties with one another. With the dawn of the age of the automobile, in fact, visits between those in the black neighborhoods and their relatives in surrounding cities and towns may well have become more, not less frequent. Jeanetta Gilliam Duvall, who grew up at Roberts Settlement in the 1920s and 1930s, later recalled such exchanges as an integral part of community life. Her family often traveled on weekends to Noblesville, combining errands together with social calls and attendance at local black churches with her Roberts kin. Relatives from Noblesville, Kokomo, and Indianapolis, in turn, often made weekend excursions of their own to Roberts Settlement. Funerals and annual revivals also served to draw back those who had moved to surrounding cities and towns. Similar patterns of visiting prevailed at the Beech as well.[5]

❦ ❦ ❦

Ironically, the closing of Beech and Roberts settlements' most dynamic period in the early twentieth century opened the door to a second phase in the communities' histories, one that has now proven even longer lived than the first. As the "golden era" of the neighborhoods receded into the more distant past, and as increasing numbers of native sons and daughters were immersed in the mainstream of northern, urban African-American life, current and former residents alike became increasingly aware of the neighborhoods' exceptional character and history. This heightened awareness, in turn, led to ongoing efforts to maintain, preserve, and cultivate the memory of the Beech and Roberts communities. The centerpiece of these efforts became (and remains) annual homecoming reunions. Dozens of families gathered each year at the site of the settlements' churches to reminisce, share picnic meals, pray together, and honor their common heritage. Stimulated in part by the homecomings, several descendants also began to collect information concerning their families' and communities' histories, and to seek ways to preserve the material culture associated with the two neighborhoods. These combined developments have created an ongoing "renascence" with an influence that goes well beyond the settlements' immediate surroundings.

As the permanence of the communities' decline became apparent, family homecomings were established in both locations then grew in structure and attendance over the next several decades. At the Beech the first homecoming occurred in 1904, about the time that the neighborhood's school and church closed. Other "basket meetings" convened over the following the ten to fifteen years, and the affair became an annual get-together held the last Sunday in August. Roberts Settlement's homecoming developed somewhat differently, reflecting the more drawn-out nature of that neighborhood's downturn. First an annual reunion developed in Noblesville among the combined members of the Roberts and Winburn families living there, perhaps as early as the 1890s. Then, on July 4, 1924, the first formal homecoming at Roberts Settlement itself was celebrated. The event subsequently became an annual affair celebrated on the Fourth of July and after several years absorbed the Roberts–Winburn gathering. At both Beech and Roberts settlements the homecomings evolved from the start around formal programs held at the neighborhood's churches followed by church lawn picnics.[6]

For much if not all of the first fifty years the annual reunions attracted large crowds year in, year out. At the height of their popularity, during a period that ran from the 1920s through the 1950s, they each drew hundreds of people annually. Moreover, as opportunities for travel improved over time, and as descendants become more widely dispersed, the numbers arriving from distant locations increased as well. Both Beech and Roberts gatherings thus gradually extended beyond their initial reach, which had been confined largely to Indiana, first drawing in those from regional centers like Chicago, Detroit, and St. Louis, and then ultimately attracting participants from both coasts as well.[7]

The homecomings had tremendous appeal because of the exceptional opportunities for fellowship they presented. Family and friends now separated by considerable distances could get together to reminisce about old times and catch up on one another's recent experiences. With specific dates set aside for reunions each year, and with large numbers usually expected to attend, conditions for such visiting could hardly have been made more favorable. Participants often arrived the week before and stayed over with those living either at or near the settlements. In Carthage during the 1940s and 1950s, for example, the homes of the Tuttles, Weavers, and Carters were always a hub of activity in the days leading up to the Beech reunion, filled with relatives dropping by from Terre Haute, Richmond, and Noblesville.[8]

On a deeper and more significant level, the homecomings' early appeal and their enduring popularity derived from the strong sense of identity and place they offered. This issue is easier to comprehend if the reunions' activities are put in the context of other contemporary gatherings and associations based on common heritage and/or ties to a given area. Historians have noted that large family reunions first gained popularity in the decades surrounding the turn of the twentieth century in response to the rapid social change then underway. Attracting mostly middle-class Protestants whose kindreds had deep roots American soil, these gatherings served not just as a chance to mingle with far-flung relatives and to honor common ancestors, but also to affirm "old-fashioned" values and beliefs seemingly jeopardized by the advent of large-scale industry, the spread of corporate capitalism, the rise of urban metropolises, and the enormous influx of immigrants from southern and eastern Europe. Selectively interpreting their families' histories, participants elevated both their pioneering forebears and the morality they associated with their forebears' character. Hence they called upon one another to emulate the rugged individualism, work ethic, familial commitment, religious fervor, and achievement of those who had preceded them. They also set themselves apart from, and above, outsiders by stressing their distinguished bloodlines, drawing upon prevailing scientific and popular thought about the biological superiority of certain racial and ethnic groups (most notably, Anglo-Saxons) over others. Associational groups like the Indiana Society of Pioneers and the Daughters of the American Revolution emphasized similar themes and motifs as well. In all these instances, selective memories of the past were used by participants to help them cope more successfully with the challenges of the present—to provide them with a more secure sense of place in a time of uncertainty.[9]

By the early twentieth century Beech and Roberts descendants had ample grounds for turning to their own forebears and their forebears' rural heritage in order to help make their way in the world. They faced even greater challenges and more uncertainty than middle-class Americans generally during the transition to modern life. They, after all, were now immersed in a northern urban setting in which whites rigidly constrained blacks' economic and social opportunities, and in which blacks were denigrated as racially inferior by virtually all whites. While neither discrimination nor ideas of white racial superiority were new to those born in the Beech and Roberts neighborhoods, their heavy weight was felt more acutely and on a much more ongoing basis in cities like Kokomo, Evansville, Indianapolis, and Chicago. The inspiration of their ancestors' own successful struggles thus served an obvious need.

The Great Migration, which began during World War I, brought tens of thousands of southern blacks each year to northern cities and made matters even more pressing and uncertain. African-American urban communities were thrown into much greater flux than before and whites grew increasingly resentful of blacks' presence as their population surged. In larger cities like Indianapolis and Chicago the negative characteristics associated with ghetto life, including strict residential segregation, inferior public services, and severe overcrowding, became much more pronounced. The Migration transformed the social milieu associated with midwestern black urban communities in other ways as well. Increasingly, those from relatively privileged northern rural neighborhoods like Beech and Roberts settlements were a minority within a minority. Ever larger numbers of black city dwellers came from markedly different educational, class, and cultural backgrounds. Given this new dynamic, Beech and Roberts settlements' distinctiveness became even more apparent to their former residents—and were deemed even more praiseworthy—with the passage of time.

This was certainly the perspective of Carl G. Roberts, whose experiences were described by E. Franklin Frazier in scholarly writings during the 1930s and 1940s. Frazier, the leading sociologist of black America at the time, interviewed Roberts at length concerning the Roberts family's history as well as Carl's experiences as a prominent black professional in Chicago during the early phases of the Great Migration. Roberts, in turn, appeared as an unnamed figure in several of Frazier's studies. He emerged at times as an archetypal representative of middle-class blacks whose ancestors were free before the Civil War, and at others as a exemplary black professional who struggled constantly to preserve the high standards of achievement, education, and respectability he had set for himself and his family. According to Frazier, Carl's ability to surmount the destructive forces of city life was due to the stable traditions and values his family had acquired over successive generations. Carl himself is quoted at length describing his family's accomplishments in both North Carolina and Indiana. In a typical passage, he noted with understated pride that:

> Our settlement [Roberts Settlement] was first established around 1823. . . . My grandfather was buried in that cemetery in 1848. . . . One of the stations of the Underground Railroad was located there. Soil was very fertile. Race relations were very good. They have had family reunions there for about thirty-seven years. . . . At one time we have had as many as eight or nine hundred people gathered there at family reunions. . . . I don't know of any colored settlement any older than that in the North. . . .[10]

By their very design Beech and Roberts homecomings evoked a similar, unaffected sense of tradition, accomplishment, and solid values. This was achieved in part through the very act of gathering at the neighborhood's churches. Even before arriving at the meetinghouses participants were immersed in a rural setting that had long been dominated by their ancestors. Seemingly everywhere stood houses, barns, and other outbuildings built by their relatives. Fields were filled with rapidly maturing corn and other crops, much as they had been for generations before. The churches themselves, well-aged but nonetheless rock solid and carefully preserved, stood as symbols of countless community gatherings, church services, baptisms, and funerals dating back to the mid-nineteenth century. Rows of tombstones in adjacent and nearby cemeteries conjured up memories and thoughts of those had passed on earlier, including most of the founding landowners of each community. Time-honored values were also conveyed through the day's activities. Picnics provided ample opportunity for fellowship and camaraderie, while formal services invariably were well-grounded in prayers and hymns that underscored the communities' deep religious commitment.

Equally critical were efforts to capture and pass along the neighborhoods' history and heritage in terms that conveyed special meaning for those in attendance. These attempts were not always made deliberately or self-consciously. And, in fact, it is likely that most shared memories were exchanged in a very casual fashion, perhaps while lingering over homemade desserts or while wandering through the community graveyards. Nor were these efforts to understand and interpret the past limited only to the homecomings themselves. Certainly efforts to trace, record, and disseminate the communities' histories extended well beyond the actual reunions. Nonetheless the homecomings were at the very center of Beech and Roberts descendants' efforts to create a useable past in two particular ways. They focused attention squarely on the neighborhoods' heritage once every year, thereby generating an ongoing, general appreciation among those attending the reunions. And they served to inspire those with a special interest in the communities' or their families' heritage, thereby stimulating additional individual initiatives to uncover, maintain, and promote their history.

An early example of the homecoming's role in promoting a deeper, richer sense of the past can be seen in a speech delivered by the Reverend Cyrus W. Roberts at the Roberts homecoming on July 4, 1925. The grandson of founding patriarch Hansel Roberts, Cyrus was a retired minister of the A.M.E. church and among the oldest surviving neighborhood natives. He used his talk to provide the first formal account of the origins of both the Roberts family and Roberts Settlement. His oration outlined the Robertses' free Negro ancestry in North Carolina, the kindred's migration to the Indiana frontier, the Roberts neighborhood's subsequent development as a frontier community, and the accomplishments of the neighborhood's most distinguished native sons and daughters. Throughout, considerable attention was paid to detailed evidence—specific dates, locations, names, events. His findings, he noted at the very outset, were based on "much investigation and research among several histories for facts and causes." The effect of this methodical rigor was to give the talk an air of authority and indisputable truth. (Tellingly, those in attendance voted favorably on a motion to have the talk "published and kept on record for future reference."[11])

Cyrus stressed three overlapping themes that would recur in subsequent accounts of both Beech and Roberts settlements. The first concerned the Roberts family's multiracial background and ties to Native Americans. While acknowledging the Robertses' Negro ancestry, little effort was made to probe the origins or significance of this African-based past. Instead, greater attention was placed on kindred's lineage with Indians, whose heritage stretched back in American history "before Columbus discovered America (if he did), or ever the Pilgrim Fathers of the May Flower [*sic*] set foot on this continent." Cyrus more specifically posited that the Robertses descended from Cherokees, a tribe he lauded for its advanced, civilized society at the time of its forced removal from North Carolina in the 1830s. Cyrus' hypothesis of a direct Roberts–Cherokee connection was apparently off target, but that was beside the point. What was most critical was the way that Roberts residents' heritage was tied to an exceptional, noble past, one that few other Americans, white or black, could claim as their own.[12]

Another significant thread in Cyrus' rending of the past involved the successful struggle to turn their rural neighborhood into a "thrifty, hard working community." In conventional fashion, Cyrus set out the names of the settlement's first pioneers, described their arrival from North Carolina and the Beech in the late 1830s, and tried to give a bit of the flavor of their struggle in the wilderness. He observed that:

> The country was new then and unimproved. At that time land was cheap . . . so that all owned their own homes. . . . The settlers built log houses to live in, to worship in, and to hold school in. . . . Some of those houses were built of round logs and some of hewn logs, flattened on two sides, corn cribs and barns in like manner. . . . Some of those old log houses were still standing until a few years ago, being replaced by more modern, or frame buildings. Meetings were also held in barns, private dwellings, and in the woods. . . . In that day we had no high school grades nor college bred teachers, but any one who could read intelligently, write legibly, and spell correctly (if they could), was qualified to teach subscription school. Later on came the "Free School." The land was cleared and improved, and after a lapse of 90 years beautiful frame houses and barns have taken their place. . . .[13]

Cyrus' descriptive narrative and rhetoric about pioneer life followed a well-worn formula. Similar passages can be found in countless midwestern county histories published in the decades surrounding the turn of the twentieth century, not to mention in innumerable speeches presented before local and state pioneer societies across much of the nation. And, in all likelihood, it probably served much the same purpose. As suggested earlier, these celebrations of hardy pioneers were as much reaffirmations of values like hard work, determination, and perseverance as they were testimonials to the pioneers' character and accomplishments. They spoke directly to their audiences' own conservative ethos. Yet even more was involved for Beech and Roberts descendants. By structuring their own history in terms that so closely paralleled those of other successful, illustrious Americans, they in effect countered prevailing notions about blacks' inferiority and insignificance in the American past. Here were *their* ancestors, participating in a saga that was as quintessentially American as any that could be imagined. This pioneer-era legacy also reinforced the notion that the communities' descendants were quite different from the African Americans migrating from the South to northern cities. At a time when most blacks were enslaved, their grandparents and great-grandparents were clearing Hoosier wilderness. Hence they could claim a sense of belonging and place inaccessible to southern immigrants.

The third major stress within Cyrus Roberts' oration was on the exemplary character and talent that Roberts Settlement had bestowed upon its residents. With effusive pride he asserted that:

> Our religious and educational facilities and opportunities have not been excelled in the past, until our religious influence and intellectual ability . . . are known and felt far and wide in every hamlet, and village, and town, and adjacent city. . . . [Today] our talent is sought and the name "Roberts Settlement" has become a synonym, not only for greatness, but also for honesty and uprightedness wherever spoken. The enlightenment of its citizenry, the expanse of its civilization, has and does today command the best talent of those who teach and those who preach. Others need not apply.

To emphasize this point, Cyrus first listed the names and professions of more than two dozen Roberts residents who had become ministers, teachers, or other professionals. Then he noted that "time would fail me to speak further in detail of all who are entitled to honorable mention in this category" of career success.[14]

As in his recitation of the Roberts family's early American roots and Roberts Settlement's frontier origins, Cyrus' comments about character and career success were directed as much to the present as to the past. Roberts Settlement's influence, he suggested, was neither ephemeral nor transitory but rather something far-reaching and potentially long lasting.

Given the vastly restricted occupational and career opportunities open to African Americans in northern cities, not to mention the broader problems associated with black urban life, these words must have been comforting and encouraging. The Robertses' educational achievements and religious ardor had allowed them to excel in the past. Presumably these same advantages would continue to serve them as well in cities and towns as in the countryside.

The thrust of Cyrus' historical interpretation was refined and extended through the actions of several other Beech and Roberts descendants in subsequent decades. At Roberts Settlement, Carl Roberts followed in Cyrus' footsteps as the community's unofficial historian. For almost a decade he investigated the Roberts family's roots, ultimately compiling a 45-foot-long genealogical chart that, in various forms, became a staple of discussion at Roberts homecomings from the 1930s onward. He also gathered together family financial papers dating from the mid-eighteenth century and letters written during the Robertses' migration to the Indiana frontier. These he donated to the Library of Congress, along with a copy of his genealogical chart. In a manuscript included with this collection, Carl reiterated much of Cyrus' history—indeed, much of Cyrus' history was quoted directly. Carl did, however, give somewhat greater emphasis to the family's free heritage, noting that "[t]here is no evidence that these people or their ancestors were ever enslaved." In doing so he further distanced the Robertses from most other African Americans.[15]

Beech Settlement acquired its own historians as well. The first was Nathan Hill, the principal of an all-black high school in southern Indiana and the grandson of pioneer Edmund Hill. In 1943 Hill published a brief, two-page overview of the neighborhood's history in the *Indiana Negro History Bulletin*. In a fashion similar to Cyrus and Carl Roberts, he focused largely on the community's frontier heritage and its successful native sons and daughters. Lawrence Carter, in turn, followed in Hill's footsteps and ultimately developed a much richer, more detailed, and more influential understanding of Beech Settlement's heritage. Carter, whose mother had grown up at the Beech, was raised in Carthage in the 1920s and 1930s and continued to return there each summer during his subsequent career as a teacher in Indiana and Ohio. For more than thirty years Carter collected all manner of Beech historical information. He scoured local histories, courthouse records, Beech cemetery tombstones, his own family's memorabilia, and a host of other sources. Most significantly, from the late 1930s through the early 1950s he interviewed more than three dozen Beech descendants, including a number of former residents, about their recollections and family lore.[16]

Lawrence Carter's efforts were never complete—his dreams of publishing a comprehensive Beech history went unfulfilled—but his impact on the community's heritage was nonetheless profound. In several ways he did more than anyone else to kindle an ongoing interest in, and appreciation of, the Beech among its descendants. Carter's extensive attempts to recapture the neighborhood's history, first of all, helped elevate its importance by making descendants more acutely aware of the neighborhood's distinguished past. Similarly, he sought to promote a continuing historical understanding by mounting modest exhibit boards at the annual homecomings that displayed old photographs and other historical information. These, in turn, became informal focal points that helped prompt reminiscences and general discussion about family and community roots. Carter was also actively involved with a handful of others in preparing the Mount Pleasant A.M.E. Church site each year for the homecoming itself, tidying up the surrounding grounds and opening up the now unused meetinghouse for the gathering. While Lawrence Carter was far from the only one working to preserve the Beech's heritage, the depth and length of his commitment made him stand out. By the end of his tenure as a driving force behind Beech homecomings—he remained active through the early 1980s—he had himself become something of a living embodiment of the community's distinguished past.[17]

↝ ↝ ↝

Family reunions in general have undergone a tremendous transformation over the last one hundred years. The vast majority of the annual reunions established in the late nineteenth and early twentieth century are now long gone. While a small proportion remained active for decades and grew larger, developing at times even into national family associations, the vast majority languished or completely lapsed after an extended period. The geographic and social mobility of reunion participants, waning interest in such gatherings over time, the splintering of branches from the main family tree, and the deaths of the reunions' moving forces all took their toll. In the 1960s, however, decline began to give way to renewal. Family reunions, never totally abandoned, came back into much greater vogue. This resurgence was driven by several discernible factors: the social turbulence of the 1960s, the growing popularity of genealogy, and a renewed emphasis on "place," especially in the years immediately following publication of Alex Haley's *Roots* (1976). The purposes and meanings attached to family reunions also changed dramatically. The conservative, moral component all but disappeared. Reunions, in the words of historian Robert M. Taylor, have become "less strident, less remonstrative, more strictly devoted to fun and fellowship." They continue to stress identity and group unity, but have stripped away much of the remaining emphasis on older values. "The primary goals are not to advance morality, race, or class, but to carry on social acquaintances," exchange genealogical information, and serve other, limited ends.[18]

Beech and Roberts settlements' homecomings have undergone somewhat analogous evolutions. After cresting in popularity during the first half of the twentieth century, both seemingly experienced prolonged periods of diminished attendance during the quarter century thereafter. The factors behind the declines were in part those associated with the eclipse of other family reunions: the deaths of the homecomings' initial organizers and leaders, and the increasing dispersion of the settlements' descendants, both geographically and socially. At the Beech, where the drop-off was most precipitous, the deaths and retirements of the neighborhood's last resident black farmers apparently took an additional toll as well. The Beech was no longer a functioning farm community, which made it all the more difficult to keep memories of the settlement alive. Its homecomings also suffered because the small towns nearest the community, especially Carthage, experienced prolonged economic declines that dramatically thinned the ranks of descendants living in close proximity. Over time, fewer and fewer people remained to help coordinate reunion activities or act as hosts for those arriving from out of town.[19]

Such downturns notwithstanding, the Roberts and Beech homecomings have demonstrated remarkable resilience, with both remaining ongoing affairs into the twenty-first century. Since the 1970s the homecomings have benefited from the "*Roots* phenomenon"—that is, the heightened interest in family history and understanding the role of one's ancestry and geographic origins in shaping personal identity. Because these emphases have dovetailed closely with long-standing homecoming themes, they have helped revitalize the get-togethers by both galvanizing the commitment of old-timers and drawing in a new generation of participants.

Overlapping with these emphases, and equally important, has been the tremendously greater understanding and appreciation of African-American history and cultural heritage that has developed among all Americans since the 1960s. In the immediate context of the homecomings, Alex Haley's book *Roots,* its adaptation for television, and the subsequent popular interest in black family heritages have been especially influential. They have fostered a broader, more inclusive way of interpreting the rural settlements' history, along with a greater appreciation of the value of having pride in one's family, kin, and community. The result has been homecomings that have continued to stress Beech and Roberts' exceptional character, but that have also managed to shift with the times and remain relevant and vital to younger participants. Some of the subtle, exclusive undertones associated with the earlier gatherings have been replaced with a more inclusive celebration of racial pride. "Alex Haley did us a very great favor when he wrote *Roots,*" one long-time participant responded to a question concerning the Roberts homecoming's enduring popularity in the 1990s. "And we have built on that."[20]

This building process has admittedly been uneven. At Beech Settlement, the Mount Pleasant Church's historical significance as the founding site of the Indiana Conference of the A.M.E. Church has become an important element in the annual gatherings. In recent decades members of the Indiana Conference without direct ties to Beech residents have attended the homecomings in large numbers, in effect transforming the gathering into a dual-purpose function commemorating Mount Pleasant as the Conference's "birthplace" as much as, if not more than, as a symbol of Beech Settlement itself. Many Beech descendants, in turn, have come to feel that the homecoming has lost its original purpose as a gathering for community residents and their descendants. The resulting controversy over the homecoming's purpose has remained largely muted, but nonetheless has dampened enthusiasm for the reunion among those with direct family ties. While perhaps fifty descendants continue to return each August, their numbers have remained steady at best. All but a few are middle-aged or older. The homecoming is by no means in danger of imminent collapse, but clearly has failed to reap the full benefits of the larger trends just noted.[21]

The Fourth of July gatherings at the Roberts church have fared much better. The reunions have retained much of their traditional emphasis on the virtually all-encompassing Roberts family and its distinguished heritage in the Old South, at the frontier, and upon subsequent generations. In this sense, the homecomings seemingly have changed very little. Yet much has changed. Responding to declining attendance, the gatherings' leaders in the early 1970s revamped the homecoming to attract a broader spectrum of participants. A wiener roast and hayride were added for younger children the evening before the main gathering, and a large canvas tent was erected to provide greater shelter during the communal picnic. To improve communication and stimulate year-round interest, a newsletter also began to be mailed at least twice yearly to descendants across the nation. Together, these efforts and the "*Roots* phenomenon" have placed the Roberts Chapel gathering on a much firmer footing. Declining attendance has given way to larger, seemingly stable crowds numbering far more than one hundred participants each year. A large proportion are families with young children.[22]

The settlement's historical heritage continues to receive strong emphasis at homecomings as well. Tangible scraps of history like Carl Roberts' lineage charts, the work of recent genealogists, and old family photographs are still passed around and lingered over, and pilgrimages to the church and adjoining cemetery still serve to jog memories and prompt discussion about an increasingly distant past. Equally significant, new efforts have been made from time to time to further enhance that appreciation. In the mid-1980s, for example, the adult children of Pauline Baltimore, who grew up at Roberts Settlements in the early twentieth century, compiled and privately published *A Children's History of Roberts Settlement.* This forty-eight-page, photocopied booklet combined previously reported historical facts about the Robertses, Pauline's own childhood memories of country life, and a workbook of related activities geared toward young readers. More recently, in the mid-1990s, a successful campaign was conducted to have the Roberts church placed on the National

Register of Historic Places. Talk of a similar campaign has begun at the Beech.[23]

It is the Beech and Roberts homecomings' ongoing stress on their historical underpinnings, in fact, that together with their longevity makes them so distinctive at the beginning of a new millennium. Other family reunions share their emphasis on self-awareness, family pride, and group unity. Arguably, however, few go to the lengths of Beech and Roberts settlements in terms of their deliberate evocation of the past, both in the formal commemorative programs held on each homecoming occasion and in myriad informal ways at the homecomings and beyond. The past continues to be used as a source of identity and as a guide for future conduct. Although the latter emphasis is often expressed more subtly than in Cyrus Roberts' day, it nonetheless remains. (The authors of the Baltimore's *Children's History* affirmed a widely held view when they noted in their introduction that "it is essential to inform our youth of their valuable heritage. Our goal . . . is to inform and instruct the future leaders of Roberts Settlement."[24])

Undoubtedly the greater emphasis on Beech and Roberts' exceptional history and heritage is well grounded in the unique challenges facing African Americans in modern American society. The ability of their forebears to confront and overcome barriers related to inequality, discrimination, and the challenges of everyday life resounds clearly even a full generation after the advances of the modern civil rights movement. The resulting sense of confidence derived from a Beech or Roberts connection is often expressed in muted, but knowing terms. "It does make me feel good, or least different," one Beech descendant observed in the mid-1990s,

> when [I] talk to people about their father coming from Tennessee or Arkansas or someplace, and I think to myself, well we were here. Even no matter whether they were black or white—I think that way because my people have been here for such a long time. We go back so far in the history of the area. . . .[25]

Intertwined with this ongoing identification with place is a special, vital sense of accomplishment and possibility. Beech and Roberts homecomings continue to attract disproportionately large numbers of African-American professionals. Those who regularly attend include more than a sprinkling of successful business people, lawyers, doctors, teachers, elected government officials, and (at Roberts Settlement) even farmers. Informal conversations are frequently peppered with talk about young descendants' progress at top-flight colleges, universities, and graduate schools, and with the latest news concerning the careers of those working in far away locations like Los Angeles, Detroit, and New York. The homecomings' formal programs, meanwhile, continue to provide ample opportunity for descendants to display their musical talents, spiritual fervor, and organizational skills. Accomplishment and talent are as much hallmarks of the settlements today as they were in past generations.

Ironically, the only clouds on the homecomings' horizon are tied to the descendants' very success and the relatively greater opportunities available to African Americans generally in recent decades. Younger Beech and Roberts descendants' pursuit of higher education and demanding careers has led them farther and farther from the rural neighborhoods. Increasingly they have tenuous ties even to their parents' hometowns, let alone to those of the settlements themselves. This physical distancing is exacerbated by the growing lapse of time between the settlements' active days and the present. Only those well into their retirement years can now recall the time when the communities' churches and schools were still active. The "specialness" of Beech and Roberts' history, meanwhile, may also have lost a bit of its edge in a second respect for those who were raised during the past generation. While the elimination of formal racial barriers to education, employment, and housing since the 1960s has not leveled the playing field for blacks in American society, it has created vastly improved opportunities. This improved environment, in turn, may make it harder for younger descendants to appreciate as deeply the challenges and achievements of their ancestors both in the Old South and at the Indiana frontier. Certainly today's descendants still confront race-related challenges that give their Beech and Roberts heritage a special resonance. Whether that resonance rings as loudly as it did for their parents and grandparents, however, is another matter.

It is worth emphasizing one final time that individuals like Carl Roberts, Lawrence Carter, and Pauline Baltimore were not guided by nostalgia alone when they celebrated Beech and Roberts settlements' "specialness." Both communities, as this study has emphasized, *were* different from those of African Americans in other, more urbanized northern settings. Members of the farm communities, for one thing, shared a free ancestry that set them apart from most other blacks. The neighborhoods' founders were mostly light-skinned descendants of racially mixed men and women who had been free before the turn of the nineteenth century, at least two full generations before most black Americans were emancipated. Because they were free at an early date, families like the Watkinses, Robertses, and Hunts were able to control their own destinies in critical ways other African Americans did not. As free people of color they enjoyed greater autonomy in matters of religion, education, and economic advancement. Well before 1865 Beech and Roberts residents were accustomed to sending their children to school, worshiping in A.M.E. and Wesleyan churches, and buying and selling farmland. The relative advantages derived from such freedom persisted well after slavery was destroyed. Compared to other northern blacks, the neighborhoods' residents in the late nineteenth century were more likely to be well educated, financially secure, and acculturated to middle-class values.

The Beech and Roberts kindreds' landownership also contributed to their distinctiveness. Before 1900 the aspirations of most African Americans were consistently dashed by economic exploitation at the hands of whites. Whether as slaves before the Civil War, as free laborers in urban settings, or as sharecroppers in the postbellum South, blacks found their lives to be adversely affected by the abuse and discrimination they faced at the workplace. In the North racially biased labor practices led to low wages, underemployment, and unemployment; few families escaped poverty—or the myriad problems associated with it. Beech and Roberts families like the Jeffries, Roberts, and Watkins kindreds, however, were able to avoid this predicament because they were farmers who held title to their own land. As freehold farmers first in the South and then in the North, they were dependent largely upon one another for their economic well being. While Beech and Roberts families were never entirely self-sufficient, they were able to shape their own economic fortunes to an extent most African Americans would have envied.

Financial security and stability, not poverty, marked the lives of most of the settlements' families. Beech and Roberts pioneers seldom parted with the rich farmland they acquired in the early 1830s. Most cleared their holdings, developed profitable farm operations, and continued to manage their own financial affairs until their final days. Those who bought or sold acreage tended to buy more than they sold. Some, like Walker Jeffries and Elias Roberts, built up considerable estates of 160 acres or more over their lifetimes. Significant problems with farming cropped up only in the late nineteenth century, when commodity prices declined steadily and farms were divided into smaller, less profitable units for the benefit of the pioneers' children and grandchildren. Yet even then outright financial distress was much more the exception than the rule.

Landownership allowed Beech and Roberts families to shape their lives in other positive, contrasting ways as well. Both neighborhood's founders, by acquiring large tracts of land and by settling near non-hostile whites, created social settings that sheltered them from much of the racial hostility and discrimination of the nineteenth century. Relative to their urban counterparts, residents of Beech and Roberts settlements were less adversely affected by acts of racial violence and patterns of segregation concerning such matters as work and education. Daily contact with whites was much more limited and much more likely to take place with neighbors who treated them in a roughly equitable fashion. Instead of blocking access to educational opportunities, for example, Quakers near both communities encouraged and supported black settlers' efforts to establish their own independent schools. With fewer race-related obstacles to confront, residents of the settlements had more freedom to shape their lives according to their own wishes.

Beech and Roberts families, of course, never fully escaped the problems and handicaps common to African Americans. The landholdings of black farmers at both locations tended to be smaller than those of surrounding whites, a legacy in large measure of their ancestors' humble beginnings as freed slaves. Smaller farms meant smaller farm surpluses and smaller inheritances for future generations. The difficulties confronting midwestern farmers in the late nineteenth century were felt more acutely at Beech and Roberts settlements because of the neighborhoods' less secure financial footing. Racial discrimination, meanwhile, always pressed down on the communities' members, even if it pressed down less severely than on urban blacks. The presence of non-hostile neighbors did not alleviate the sufferings caused by racially biased laws concerning voting rights, funds for public schools, or the legal standing of blacks before local courts. Beech and Roberts residents were second-class citizens, if citizens at all, and could often do little to make up for that handicap. The presence of non-hostile neighbors also did little to shelter the settlements' residents from informal acts of prejudice and discrimination, especially beyond the neighborhoods' immediate vicinities. Insults and slights marred everyday interactions with whites, with residents expected to accept their lot in life with little protest. The lynching of Billy Keemer stood as a reminder of the danger inherent in challenging white expectations.

Given the constant difficulties they confronted, the most remarkable thing about the people of Beech and Roberts settlements was not their free black ancestry or their ownership of land per se. Rather, it was the fact that over succeeding generations they were able to protect and maintain their relatively enviable position among African Americans. Repeatedly they faced and overcame extremely troubling, if not threatening, situations. In the early nineteenth century the neighborhoods' founders confronted declining farm prospects and deteriorating race relations in the Old South. Migrating to the northern frontier, they markedly improved the fortunes of both themselves and their children. A half century later a new generation of Beech and Roberts residents overcame a somewhat similar, if less dire, predicament. Faced again with limited farm prospects, a significant number migrated to urban centers and joined the ranks of teachers, ministers, and other black professionals. Some were more successful than others, to be sure, and many accepted less secure and less prestigious occupations. Nonetheless the point remains: the good fortune of one generation had been kept intact and passed on to the next.

Beech and Roberts residents engaged in the same ceaseless struggle as all black Americans. Their advantages increased the odds that they might wage their struggle successfully—that they might move ahead socially and economically in an inequitable and unjust society—but the outcome of their struggles was never guaranteed. The fact that families like the

Robertses repeatedly overcame adversity and improved their fortunes is a testament to the men and women of Beech and Roberts settlements. And, in the end, it explains the continuing interest in the communities' past more than any other factor. The settlements' late twentieth century descendants, confronting their own unique challenges both as individuals and as African Americans, have ample reason to nurture and extend the extraordinarily rich heritage they have inherited.

APPENDIX

The Southern Origins of 1840 Beech and Roberts Household Heads

In order to assess the pre-migration backgrounds of early Beech and Roberts settlement pioneers, an effort was made to trace the previous southern residences of
the sixty-eight household heads at the two communities in 1840. Those traced
included sixty-three black householders in Ripley Township, Rush County, Indiana (Beech Settlement), and five black householders in Jackson and Adams townships, Hamilton County, Indiana (Roberts Settlement).

As with any attempt to trace the origins of 1840 household heads, the effort
was hampered by the limited information available in early United States census
returns. In 1840 census enumerators recorded only the name of the household
head, the composition of his/her household by race, gender, and age range of each
individual, and the number of individuals in the household pursuing any of seven
broad occupational categories. For the Elijah and Kessiah Roberts family at Roberts Settlement, for example, the census indicates only that the household was
headed by Elijah Roberts, that three individuals were engaged in agricultural pur-
suits, and that the household comprised eleven individuals: a free black man and
woman, each 36–55 years old; two free black boys, ages 10–23; two free black
girls, aged 10–23; four free black boys, under the age of 10; and one free black girl
under the age of 10. Unlike the case with later censuses, no indication is given of
the names of the other individuals in the household, the birthplace(s) of household members, the specific occupation of each adult, the value of the household
head's real estate holdings, or other data which might help further identify the
individual and his/her family. Given this sketchiness, it is often difficult to determine with confidence whether an individual mentioned in another source is actually the same as that found in the 1840 census. Little evidence exists in the census
either to confirm or reject the possibility that tax, land, probate, census, or other
pre-1840 records for *an* Elijah Roberts in, say, North Carolina are those of *the*
Elijah Roberts who moved to Roberts Settlement.

Despite such difficulties, almost two-thirds (43 of 68, or 63.2 percent) of the
1840 heads have been traced using sets of criteria that firmly tied the heads to
both a southern county and Beech/Roberts settlements (see Table 19). The previous southern residences of eight additional heads (11.8 percent) were indicated
by sources that could not be verified with the same degree of confidence; their
origins thus are probably, though not certainly, known. Altogether, the premigra-

TABLE 19

Results of Tracing Southern Origins of 1840
Household Heads from Beech and Roberts Settlements

	No. of heads	% of total
Traced with certainty	43	63.2
Probable origins	8	11.8
Origins unknown	17	25.0
Total	68	100.0

Sources: Census manuscripts, Rush and Hamilton counties; Jonathan Roberts Collection, Library of Congress, Washington, D.C.; Lawrence Carter Collection, Indiana Historical Society Library, Indianapolis; Eastern Cherokee Indian Claims, Record Group 54, National Archives and Records Service, Washington, D.C.; marriage, land, tax, and probate records, Northampton and Halifax counties, North Carolina, North Carolina State Archives, Raleigh; marriage, land, tax records and free Negro register, Greensville County, Virginia, Virginia State Library, Richmond; Carter G. Woodson, *Free Negro Heads of Families in the United States in 1830* (Washington: Association for the Study of Negro Life and History, 1925); Helen Tunnicliff Catterall, *Judicial Cases Corncerning American Slavery and the Negro*, 5 vols. (Washington, D.C.: Carnegie Institute, 1926–36), 5:33–34; Thomas T. Newby, *Reminiscences* (Carthage, Ind.: n.p., 1916), 16–17; *Atlas of Rush County, Indiana . . . History, Statistics, Illustrations* (Chicago, 1879; reprint ed. Knightstown, Ind.: Bookmark, 1979), 67; deeds, N:400. Recorder's Office, Rush County Courthouse, Rushville, Indiana.

tion homes of fifty-one heads (75.0 percent) could be located with varying degrees of satisfaction.

In twenty-nine instances the previous residence of an 1840 household head has been determined through contemporary sources that unequivocally indicate the location. A dozen letters exchanged between members of the Roberts kin network in both Indiana and North Carolina during the 1830s, for instance, reveal that more than twenty of the heads were natives of Northampton County, North Carolina. Similarly, free papers, court documents carried by free Negroes to vouch that they were free people, still exist for a small number of 1840 household heads and list their holder's county of residence prior to the move North. In each case the tie between one of the frontier communities, on the one hand, and a southern location, on the other, is clear and convincing.

The previous residences of ten other 1840 heads have been traced by using a combination of primary and secondary sources. In all of these instance local and family history materials gathered in the late nineteenth and twentieth centuries indicate the southern counties of black pioneers, while primary source materials from the period before 1840 verify the accuracy of the after-the-fact accounts. Much of the family history data comes from claims filed by Beech and Roberts pioneers' descendents in 1906 for monies owed those who could prove Cherokee ancestry. (Their applications were rejected, albeit on grounds totally unrelated to the veracity of the information they submitted.) One claim, for instance, notes that 1840 Beech householder Benjamin James came to Indiana from Halifax County, North Carolina; the claim is supported by the 1830 census for Halifax, which lists Benjamin James, free black, among the county's household heads.

In the final four firmly established cases, census data from 1850 was combined with evidence from pre-1840 local records. In each instance the state of the head's birth was found in the 1850 census manuscripts, while the county of origin was located through public records from the principal areas of migration (northeastern and north central North Carolina, southeastern Virginia). Goodwin Hunt, for example, was listed as a Virginia native in the 1850 census for Ripley Township, Rush County, Indiana (Beech Settlement); tax and marriage records, along with the Free Negro Register from Greensville County, Virginia identified him as a Greensville resident. Evidence from the public records leaves little doubt about the definitiveness of the match in at least two of the four cases. In the case of Goodwin Hunt local tax records note that he emigrated from the county at the same time (1834) as several other Beech Settlement pioneers from Greensville. Records concerning General Tootle of Northampton County, in a similar fashion, include a marriage license for General and his first known wife, Martha, that leaves little uncertainty about General's county of origin.

The likely southern origins of eight additional 1840 household heads are indicated by sources that cannot be verified with as reasonable a degree of confidence. In four instances local or family history sources note the previous county of residence, but no supporting evidence from primary sources from that county has been found. According to a 1906 Cherokee claim application, for example, the Keemer family migrated to Beech Settlement from Halifax County, North Carolina. While such a migration appears probable—at least eight families came from the area—no substantiation for the claim has been found. In four cases a reverse situation exists: tax, census and other records from the principal counties of migration note the presence of free Negroes with the same names as 1840 household heads, but no additional materials show that the individuals in fact were the persons in question. Several documents from the early 1830s tie Edwin Jones to Greensville County, for example, but there is no firm proof that he is the same man by that name living at Beech Settlement in 1840.

NOTES

INTRODUCTION

1. The comments by Wright and DuBois appear in Richard Wright, Jr., "Negro Rural Communities in Indiana," *Southern Workman* 37 (March 1908): 158–72; and W. E. B. DuBois, "Long in Darke," *Colored American Magazine* 17 (November 1909): 553–55.

2. U.S. Bureau of the Census, *Ninth Census* (Washington, D.C., 1872), 1: 108–21, 123–31, 168–76, 287–95; *Tenth Census* (Washington, D.C., 1883), 1: 130–55, 212–13, 285–302, 366–75, 417–25; *Twelfth Census* (Washington, D.C., 1901), 1: 613–16, 623–24, 633–36, 645–46.

3. Ibid.

4. No comprehensive, detailed analysis has been attempted of blacks in the rural Old Northwest. The overview in this and the following three paragraphs is informed by many sources, including Emma Lou Thornbrough, *The Negro in Indiana before 1900: A Study of a Minority* (Indianapolis: Indiana Historical Bureau, 1957); David Gerber, *Black Ohio and the Color Line, 1860–1915* (Urbana: University of Illinois Press, 1976); Juliet E. K. Walker, *Free Frank: A Black Pioneer on the Antebellum Frontier* (Lexington: University Press of Kentucky, 1983); George K. Hesslink, *Black Neighbors: Negroes in a Northern Rural Community*, rev. ed. (Indianapolis: Bobbs Merrill, 1974); Benjamin C. Wilson, *The Rural Black Heritage between Chicago and Detroit, 1850–1929: A Photograph Album and Random Thoughts* (Kalamazoo: Western Michigan University Press, 1985); Zachary Cooper, *Black Settlers in Rural Wisconsin* (Madison: State Historical Society of Wisconsin, 1977); John Wesley Lyda, *The Negro in the History of Indiana* (Coatesville, Ind., ca. 1953); Carl Chester Lyles, *A History of Lyles Station, Indiana* (Evansville, 1973); Coy D. Robbins, *Forgotten Hoosiers: African Heritage in Orange County, Indiana* (Bowie, Md.: Heritage Books, 1994); Xenia Cord, "Black Rural Settlements in Indiana before 1860," in Wilma Gibbs, ed., *Indiana's African-American Heritage: Essays from Black History News & Notes* (Indianapolis: Indiana Historical Society, 1993), 99–110; Wright, "Negro Rural Communities"; DuBois, "Long in Darke"; Roma Jones Stewart, "The Migration of a Free People: Cass County's Black Settlers from North Carolina," *Michigan History* 71 (1987): 34–38; Harold B. Fields, "Free Negroes in Cass County before the Civil War," *Michigan History* 44 (1960): 375–83; Leonard U. Hill, "John Randolph's Freed Slaves Settle in Western Ohio," *Cincinnati Historical Society Bulletin* 23 (1965): 179–87; Frank F. Mathias, "John Randolph's Freedmen: The Thwarting of a Will," *Journal of Southern History* 39 (1973): 263–72; Wilhemena Robinson, "The Negro in the Village of Yellow Springs, Ohio," *Negro History Bulletin* 29 (1966): 103–12; James H. Rodabaugh, "The Negro in the Old Northwest," in O. Fritiof Ander, ed., *In the Trek of the Immigrants: Essays Presented to Carl Wittke* (Rock Island, Ill.: Augustana College Library, 1968), 219–39; idem, "The Negro in Ohio," *Journal of Negro History* 31 (1946): 9–29.

5. T. H. Breen and Stephen Innes, *"Myne Owne Ground": Race and Freedom on Virginia's Eastern Shore, 1640–1676* (New York: Oxford University Press, 1980), 6; Loren Schweninger, *Black Property Owners in the South, 1790–1915* (Urbana and Chi-

cago: University of Illinois Press, 1990), 15–16. Similar emphases are found in several other studies, including Elizabeth Rauh Bethel, *Promiseland: A Century of Life in a Negro Community* (Philadelphia: Temple University Press, 1981), and Orville Vernon Burton, *In My Father's House Are Many Mansions: Family and Community in Edgefield, South Carolina* (Chapel Hill: University of North Carolina Press, 1985).

1. SOUTHERN ORIGINS, CA. 1760–1830

1. Willis migrated to Ripley Township, Rush County, Indiana, the site of Beech Settlement, in the spring of 1829 but had doubts about the move for some time thereafter. His homesickness for Northampton grew so great that he returned for a visit in the spring of 1830. References to his longing for former friends and his plans to return are found in Thomas Clifton and James Davis to Willis Roberts, 1 February 1830, and James L. Roberts to Willis Roberts, ca. 15 February 1830, Jonathan Roberts Collection, Library of Congress, Washington D.C.

2. A full description of the methods and sources used to trace the 1840 household heads is found in the appendix.

3. Rosser Howard Taylor, *Slaveholding in North Carolina: An Economic View*, James Sprunt Publication Series, vol. 18, no. 2 (Chapel Hill: University of North Carolina Press, 1926), 12–18; Harry Roy Merrens, *Colonial North Carolina in the Eighteenth Century, A Study in Historical Geography* (Chapel Hill: University of North Carolina Press, 1964), 63, 66–68, 74–81, 108–24 passim; E. Carl Witt, ed., *Footprints in Northampton, 1741–1776–1976* (Northampton County [N.C.] Bicentennial Committee, 1976), 2, 5; Allan Kulikoff, *Tobacco and Slaves: The Development of Southern Cultures in the Chesapeake, 1680–1800* (Chapel Hill: University of North Carolina Press, 1986), 141; Marvin L. Michael Kay and Lorin Lee Cary, "A Demographic Analysis of Colonial North Carolina with Special Emphasis on the Slave and Black Populations," in Jeffrey J. Crow and Flora J. Hatley, eds., *Black Americans in North Carolina and the South* (Chapel Hill: University of North Carolina Press, 1984), 73–87; U.S. Bureau of the Census, *Heads of Families at the First Census of the United States . . . 1790 North Carolina* (Washington, D.C.: Government Printing Office, 1908), 9, 72–76. The population estimate for Northampton County in the 1760s is based on a 1762 tax list, which included 1,109 white and 1,171 black taxables; see Witt, ed., *Footprints in Northampton*, 5. This estimate is in line with later census reports, which noted 8,230 residents in 1786 and 9,992 in 1790. The estimate of the proportion that was enslaved is based on that for the northern inner coastal plains counties, which includes Northampton and demographically similar areas, given in Kay and Cary, "Demographic Analysis," 82–83.

4. Witt, ed., *Footprints in Northampton*, 2, 5; U.S. Census, *1790 North Carolina*, 9, 72–76. In Northampton County, 526 of 1,113 household heads (47.3 percent) were listed as without slaves in 1790; an additional 255, or 22.9 percent, were listed as having one to three slaves. Forty-six householders owned between twenty and forty-nine slaves.

5. U.S. Census, *1790 North Carolina*, 72–76; Kay and Cary, "Demographic Analysis," 87–90, 109–10; Paul Heinegg, *Free African Americans of North Carolina and Virginia* (Baltimore: Genealogical Publishing, 1994), 6. The estimate for Northampton's free black population is based on the assumption that free blacks accounted for 4 percent of the county's overall population in the 1760s.

6. Ira Berlin, *Slaves without Masters: The Free Negro in the Antebellum South* (New York: Oxford University Press, 1974), 3–4; Joel Williamson, *New People: Miscegena-

tion and Mulattoes in the United States (New York and London: Oxford University Press, 1980), 6–14; Schweninger, *Black Property Owners in the South,* 17; Jeffrey J. Crow, *The Black Experience in Revolutionary North Carolina* (Raleigh: North Carolina Department of Cultural Resources, 1977), 30; Heinegg, *Free African Americans;* Kay and Cary, "Demographic Analysis," 103, 106–108; lists of Continental Army drafts from Northampton County, n.d. [1779] and 1780, North Carolina State Archives (NCSA), Raleigh; files of John Roberts (S7402), Drew Tann (S19484), John Winburn (S7937), Drury Walden (R11014), Lemon Land (W20401), Jeremiah James (W467), in Revolutionary War Pension Application Files, Record Group 15, National Archives and Records Service, Washington, D.C.

Heinegg's detailed analysis of local, colonial, and state records has enabled him to trace the origins of more than four-fifths of the free people of color listed in the 1790 and 1800 census for North Carolina and Virginia. While no attempt has been made to quantify the results of his well-documented genealogical study, he clearly documents the fact that hundreds of free blacks settled in Northampton and surrounding counties prior to the Revolution.

A cursory examination of a list of thirty-three Continental Army recruits from Northampton in 1780 disclosed the names of at least three free blacks: Philip Byrd, John Haithcock, and Micajah Walden. A similar examination of a list for 1779 showed the name of three other freedmen, Isaac Scott, Sampson Morgan, and Christian Stewart, among eleven recruits. A more thorough comparison of the lists with the 1790 census might readily disclose the names of additional free people of color.

A more careful comparison of the 1790 census from Northampton with Revolutionary War pension applications revealed the names of six other free black men who served in the war: John Roberts, Drew Tann, John Winburn, Drury Walden, Lemon Land, and Jeremiah James.

Drawing upon other sources, Paul Heinegg has found evidence of Revolutionary War service by several additional free blacks from the county. See Heinegg, *Free African Americans.*

7. Edgar C. Conkling, "Roberts Settlement: A Mixed-Blood Agricultural Community in Indiana" (M.A. thesis, University of Chicago, 1957), 17–18; Carl Roberts, "Explanatory Notes," unpublished manuscript in Jonathan Roberts Collection, Library of Congress; Cyrus W. Roberts, "History of Roberts Settlement," *Noblesville [Ind.] Daily Ledger,* 25 July 1925.

Accounts of the Roberts family's early history have varied considerably over the past century, with early discussions containing no hint of the family legend. The first published history, written by Cyrus W. Roberts in 1925, notes that the family migrated to Indiana from the Northampton–Halifax area; it also stresses that the family intermarried with Cherokees in the area. No mention is made of specific African ancestors. Detailed notes on the family's history written in the 1930s by Carl G. Roberts, who devoted considerable study to the group's past, reiterate much of Cyrus Roberts' findings and emphasize that there is no evidence of the family's enslavement. While noting that those who came to Indiana "were free people of mixed Cherokee Indian, Welsh, and Negro blood," he, too, fails to mention an African ancestor.

An account written by Edgar Conkling in the early 1950s based upon interviews with Carl Roberts, however, provides a much more detailed explanation of the family's origins. According to Conkling, the family legend holds that:

> the founder of the Roberts family was born in Africa and came to this country as the valet of a Lord Roberts, who owned a plantation in North Caro-

lina. Family tradition holds that this legendary ancestor was not a slave but was instead a servant who also acted as [an] overseer to Lord Roberts' several slaves. . . . Lord Roberts at last returned for a visit to his native England, where he became ill and died. Since he had no family or heirs, his African overseer assumed proprietorship of the plantation. The new owner then took over his predecessor's name and married a Cherokee Indian woman. . . .

No effort has been made to conclusively prove or disprove this legend. It should be noted, however, that no mention of a Lord Roberts is found in Northampton County land, tax, and probate records; William L. Saunders, ed., *Colonial Records of North Carolina,* 10 vols. (Raleigh: P. M. Hale and Josephus Daniel, 1886–1890); or in the Roberts genealogy compiled in Heinegg, *Free African Americans.*

8. Winthrop Jordan, *White over Black: American Attitudes towards the Negro 1550–1812* (Chapel Hill: University of North Carolina Press, 1968; reprint ed., Baltimore: Pelican Books, 1969), 71–82; Edmund S. Morgan, *American Slavery, American Freedom: The Ordeal of Colonial Virginia* (New York: W. W. Norton and Co., 1975), 154–57; Breen and Innes, *"Myne Owne Ground"*; Heinegg, *Free African Americans,* 3, 5, and 23–641 passim; Ross M. Kimmel, "Free Blacks in Seventeenth-Century Maryland," *Maryland Historical Magazine* 71 (1976): 19–25; Nicholls, "Passing through This Troublesome World: Free Blacks in the Early Southside," *Virginia Magazine of History and Biography* 92 (1984): 52–53; Crow, *Revolutionary North Carolina,* 30; John Henderson Russell, *The Free Negro in Virginia, 1619–1865* (Baltimore: Johns Hopkins University Press, 1913), 16–41. Heinegg, the leading authority on the origins of Virginia and North Carolina free black families, concluded that most traced their free heritage to white servant women; Kimmel noted a similar pattern in Maryland.

9. J. Leitch Wright, Jr., *The Only Land They Knew: The Tragic Story of the American Indians in the Old South* (New York: Free Press, 1981), 248–78; E. Franklin Frazier, *The Free Negro Family* (Nashville: Fisk University Press, 1932; reprint ed., New York: Arno Press, 1968), 13; E. Franklin Frazier, *The Negro Family in the United States* (Chicago: University of Chicago Press, 1939), 215–45; Douglas W. Boyce, "Iroquoian Tribes of the Virginia–North Carolina Coastal Plain," in William Sturtevant, ed., *Handbook of North American Indians,* vol. 15 (Washington, D.C.: Smithsonian Institution, 1978), 282–89; Christian F. Feest, "Virginia Algonquians," in Sturtevant, ed., *North American Indians,* vol. 15, 253–70; Brewton Berry, "Marginal Groups," in Sturtevant, ed., *North American Indians,* vol. 15, 290–95; Theda Perdue, *Native Carolinians: The Indians of North Carolina* (Raleigh: North Carolina Department of Cultural Resources, 1985), 25–31; Stanley A. South, *Indians in North Carolina* (Raleigh: North Carolina Division of Archives and History, 1959); Witt, ed., *Footprints in Northampton,* 6; Heinegg, *Free African Americans,* 16–21; Russell, *Free Negro in Virginia,* 127–30; Williamson, *New People,* 13; free papers of Dolphin Roberts, Jonathan Roberts Collection.

Roberts family tradition variously claims the family's Indian heritage to be that of Cherokees. It seems unlikely that James' mother was descended from that group, however, since they did not have a sizable presence in eastern Virginia or North Carolina.

The family's seemingly mistaken emphasis on this specific tribe is easily understood. In part, it reflects a common tendency of Indian-descended African Americans to presume that their Native American ancestry originates with the Cherokees and Seminoles, two larger groups widely known to the general public and groups often associated with African Americans. E. Franklin Frazier noted this tendency in the

1930s. The Robertses undoubtedly also have associated their kindred with Cherokees because of claims filed in the early twentieth century by several Roberts and Beech residents for a portion of the funds owed by the United States government to Cherokee descendants. Government officials dismissed these claims, but did note that many of the claimants had Indian physical features. For typical claims by those of Roberts Settlement, see the files of Minnie Gilliam (27926) and Fletcher Roberts (27065), Eastern Cherokee Indian Claims, Record Group 54, National Archives and Records Service, Washington, D.C.

10. Land deed books, Northampton County, 3:408, available on microfilm at NCSA; will of James Roberts, 3 March 1803, in wills, Northampton County, NCSA; tax list, 1780, in tax records, Northampton County, NCSA; *1790 North Carolina*, 73; genealogical charts, Jonathan Roberts Collection. Roberts family history materials in the Jonathan Roberts Collection, which correspond closely to census, probate, and other public records, disclose only the names of James and Ann's male offspring. James' will gives only limited, if any, additional information concerning his family. It mentions his wife Ann, grandson Willis, sons Elias and Claxton, and three individuals whose ties are not explicitly stated: Jonathan Roberts, William Roberts, and Mary Scott. Jonathan and William Roberts were probably his sons, while Mary Scott may have been a daughter or daughter-in-law.

11. Merrens, *Colonial North Carolina*, 63; land deed books, Northampton County, 3: 408, 6: 331, 8: 227, 10: 233, 340, 407, NCSA; will of James Roberts, Northampton County, NCSA.

Land deed books are subject to error because an uncertain number of transactions were not registered with local officials; any estimation of total holdings based on deeds is liable to reflect such underreporting. Tax records, while also subject to various forms of error, are generally a more reliable source for gauging real estate ownership. Available tax lists for Northampton County before 1840, however, cover only the years 1780 and 1823–1838. The land deed records related to the Robertses and other free black families in Northampton County apparently provide only a rough measure of their holdings. A comparison of holdings based on land deeds with holdings reported in probate records and later tax lists shows a small, though troublesome number of discrepancies. Land deed records for James Roberts, for example, indicate that he made three purchases totaling 570 acres between 1765 and 1785, while selling land totaling 375 acres between 1790 and 1797. Thus he would have owned 195 acres in 1803, the date at which he made out his last will; the will itself, however, describes James' estate as totaling 325 acres. The statement above that James' purchases totaled roughly 700 acres takes into account the apparent omission in deed records of a transaction in which James purchased an additional 130 acres.

12. Francis Grave Morris and Phyllis Mary Morris, "Economic Conditions in North Carolina About 1780: Part I, Landholdings," *North Carolina Historical Review* 16 (1939): 128–29; Cornelius Oliver Cathey, *Agricultural Developments in North Carolina, 1783–1860*, James Sprunt Publication Series, vol. 38 (Chapel Hill: University of North Carolina Press, 1956), 48; Nicholls, "Passing through This Troublesome World," 65–69; Berlin, *Slaves without Masters*, 58–64; Heinegg, *Free African Americans*, 7–10.

Cathey estimates that in 1783 one-fourth of landowners held 1 to 100 acres; one-fourth held 101 to 200 acres; one-fourth held 201 to 400 acres; and one-fourth held more than 400 acres. The Morrises, in a more detailed analysis of tax lists from 26 of 48 counties from 1777 to 1784, found that 47.5 percent of freeholders owned 1 to 200 acres; 25.8 percent owned 201 to 400 acres; and 26.6 percent more than 400 acres. In adjacent Halifax County, the Morrises noted, landholdings were somewhat more concentrated than in the state as a whole: 41.6 percent held 200 or less acres; 26.9 percent 201 to 400 acres; and 31.5 percent more than 400 acres. No estimate is available for Northampton County. Conditions in the adjacent Southside region of Virginia were broadly similar; see Kulikoff, *Tobacco and Slaves*, 155–56.

Heinegg provides a more positive assessment of free blacks' economic status than most other historians, claiming that most families in several North Carolina counties owned their own land. His individual genealogical accounts support the view that landownership may have been more widespread than is conventionally believed; whether they demonstrate that a majority of individual families held land, however, is difficult to determine without further analysis.

13. Michael Merrill, "Cash Is Good to Eat: Self-Sufficiency and Exchange in the Rural Economy of the United States," *Radical History Review* 3 (1977): 42–71; Leonard P. Curry, *The Free Black in Urban America, 1800–1850: The Shadow of the Dream* (Chicago: University of Chicago Press, 1981),16–35; Berlin, *Slaves without Masters*, 58–64; Nicholls, "Passing through This Troublesome World," 53.

14. Breen and Innes, *"Myne Owne Ground,"* 6, 78–80, 110–14; Heinegg, *Free African Americans*, 8. Heinegg observes that in mid-eighteenth century North Carolina, settlers were more concerned with social class than race, and specifically that wealthy mixed-race families were listed sometimes as mulattoes, and sometimes as whites.

For other views on the special meaning of landownership for free blacks, see Schweninger, *Black Property Owners*, 15–16; Orville Vernon Burton, *In My Father's House Are Many Mansions: Family and Community in Edgefield, South Carolina* (Chapel Hill: University of North Carolina Press, 1985), 205–206.

15. For evidence of the Robertses' early transactions, see the account books of Jonathan and Willis Roberts, Jonathan Roberts Collection; land deeds, Northampton County, 3: 408, 6: 331, 10: 407, NCSA; estate papers of Kinchen Roberts, NCSA. On the positive relations between at least some colonial North Carolina free blacks and their white neighbors, see Crow, *Revolutionary North Carolina*, 32, and Heinegg, *Free African Americans*, 6.

16. *1790 North Carolina*, 73; Carl Roberts, "Explanatory Notes," 2, Jonathan Roberts Collection; account books, Jonathan Roberts Collection; Schweninger, *Black Property Owners*, 22–25; John Hope Franklin, *The Free Negro in North Carolina, 1790–1860* (Chapel Hill: University of North Carolina Press, 1943),159–61, 184–85, 234–37; R. Halliburton, Jr., "Free Black Owners of Slaves: A Reappraisal of the Woodson Thesis," *South Carolina History Magazine* 76 (1975): 129–42; Philip J. Schwarz, "Emancipators, Protectors, and Anomalies: Free Black Slaveowners in Virginia," *Virginia Magazine of History and Biography* 95 (1987): 317–38; Michael P. Johnson and James L. Roark, *Black Masters: A Free Family of Color in the Old South* (New York: W. W. Norton, 1984), 23. Carl Roberts states that "There is no evidence that [the Robertses in Northampton County] or their ancestors were ever enslaved."

Recent historians have disagreed over the extent to which free black slaveholders held slaves for exploitative or fraternal/benevolent purposes. Halliburton emphasizes the former in a study of South Carolina, while Schwarz stresses the latter in a study of Virginia.

Johnson and Roark offer an insightful discussion of how the use of slaves by free black William Ellison aided Ellison in his efforts to establish himself in a rural South

Carolina district in the 1820s. "By showing that he did not hesitate to own, use, and exploit slave labor," Johnson and Roark note, Ellison "demonstrated to local whites that, although he was a Negro, although he had only recently been a slave himself, he was no more antislavery than they were—namely, not at all."

17. Berlin, *Slaves without Masters,* 7–10, 57–58; Crow, *Revolutionary North Carolina,* 30–33; Heinegg, *Free African Americans,* 2–9; Williamson, *New People,* 13; Jordan, *White over Black,* 167–74.

18. Carl G. Roberts, marginal comment included in transcription of Roberts family letters, Jonathan Roberts Collection. James Oliver Horton provides a similar line of argument to explain the more favorable treatment whites afforded mulattoes relative to blacks in antebellum Cincinnati; see Horton, "Shades of Color: The Mulatto in Three Antebellum Northern Communities," *Afro-Americans in New York Life and History* 19 (1986): 37–59, esp. 54–56.

19. Land deeds, Northampton County, 5: 321, 10: 66, 10: 233, 13: 33, NCSA; will of James Roberts, will records, NCSA. Land deed records list John Roberts as selling 106 acres in 1797; his only purchase, according to the deeds, was of 6 acres in 1779.

20. *1790 North Carolina,* 73; U.S. census manuscripts for Northampton County, 1800–1820, available on microfilm at Indiana State Library, Indianapolis; genealogical materials, Jonathan Roberts Collection, Library of Congress; will of James Roberts, will records, Northampton County, NCSA; undated tax list, ca. 1810–1816, Northampton County, NCSA; land deed record, Northampton County, 10:362, NCSA; file of John Roberts (S7402), Revolutionary War Pension Application Files, Record Group 15, National Archives and Records Service; Kulikoff, *Tobacco and Slaves,* 85–92, 158–61, 173, 187; Phillip J. Greven, Jr., *Four Generations: Population, Land, and Family in Colonial Andover, Massachusetts* (Ithaca: Cornell University Press, 1970); Daniel Scott Smith, "Parental Power and Marriage Patterns: An Analysis of Historical Trends in Massachusetts," *Journal of Marriage and the Family* 35 (1973): 419–28; Robert A. Gross, *The Minutemen and Their World* (New York: Hill and Wang, 1976).

21. Cathey, *Agricultural Development,* 48–49; Lewis Cecil Gray, *History of Agriculture in the Southern United States to 1860,* vol. 2 (New York: Peter Smith, 1941), 889, 912–14; Guion Griffis Johnson, *Ante-bellum North Carolina: A Social History* (Chapel Hill: University of North Carolina Press, 1937), 38–41; U.S. Bureau of Census, *A Century of Population Growth from the First Census of the United States to the Twelfth, 1790–1900* (Washington, D.C.: Government Printing Office, 1909), 204–205; idem, *Return of the Whole Number of Persons Within . . . the United States . . . Second Census* (Washington, D.C.: W. Duane and Son, 1802), 69, 74; idem, *Aggregate Amount of Each Description of Persons Within the United States . . . 1810* (Washington, D.C., 1811), 54a, 75a; idem, *Census for 1820* (Washington, D.C.: Gales and Seaton, 1821), 24–25; idem, *Fifth Census, or Enumeration of the Inhabitants of the United States, 1830* (Washington, D.C.: Duff Green, 1832), 25 a; idem, *Abstract of the Returns of the Fifth Census . . .* (Washington, D.C.: Duff Green, 1832), 16, 19; receipts of Claxton, William, and Willis Roberts, 23 February 1810, and Willis Roberts, 19 October 1820, and 6 December 1828.

22. Census, Northampton County, 1800–1820; Cathey, *Agricultural Development,* 49; land deed books, Northampton County, 17:45, 20:51, NCSA; land deeds of Ransom Roberts and James Roberts, Jonathan Roberts Collection; will of Jonathan Roberts, will records, Northampton County, NCSA; tax lists, 1823–35, Northampton County, NCSA. Land indentures for Jonathan's sale of land to Ransom and James are

included in Jonathan Roberts Collection, but apparently were not registered with local authorities.

23. Jordan, *White over Black,* 315–582; Duncan J. MacLeod, "Toward Caste," in Ira Berlin and Ronald Hoffman, eds., *Slavery and Freedom in the Age of the American Revolution* (Charlottesville: University Press of Virginia, 1983), 230–35; Sylvia Frey, *Water from the Rock: Black Resistance in a Revolutionary Age* (Princeton: Princeton University Press, 1991), 223–42, esp. 240–42; Jeffrey J. Crow, "Slave Rebelliousness and Social Conflict in North Carolina, 1775 to 1802," *William and Mary Quarterly* 37 (1980): 79–102; Crow, *Revolutionary North Carolina,* 87–95.

24. Jordan, *White over Black,* 407–14, 575–82; Berlin, *Slaves without Masters,* 79–107, 184–92, 199–212; Franklin, *Free Negro in North Carolina,* 58–74, 184–89; David Dodge, "Free Negroes of North Carolina," *Atlantic Monthly* (January 1886): 20–30.

25. Franklin, *Free Negro in North Carolina,* 60–72, 184–89. Quote is from the 1795 statute as cited in Franklin, p. 60.

26. *1790 North Carolina,* 72–76; Herbert Aptheker, *American Negro Slave Revolts* (New York: Columbia University Press, 1943; reprint ed., New York: International Publishers, 1963), 231, 244–47, 277; census, Northampton County, 1820; slave patrol order of September 1830, slave records, Northampton County, NCSA.

27. Johnson, *Ante-bellum North Carolina,* 510–13, 516–17, 519–20; Charles Edward Morris, "Panic and Reprisal: Reaction in North Carolina to the Nat Turner Insurrection, 1831," *North Carolina Historical Review* 62 (1985): 33–37; Frankfort, Kentucky *Guardian of Freedom,* 7 July 1802, 3.

28. Edgar Conkling, "Roberts Settlement," 24; Roberts, "History of Roberts Settlement"; Lawrence Carter, unpublished, untitled notebooks on history of Beech Settlement, 4 vols., Indiana Historical Society Library, Indianapolis; letter of James L. Roberts to Willis Roberts, n.d. [February 1830], Jonathan Roberts Collection, Library of Congress. The spelling, capitalization, and punctuation of this and subsequently cited letters from the Jonathan Roberts Collection have been modernized; no alteration has been made of the writers' grammar, syntax, or choice of words.

29. Letter, James L. Roberts to Willis Roberts, n.d. [February 1830], Jonathan Roberts Collection.

30. File of Drewry Walden (R11014), Revolutionary War Pensions, NARS; tax list, 1780, Northampton County, NCSA; land deed book, Northampton County, 10: 204, 10: 316, 13: 155, 13: 195, 20: 51, NCSA; tax lists, 1823–1835, Northampton County, NCSA; Heinegg, *Free African Americans,* 603–605, 608–609.

31. Will of Drewry Walden, Northampton County, NCSA; file of Drewry Walden (R11014), Revolutionary War Pensions, NARS; census manuscripts, 1800–1820, Northampton County; tax lists, 1823–35, Northampton County, NCSA.

32. *1790 North Carolina,* 61–66, 72–76; 1780 tax list, Northampton County, NCSA; Heinegg, *Free African Americans,* 61–78, 125–30, 449–54, 526–35.

33. Will and estate records of John Bass and James Byrd, Northampton County, NCSA; tax lists, 1823–35, Northampton County, NCSA.

34. U.S. Census, *A Century of Population Growth,* 204–205; idem, *Second Census,* 69, 74; idem, *Aggregate . . . 1810,* 54a, 75a; idem, *Census for 1820,* 24–25; file of John Winburn (S7937), Revolutionary War Pensions, NARS; *1790 North Carolina,* 65; claim applications of Thadeus Winburn (27032) and Bryant Brooks (39150), Eastern Cherokee Claims, NARS; land deeds, Halifax County, 14: 195, 18: 832, 19: 288, 21: 422, 22: 51, 245: 307, NCSA; wills of Thomas Winburn and Lucy Murry, will records, Halifax County, NCSA; Heinegg, *Free African Americans,* 351–59, 638–39.

The names of John Winburn and Benjamin James are listed next to one another in the 1790 census, indicating the close proximity of their residences. Government agents in 1908 noted that Bryant Brooks, the grandson of Benjamin James, showed "strong Indian (& Negro) descent." No tax records and few probate records for the late eighteenth and early nineteenth centuries have survived for Halifax County.

Population figures for Halifax County, 1790–1820, parallel those from Northampton:

	1790	1800	1810	1820
Total	14,310	13,563	15,620	17,237
Whites	7,170 (50%)	5,920 (44%)	5,760 (37%)	6,371 (37%)
Slaves	6,697 (47%)	7,020 (52%)	8,624 (55%)	9,450 (55%)
Free blacks	443 (3%)	623 (5%)	1,236 (8%)	1,551 (9%)

35. Tax lists, 1823–1838, Northampton County, NCSA; U.S. census manuscripts, Northampton and Halifax counties, 1830, available on microfilm, Indiana State Library. Two factors make it impossible to calculate precisely the number and proportion of households located in a specific militia district. Northampton tax records, for one, list taxable males and landowners, not households per se. For another, taxable individuals, especially those who were young and landless—a growing group in the 1820s and early 1830s—often migrated from area to area in search of work and land to buy or rent. Nonetheless, roughly three-quarters of those listed from the free black kindreds resided in Districts 3 and 4 throughout the 1820s and early 1830s. In 1826, for example, 18 out of 25 (72%) were reported in the two districts.

36. Master index of North Carolina marriage bonds, 1741–1868, available on microfiche, NCSA.

37. Johnson, Ante-bellum *North Carolina,* 203–205; Raymond A. Winslow, Jr., "Marriage, Divorce, and Vital Statistics," in *North Carolina Research: Genealogy and Local History* (Raleigh: North Carolina Genealogical Society, 1980), 131–37; genealogical materials, Jonathan Roberts Collection; wills of Jonathan Roberts, Martha Walden, Winnifred Newsom, Nathaniel Newsom will records, Northampton County, NCSA. More detailed analysis of marriage bond patterns is precluded by the fact that small numbers of whites in Northampton and Halifax shared the surnames of the families that migrated to Beech and Roberts settlement, as well as the failure of the bonds to indicate the race of those to be married. In some instances inferences could be based on the names of the marriage party and the bondsmen, who were usually friends or kin of the groom. Those involving members of the Byrd, James, and Walden families, for example, apparently referred to free blacks; all 17 households headed by individuals with those names in Northampton and Halifax counties in 1820 were free blacks. In other instances the choice was less clear cut; only 2 of 10 Bass families were listed as whites in 1820. Overall, 56 of 74 households (75.7 percent) sharing the names of the principal Beech and Roberts families—Bass, Byrd, James, Newsom, Roberts, Walden, Winburn—in Northampton and Halifax counties in 1820 were headed by free blacks.

38. Marriage bonds of Hansel and Priscilla Roberts, James and Martha Roberts, Watts and Elizabeth Roberts, index to marriage bonds, NCSA; Kulikoff, *Tobacco and Slaves,* 252–55; E. H. Fitchett, "The Traditions of the Free Negro in Charleston, South Carolina," *Journal of Negro History* 25 (1940): 139–42; Johnson, *Ante-bellum*

North Carolina, 191. The Winburn and James kindreds, in Halifax County, appear also to have been closely allied. Four Winburn–James weddings took place between 1816 and 1830, including two between couples who would migrate to Beech Settlement in the early 1830s.

39. Index to marriage bonds, NCSA; *Heads of Families,* 61–65, 72–76.

40. Heinegg, *Free African Americans,* 8, 70, 75; Carter, notebooks, 1: 30–34; Carl G. Roberts, marginal comment included in transcription of Roberts family letters, Jonathan Roberts Collection; Conkling, "Roberts Settlement," 21–22; Frazier, *Negro Family in the United States,* 519–20.

Heinegg notes that several Bass family members in Northampton County married whites; many subsequently adopted white identities. Carl Roberts, in a marginal comment, indicates that James Roper, who is listed in the 1790 census as a white, "intermarried with the Roberts family." Conkling, whose discussion is based largely on interviews with Carl Roberts, notes that the Roberts family in the late eighteenth century began intermarrying with families who migrated to Northampton and Halifax counties from Virginia about that time. In an interview with E. Franklin Frazier, Carl Roberts noted that his grandmother, Kessiah Corbin, was a slave who had been purchased, married, and freed by his grandfather, Elijah Roberts.

41. Tiara Sudarkasa, "African and Afro-American Family Structure: A Comparison," *Black Scholar* 11 (1980): 37–60; Kulikoff, *Tobacco and Slaves,* 347, 374; John W. Adams and Alice B. Kasakoff, "Factors Affecting Endogamous Group Size," in Moni Nag, ed., *Population and Social Structure* (The Hague: Mouton Publishers, 1973), 147–74; John W. Adams and Alice B. Kasakoff, "Migration and the Family in Colonial New England: The View from Genealogies," *Journal of Family History* 9 (1984): 28–29; Heinegg, *Free African Americans.*

For the influence of African cultural beliefs on family ties among Afro-Americans in the twentieth century South see Demitri B. Shimkin, Gloria Jean Louie, and Dennis A. Frate, "The Black Extended Family: A Basic Rural Institution and a Mechanism of Urban Adaptation," in Demitri B. Shimkin, Edith Shimkin, and Dennis A. Frate, eds., *The Extended Family in Black Societies* (The Hague: Mouton Publishers, 1978), 66–73, 112–30; for the same influence among slaves in the antebellum South, see Herbert Gutman, *The Black Family in Slavery and Freedom, 1750–1925* (New York: Random House, 1976), 87–93, 113–14, 131–38.

A cursory examination of Heinegg's genealogical data for North Carolina and Virginia reinforces the view that free people of color throughout northeastern Virginia and southeastern Virginia were well acquainted and shared a common identity with one another.

42. Wills of James Roberts, John Bass, Jonathan Roberts, Drewry Walden, Michael Walden, Martha Walden; estates of Kinchen Roberts, James Roberts, Jr., James Roberts (son of Jonathan), John Walden, James Byrd, Jesse Byrd, Solomon Byrd, Moses Byrd, Phillip Byrd. All in records of Northampton County, NCSA.

43. Estates of Jesse Byrd, Kinchen Roberts in Northampton County, NCSA.

44. Eighteenth century inheritance customs in nearby Virginia are described in Kulikoff, *Tobacco and Slaves,* 188–93.

45. Wills of James Roberts, John Bass, Jonathan Roberts, Drewry Walden, Michael Walden, Martha Walden; estates of Kinchen Roberts, James Roberts, Jr., James Roberts (son of Jonathan), John Walden, James Byrd, Jesse Byrd, Solomon Byrd, Moses Byrd, Phillip Byrd; estate sales and inventory records of Dempsey Winburn,

James Roberts (son of Jonathan), John Bass, Drewry Walden, Council Bass, Jesse Byrd, James Byrd, Kinchen Roberts. All in Northampton County, NCSA.

46. Franklin, *Free Negro in North Carolina*, 82–84, 153–55; Arlene Eakle, "American Court Records," in Arlene Eakle and Johni Cerny, eds., *The Source: A Guidebook of American Genealogy* (Salt Lake City, 1984); Heinegg, *Free African Americans*, 355. Collecting debts owed to a decedent was especially difficult. Heinegg notes a revealing anecdotal comment written by William Gray, the executor for the estate of Frederick James, from adjacent Bertie County. In his inventory of the estate Gray wrote that there were "Sundry Book accts (the amt. unknown) all of which are Extremely doubtful—as the Testator was a colored man & there is no legal way to prove them."

47. John Hope Franklin discusses one instance in which a free Negro testator clearly had established a patron-client relationship with her attorney and executor. See Franklin, *Free Negro in North Carolina*, 153. The warmth of Willis Roberts' ties with James Davis, Wyatt Brantley, Thomas Clifton and other white neighbors can be seen in letters written shortly after Willis' move to the frontier. See letters of 1 February 1830, 9 January 1831, 10 July 1831, and 22 August 1831, Jonathan Roberts Collection.

48. Letters of n.d. [1 February 1830], 9 January 1831, Jonathan Roberts Collection; file of Drewry Walden (R11014), Revolutionary Pensions, NARS; Witt, ed., *Footprints in Northampton*, 7, 9; Larry E. Tise, "North Carolina Methodism from the Revolution to the War of 1812," in O. Kelly Ingram, ed., *Methodism Alive in North Carolina* (Durham, N.C.: Duke Divinity School, 1976), 43–46; Donald G. Mathews, "North Carolina Methodists in the Nineteenth Century: Church and Society," in Ingram, *Methodism Alive*, 59–66; Grady L. E. Carroll, ed., *Francis Asbury in North Carolina: The North Carolina Portions of "The Journal of Francis Asbury"* (Nashville: Parthenon Press, 1964).

49. Witt, ed., *Footprints in Northampton*, 10–11; slave patrol orders, 1830, slave records, Northampton County, NCSA; Franklin, *Free Negro in North Carolina*, 174–82; Berlin, *Slaves without Masters*, 285–86, 296–97.

50. Receipts of 22 December 1801, 6 April 1804, 16 January 1828, 17 December 1828, account book, Jonathan Roberts Collection; Franklin, *Free Negro in North Carolina*, 164–69; Berlin, *Slaves without Masters*, 74–78, 303–306.

51. Tax lists, 1825–31, Northampton County, NCSA; marriage bond of General Tootle, Halifax County, marriage bond index, NCSA; Carter G. Woodson, *Free Negro Heads of Families in the United States in 1830* (Washington: Association for the Study of Negro Life and History, 1925), 117; Heinegg, *Free African Americans*.

52. U.S. Census, *A Century of Population Growth*, 204–205; idem, *Second Census*, 69, 74; idem, *Aggregate . . . 1810*, 54a, 75a; idem, *Census for 1820*, 24–25; census manuscripts, Greensville County, 1810–1820; personal and property tax records, Greensville County, available on microfilm, Virginia State Library, Richmond.

Greensville's slower rate of population growth for free blacks relative to Northampton and Halifax apparently reflected the group's out-migration from the former to the latter, and from southern areas of Virginia to areas just south of the Virginia–North Carolina border in general. For discussion of the broader free black migration from southern Virginia to northern North Carolina, see Dodge, "Free Negroes of North Carolina," 23–24, and Heinegg, *Free African Americans*, passim.

For discussion of the general conditions facing Virginia's free black population in the nineteenth century, see John H. Russell, *The Free Negro in Virginia, 1619–1865*,

Johns Hopkins University Studies in Historical and Political Science, series 31, no. 3 (Baltimore: Johns Hopkins University Press, 1913), 88–177; Berlin, *Slaves without Masters*, 91–99, 181–92, 199–212; Nicholls, "Passing through This Troublesome World," 50–70.

Population of Greensville Co., 1790–1820:

	1790	1800	1810	1820
Total	6,362	6,727	6,853	6,858
Whites	2,530 (40%)	2,398 (36%)	2,254* (NA%)	2,056 (30%)
Slaves	3,620 (57%)	4,116 (61%)	4,599* (NA%)	4,512 (66%)
Free blacks	212 (3%)	213 (3%)	.....* (NA%)	290 (4%)

*The aggregate number of free blacks apparently was combined with that of slaves and/or whites in 1810.

53. Census manuscripts, Greensville County, 1810–1820; free Negro register, marriage, probate, tax, and land deed records, Greensville County, available on microfilm, Virginia State Library.

54. Interview with Robert Forest Hazel, 13 July 1997; email correspondence, Robert Forest Hazel to Stephen Vincent, 9 September 1997; Robert Forest Hazel, "The Andrews Jeffries Line: Greensville Co., Virginia to Alamance Co., North Carolina," unpublished report presented to Recognition Committee, North Carolina Commission of Indian Affairs, Department of Cultural Resources, Raleigh, North Carolina; tax records and free Negro register, Greensville County.

The Jeffries family's Occaneechi heritage has been thoroughly documented by Robert Forest Hazel. Hazel, an independent researcher, has done an extensive investigation for the Occaneechi of Alamance County, North Carolina, as part of the group's efforts to gain formal recognition from the State of North Carolina. His work has included tracing the Jeffries family's lineage and history in Greensville, Alamance, and several Ohio, Indiana, and Michigan locations, and leaves little doubt about the family's Native American heritage. Sources for Hazel's investigation have included Greensville tax, probate, and other local public records; Revolutionary War pension applications; nineteenth century court testimony concerning the family's Indian ancestry; published local histories from the late nineteenth century; and a late nineteenth century U.S. Senate investigation of Native Americans in Alamance. I am deeply indebted to Mr. Hazel for sharing this information.

55. Property and personal tax lists, Greensville County, VSL.

56. Census manuscripts, 1830, Halifax County; free Negro register, personal and property tax lists, Greensville County, VSL; claim application of Lewis H. Winburn (35724), Eastern Cherokee Claims, NARS; purchase of Anthony Clark, in U.S. public land entry books, Indianapolis office, vol. 5, available on microfilm, Indiana State Archives, Indianapolis. Edwin Jones, Marmajake Turner, and Jeremiah Powell were householders mentioned in Greensville records; Anthony Clark was listed in the 1830 census; and William Keemer was noted as a Halifax resident in a Cherokee claim application filed by Lewis Winburn, his son-in-law. Clark purchased forty acres at Beech Settlement in 1833.

57. For overviews of the topic of free people of color in the North and the South,

see Leon F. Litwack, *North of Slavery: The Negro in the Free States, 1790–1860* (Chicago: University of Chicago Press, 1961), and Berlin, *Slaves without Masters*. The theme of unfulfilled promise and bitter disappointments helps shape the perceptive discussion in Gary Nash, *Forging Freedom: The Formation of Philadelphia's Black Community, 1720–1840* (Cambridge, Mass.: Harvard University Press, 1988).

2. MIGRATION TO THE FRONTIER, CA. 1820–1840

1. Lawrence Carter, unpublished notebooks on history of Beech Settlement (4 vols.), I:101, available on microfilm, Indiana Historical Society Library, Indianapolis.

2. Allan Kulikoff, "Migration and Cultural Diffusion in Early America, 1600–1860: A Review Essay," *Historical Methods* 19 (1986): 164–65; John Mack Faragher, *Sugar Creek: Life on the Illinois Prairie* (New Haven: Yale University Press, 1986), 46–52; Jon Gjerde, *From Peasants to Farmers: The Migration from Balestrand, Norway to the Upper Middle West* (Cambridge: Cambridge University Press, 1985); Robert C. Ostergren, *A Community Transplanted: The Trans-Atlantic Experience of a Swedish Immigrant Settlement in the Upper Middle West, 1835–1915* (Madison: University of Wisconsin Press, 1988); Walter Kamphoefner, *The Westfalians* (Princeton: Princeton University Press, 1987).

3. The hopeful aspirations of those from Northampton County are expressed implicitly in the Roberts family letters, Jonathan Roberts Collection, Library of Congress. See especially the letter of James L. Roberts to Willis Roberts, n.d. [February 1829].

4. Berlin, *Slaves without Masters*, 99–101, 165–68; Walker, *Free Frank*, 62–68, 72–74. For a general discussion of kidnapping see Carol Wilson, *Freedom at Risk: The Kidnapping of Free Blacks in America* (Lexington: University of Kentucky Press, 1994); for a detailed overview of kidnapping in one northern frontier state, see Thornbrough, *Negro in Indiana*, 99–108.

5. Breen and Innes, *"Myne Owne Ground,"* 107–109; Heinegg, *Free African Americans*, 4–6; files of Drew Walden (R11014), John Roberts (S7402), Mark Murry (R7523) and Jeremiah James (W467), Revolutionary War Pension Application Files, Record Group 15, National Archives and Records Service, Washington D.C. Information concerning western migration patterns comes largely from Revolutionary War pension files. Mark Murry, whose kin had intermarried with the Winburns of Halifax County, moved to Wilson County, Tennessee, in 1810; Jeremiah James migrated to Nashville; Drew Walden's kin went in various directions following his death, with some moving to Tennessee, and others to Ohio and Indiana. A small number of early Beech Settlement pioneers appear to have settled in Tennessee before moving to the Northwest after 1830. The households of Alexander and Drew Moss, 1840 Beech householders, were listed in Sullivan County, Tennessee, in 1830; see Woodson, *Free Negroes in 1830*, 161.

6. R. Carlyle Buley, *The Old Northwest, Pioneer Period, 1815–1840*, 2 vols. (Indianapolis: Indiana Historical Society, 1950; reprint ed., Bloomington: Indiana University Press, 1983), I: 109–15, II: 43–100; Rodabaugh, "Negro in Northwest," 221–24; Eugene H. Berwanger, *The Frontier against Slavery: Western Anti-Negro Prejudice and the Slavery Extension Controversy* (Urbana: University of Illinois Press, 1967), 19–29; Ira Berlin, "The Structure of the Free Negro Caste in the Antebellum United States," *Journal of Social History* 9 (1975–1976): 302. An important source of information concerning the Northwest may have been local Quakers, who were attempting to remove their slaves from North Carolina, including Northampton County, to the

Northwest, Liberia, and other areas in the 1820s and early 1830s. See the discussion on pp. 32–35.

7. U.S. Bureau of the Census, *Negro Population 1790–1915* (Washington, D.C.: Government Printing Office, 1918), 45; Rodabaugh, "Negro in Northwest," 221–24; Berwanger, *Frontier against Slavery,* 19–29; Faragher, *Sugar Creek,* 46–49. The white population of the Old Northwest in 1820 was 785,028, while that of blacks totaled 7,691.

8. Charles Thomas Hickok, *The Negro in Ohio, 1802–1870* (Cleveland, 1896; New York: AMS Press, 1975), 40–46; Thornbrough, *Negro in Indiana,* 120–22, 125.

9. Personal tax lists, 1816–39, Greensville County, available on microfilm at the Virginia State Library, Richmond; U.S. public land entry books for Indianapolis Land Office, vol. 5, Indiana State Archives, Indianapolis; Woodson, *Free Negroes in 1830,* 126; family genealogy of Murphy White, unpublished papers in possession of Murphy White, Noblesville, Ind., photocopy in possession of author; tax lists, 1823–39, Northampton County, North Carolina State Archives, Raleigh; free papers of Elijah Roberts, 8 March 1820, Jonathan Roberts Collection, Library of Congress, Washington, D.C.; Irven Armstrong, "Negro Pioneers: First Settlers Came into Indiana in 1820," *Indianapolis Recorder,* V-J Day Edition, 7 July 1945, 3:13, 17.

The precise dates of departure for most of those who would come to Beech and Roberts settlements, along with the pioneers' locations before coming to the Indiana communities, are a matter of some dispute. Local histories are often at odds with information derived from census, tax, and other public records. The discussion provided here is based upon local histories where they agree with primary sources, and upon inferences from the primary sources themselves. Personal tax records are especially helpful in determining the dates of departure; when individuals left their homes, county officials struck their names from the register, and at times noted "removed" or "moved away." Hence, in Greensville John Watkins' name was removed after 1820, and Macklin, Sarah, and other Jeffries family members' names were struck out after 1825. In Northampton County, Elijah Roberts' name is not listed after 1825, and John and Anthony Roberts' names disappear after 1824. John Watkins listed Montgomery County as his place of residence when purchasing land at Beech Settlement in 1833; this is at odds with Armstrong's account that describes him as coming to Beech in the late 1820s.

10. Philip J. Grevens, Jr., *Four Generations: Population, Land, and Family in Colonial Andover, Massachusetts* (Ithaca, N.Y.: Cornell University Press, 1970), esp. 155–72; John W. Adams and Alice Bee Kasakoff, "Migration and the Family in Colonial New England: The View from Genealogies," *Journal of Family History* 9 (1984): 24–43; Gjerde, *Peasants to Farmers,* 119–23; Ostergren, *A Community Transplanted,* 111–14, 125–28; Robert E. Bieder, "Kinship as a Factor in Migration," *Journal of Family and Marriage* 35 (1973): 434–36.

11. James E. Davis, *Frontier America, 1800–1840: A Comparative Demographic Analysis of the Settlement Process* (Glendale, Calif.: Arthur H. Clark, 1977), 121–28. Davis found that blacks in 1820 accounted for .6 percent of settlers in a sampling of northern counties that experienced a rise in their population density from less than two persons per square mile to two to six persons per square mile from 1810 to 1820; in 1830, using the same rise in density formula, he found blacks accounted for only .4 percent of the population in his sampling. He notes that "blacks simply lacked the economic clout necessary to make the trek, the protection of law during the settlement process, and overall positive reinforcements and encouragements." Davis fails,

however, to consider the strategies employed by free blacks to insure their safety, strategies that necessitated migration somewhat later than whites.

Free Frank McWhorter, a free black migrating from Kentucky to Illinois in 1831, utilized a somewhat different strategy than those who came to Beech and Roberts settlements. His caution, however, was strikingly similar. See Walker, *Free Frank*, 62–68, 72–74.

12. Roberts, "Explanatory Notes," 6; and correspondence of Willis Roberts, 1828–1834: both located in Jonathan Roberts Collection.

13. Roberts, "Explanatory Notes," 6; United States Census manuscripts for Rush County, Indiana, 1830, available on microfilm at Indiana State Library, Indianapolis.

14. Sarah Newby, unpublished, undated notes on history of Ripley Township Friends, located on microfilm in Ripley Township Collection at Rushville (Indiana) Public Library; W. Howard Winslow, "A History of Walnut Ridge Quarterly Meeting," unpublished manuscript, dated May 1909, located in Ripley Township collection; "History of Carthage Friends Church," unpublished, undated manuscript located at Indiana State Library, Indianapolis; *History of Rush County, Indiana* (Chicago, 1888; reprint ed., Knightstown, Ind.: Eastern Indiana Publishing, 1966), 338, 339, 657–60; Abraham Lincoln Gary and E. B. Thomas, ed., *Centennial History of Rush County, Indiana,* 2 vols. (Indianapolis: Historical Publishing, 1921), 1: 239, 240.

15. Hiram Hilty, *Toward Freedom For All: North Carolina Quakers and Slavery* (Richmond, Ind.: Friends United Press, 1984), 1–39; Peter Kent Opper, "North Carolina Quakers: Reluctant Slaveholders," *North Carolina Historical Review* 52 (1975): 37–39; Stephen Weeks, *Southern Quakers and Slavery: A Study in Institutional History* (Baltimore: Johns Hopkins University Press, 1896), 206–25; [Meeting for Sufferings of the North Carolina Yearly Meeting], *A Narrative of Some of the Proceedings of North Carolina Yearly Meeting on the Subject of Slavery within Its Limits* (Greensboro: Swaim and Sherwood, 1848), 5–22. A general overview of American Quakers' broader struggles against slavery is found in Thomas E. Drake, *Quakers and Slavery in America* (New Haven: Yale University Press, 1950; reprint ed., Gloucester, Mass.: Peter Smith, 1965).

16. Hilty, *North Carolina Quakers and Slavery,* 41–88; Opper, "Reluctant Slaveholders," 40–58; *Narrative of the North Carolina Meeting,* 11–40; Meeting for Sufferings Correspondence, Quaker Collection, Guilford College.

17. Hilty, *North Carolina Quakers and Slavery,* 29–41, 70, 81–85; letter, Nathan Mendenhall to Asa Folger, 16 July 1826, in Meeting for Sufferings Correspondence, Guilford College.

18. Jordan, *White over Black,* 482–582; Hilty, *North Carolina Quakers and Slavery,* 39–41. For the persistence of negative racial stereotypes among North Carolina and Indiana Quakers, respectively, see Hilty, *North Carolina Quakers and Slavery,* 89–100, 107–108; and William Tallack, *Friendly Sketches in America* (London: A. W. Bennett, 1861), 52–53, 231–32.

19. Letters of Samuel Charles to Jeremiah Hubbard and Harry Ballenger, 10 August 1826, and William Talbert to Nathan Mendenhall, 12 November 1826, Meeting for Sufferings Correspondence, Guilford College; minutes, Meeting for Sufferings, Indiana Yearly Meeting, located in Quaker Collection, Earlham College; letters of Robert Parker, Josiah Parker, William Parker, and William Flanner, located in Josiah Parker Papers, Quaker Collection, Earlham College. Quote is from Charles' letter to Hubbard and Ballenger.

20. Receipt of Jonathan Roberts, 3 November 1815, Jonathan Roberts Collection, Library of Congress; declaration of Micajah Binford concerning free heritage of Anthony and Elizabeth Roberts, Rush County, Indiana Court Order Books, located in Clerk's Office, Rush County Courthouse, Rushville, Indiana.

21. Minute book of North Carolina Friends Meeting for Sufferings, November 1826, August 1828, November 1832, November 1833, November 1834, November 1835, Quaker Collection, Guilford College; letter of Josiah Parker to Richard Mendenhall and Phineas Albertson, 14 January 1827, Meeting for Sufferings Correspondence, Guilford College; account book of Josiah Parker and letter of William Parker to Josiah Parker, 26 July 1826, Josiah Parker Papers.

22. Minutes, Rich Square Monthly Meeting, February 1826, located in Quaker Collection, Guilford College; William Wade Hinshaw, *Encyclopedia of American Quaker Genealogy*, 7 vols. (Ann Arbor: Edwards Bros., 1936–1972), I: 205; "Historical Sketch, Binford Family," unpublished, undated manuscript located on microfilm in Ripley Township Collection, Rushville Public Library; *History of Rush County*, 555–56; letter of William Parker to Josiah Parker, 8 October 1828, Josiah Parker Papers, Earlham College. Apparently alluding to a recent journey he had made from Northampton to Ripley Township, William Parker noted on 8 October 1828 that "several that came on with me have had the ague and fever *James Roberts* among them . . ." [emphasis added].

23. Census manuscripts, Rush County, 1830; Thomas T. Newby, *Reminiscences* (Carthage, Ind., 1916), 17; land deed books, Rush County, Indiana, located in Recorder's Office, Rush County Courthouse, Rushville, Indiana; United States Census manuscripts, Rush County, Indiana, 1840, available on microfilm at Indiana State Library, Indianapolis.

Two of the fourteen households in 1830 were headed by members of the McCowan family, which purchased Rush County land outside of Ripley Township. Only the Carys and Robertses among the remaining twelve were listed as Ripley Township householders in 1840.

24. Land deeds, Rush County; Buley, *Old Northwest,* I: 95–99, II: 148–53; Percy Wells Bidwell and John I. Falconer, *History of Agriculture in the Northern United States* (Washington, D.C.: Carnegie Institution, 1925), 154–55; Katherine Mandusic McDonell, "Landholding Patterns in Hamilton County, Indiana, 1821–1840," paper prepared for research department, Conner Prairie Pioneer Settlement, Noblesville, Ind., 1982, 19–20.

25. Land deeds, Rush County; census manuscripts, Rush County, 1840; founding agreement, [Mount Pleasant] Methodist Church, 18 July 1832, in Jonathan Roberts Collection.

One gauge of the Beech Settlement's population by the summer of 1832 is found in the founding agreement for the Beech area's first church, which lists the names of at least forty-three individuals. Included in the list are the names of five individuals who would later buy government lands; presumably some settled on their homesteads before their purchases.

26. U.S. land entry books, vol. 5, Indiana State Archives; Woodson, *Free Negroes in 1830,* 126; *Atlas of Rush County,* 67; land deeds, Rush County; Willard Heiss, ed., *Abstracts of the Records of the Society of Friends in Indiana,* 7 vols. (Indianapolis: Indiana Historical Society, 1962–1975); Thomas C. Hill, "Quaker Meetings in Southwest Ohio," paper in Quaker Collection, Earlham College, Richmond, Indiana. Land en-

try books note the previous residences of John Watkins, General Tootle, Alexander Moss, Drewry Moss, and Hugh Bobson.

27. Sarah Newby, notes, 16–17; tax lists and land deed indexes, Randolph County, North Carolina State Archives, Raleigh.

Suggestions that Emsley Lassiter and David Winslow may have been members of Quaker-held kindreds include surnames common to Friends and prior settlement near Friends in Randolph County, North Carolina. Randolph County tax and land records provide few clues about the Lassiter and Winslow families' backgrounds; apparently they had not lived in the area as free people of color over an extensive period of time.

28. Carter, notebooks, 1:78 and passim, Lawrence Carter Collection; Conkling, "Roberts Settlement," 22–24.

29. Gjerde, *From Peasants to Farmers*; Kamphoefner, *Westfalians*.

30. Dodge, "Free Negroes of North Carolina," 24; Stephen Oates, *The Fires of Jubilee: Nat Turner's Fierce Rebellion* (New York: Harper and Row, 1975); Morris, "Panic and Reprisal," 29–52; tax lists, Greensville County, 1833–35. Quote is from Dodge, who lived in North Carolina during the antebellum period.

The out-migration of free blacks from Virginia after the Turner affair went well beyond Greensville, and included many landowners and others of substantial means. See Luther Porter Jackson, *Free Negro Labor and Property Holding in Virginia, 1830–1860* (New York: D. Appleton-Century, 1942), 112–14; Aptheker, *American Negro Slave Revolts*, 323; and Carl Lane and Rhoda Freeman, "John Dipper and the Experience of the Free Black Elite, 1816–1836," *Virginia Magazine of History and Biography* 100 (October 1992): 500–505.

31. Roberts family letters, Jonathan Roberts Collection. Letters quoted are those of Hansel Roberts to Willis Roberts, 10 July 1831; Hansel and Ransom Roberts to Willis and James L. Roberts, 17 March 1833; Grey Walden et al. to Dolphin Roberts et al., 20 April 1834.

32. Letter of Willis and James L. Roberts to Hansel and Elias Roberts, 22 August 1831, Jonathan Roberts Collection.

33. Carter, notebooks, 1: 25, 72, and passim, Lawrence Carter Collection; Lyda, *Negro in Indiana*, 23–24; Armstrong, "Negro Pioneers," 17; letter of Richard Roberts to Anthony Roberts, 6 September 1833, Jonathan Roberts Collection. The increased danger of kidnapping that free blacks faced while traveling is noted in Wilson, *Freedom at Risk*, 43.

34. *History of Rush County*, 338, 657–60; Wayne E. Kiefer, *Rush County, Indiana: A Study in Rural Settlement Geography*, Indiana University Geographic Monograph Series, vol. 2 (Bloomington: Indiana University Press, 1969), 26–34; land deeds, Rush County.

35. Land deeds, Rush County. Deed records indicate that land was sold among Beech Settlement farm owners in the late 1830s at roughly the same prices paid by blacks to whites. Thus it appears free blacks who purchased land in the late 1830s bought it at fair prices. Whether or not whites expressed a reluctance to sell to free blacks, probably a more important issue, is not discernible from transfer records.

36. Conkling, "Roberts Settlement," 24–26. Out-migration from the Beech to other farm communities continued through the end of the nineteenth century; see chaps. 3–5.

37. Obituary of Wade Roberts in Syracuse *True Wesleyan*, 12 September 1855;

newspaper clipping without citation of obituary, Martha Roberts, ca. February 1869, in Jonathan Roberts Collection, Library of Congress; Conkling, "Roberts Settlement," 24–26. The initial journey to Hamilton County is recounted in Conkling, who mistakenly gives the date as 1832.

The obituary of early Roberts Settlement pioneer Martha Roberts notes that her father, Hansel Roberts, led the family to Indiana in the spring of 1835; they arrived in May and moved to Roberts Settlement in October of the same year. Wade Roberts' obituary also notes that the family settled briefly in Rush County in 1835 before moving permanently to Hamilton County. The dating of the journey provided here is based on the arrival of Hansel in Indiana in May 1835 and the first purchase of land at Roberts Settlement in July 1835.

No firsthand account remains of those accompanying Hansel in the spring of 1835. The individuals discussed all bought land at Roberts Settlement before early 1837; most presumably either joined Hansel in his first trip or followed shortly thereafter.

38. U.S. public land survey field notes for Indiana, vol. 3, pt. 2, pp. 100–101, in Indiana State Archives; Augustus Finch Shirts, *A History of the Formation, Settlement and Development of Hamilton County, Indiana, from the Year 1818 to the Close of the Civil War* (1901), 58–59, 149–52, 156–60, 164, 204–12; John F. Haines, *History of Hamilton County, Indiana* (Indianapolis: Bowen, 1915), 149, 151.

39. Conkling, "Roberts Settlement," 24–26; land deed records, Hamilton County, Recorder's Office, Hamilton County Courthouse, Noblesville, Indiana; U.S. census manuscripts, Hamilton County, Indiana, 1840, available on microfilm, Indiana State Library. Jonathan Roberts, Henry Winburn, Dolphin Roberts, Guilford Brooks, and Elias Roberts purchased land at Roberts Settlement before 1840, but do not appear in 1840 census manuscripts for either Jackson and Adams townships, Hamilton County (Roberts Settlement) or Ripley Township, Rush County (Beech Settlement). Possibly some may have been living within the households of others at Beech or Roberts settlements; a more likely possibility, however, is that they were living at one of the communities as householders, but were overlooked by census enumerators.

40. Land deeds, Hamilton County; census, Rush County, 1840 and Hamilton County, 1850, available on microfilm, Indiana State Library; probate records of Bryant Walden, Rush County Clerk's Office.

41. Douglass C. North, *The Economic Growth of the United States, 1790–1860* (Englewood Cliffs, N.J.: Prentice-Hall, 1961; reprint ed., New York: W. W. Norton, 1966), 198–208, 256, 259; Buley, *Old Northwest*, II: 268–99 passim; John D. Barnhart and Donald F. Carmony, *Indiana from Frontier to Industrial Commonwealth*, 2 vols. (New York: Lewis Historical Publishing Co., 1954), I: 172–75, 226–27.

42. Jackson, *Free Negro Labor and Property Holding*, esp. chap. 2; Schweninger, *Black Property Owners*, 71–75.

43. V. P. Franklin, *Black Self-Determination: A Cultural History of African-American Resistance* (2nd ed., Brooklyn: Lawrence Hill, 1992), esp. 127–44. The literature on African-American migration is rich, voluminous, and understandably gives its greatest emphasis to the Great Migration. Among the more notable recent works are Walker, *Free Frank*; Nell Irvin Painter, *Exodusters: Black Migration to Kansas after Reconstruction* (New York: Knopf, 1977; reprint ed., Lawrence: University Press of Kansas, 1986); Peter Gottlieb, *Making Their Own Way: Southern Blacks' Migration to Pittsburgh, 1916–1930* (Urbana: University of Illinois Press, 1987); James R. Grossman,

Land of Hope: Chicago, Black Southerners, and the Great Migration (Chicago: University of Chicago Press, 1989); Carole Marks, *Farewell—We're Good and Gone: The Great Black Migration* (Bloomington: Indiana University Press, 1989); Joe William Trotter, Jr., ed., *The Great Migration in Historical Perspective: New Dimensions of Race, Class, and Gender* (Bloomington: Indiana University Press, 1991); Nicholas Lemann, *The Promised Land: The Great Black Migration and How It Changed America* (1991; reprint ed., New York: Vintage Books, 1992).

44. U.S. Bureau of the Census, *Ninth Census* (Washington, 1872), 1: 108–21, 123–31, 168–76, 287–95; Jackson, *Free Negro Labor and Property Holding,* 112–14; Gregory S. Rose, "Quakers, North Carolinians, and Blacks in Indiana's Settlement Pattern, *Journal of Cultural Geography,* 7 (1986): 35–46; David A. Gerber, *Black Ohio and the Color Line, 1860–1915* (Urbana: University of Illinois Press, 1976), 16–18; Wright "Negro Rural Communities in Indiana," *Southern Workman* 37 (March 1908): 158–64; Thornbrough, *Negro in Indiana,* 32–36; Cord, "Black Rural Settlements," 99–110; Stewart, " Migration of a Free People," 34–38; Wilson, *Rural Black Heritage,* 29, 36–37.

3. PIONEER LIFE, CA. 1830–1850

1. U.S. public land survey plats and research field notes, T15 R8, T15 R9, T20 R3, T20 R4, located in Indiana State Archives, Indianapolis; Shirts, *Hamilton County to the Civil War,* 27–28, 156–57; Carter, notebooks, I:58 (quote); Newby, notes; Thomas T. Newby, *Reminiscences,* 35–38.

2. McDonell, "Landholding Patterns," 44; Kiefer, *Rush County, Indiana,* 34–37.

3. Land deeds, Rush and Hamilton counties.

4. Ibid.; McDonell, "Landholding Patterns," 44; land entry book, Rush County, Recorder's Office, Rush County Courthouse.

5. U.S. census manuscripts, 1840, Rush and Hamilton counties, available on microfilm at Indiana State Library. A comparison of Rush County land deeds and 1840 census manuscripts indicates that only twenty-one of sixty-three black householders (33 percent) held land in Ripley Township in 1840. The position of the landless was somewhat less strained than this might suggest because at least three blacks owned land at the Beech but were not reported as householders; included in this group were Sarah Jeffries, Sarah Jones, and Margaret McDuffey. They apparently were considered as household members of other black-headed households, or their households were overlooked by census takers. If they were members of the sixty-three households, then twenty-four of sixty-three households (38 percent) would have included landowners.

Three other Beech householders in 1840—Bryant Walden and Stephen and Richard Roberts—owned land at Roberts Settlement but were not Ripley Township farmowners.

6. Land deeds, Rush and Hamilton counties; tax lists, 1823–1835, Northampton County, located at North Carolina State Archives (NCSA), Raleigh; tax lists, 1823–1835, Greensville County, located on microfilm at Virginia State Archives, Richmond. No tax lists have survived from Halifax County, North Carolina, the previous home of two landowners, both members of the Winburn family, at Beech Settlement in 1840.

7. Berlin, *Slaves without Masters,* 244–46; Schweninger, *Black Property Owners,* 71–75; Jackson, *Free Negro Labor,* chap. 2.

8. Jackson, *Free Negro Labor*, 105–106; Berlin, *Slaves without Masters*, 245–46, 249; land deeds, Rush and Hamilton counties; tax lists, Northampton and Greensville counties; will and estate record of Drewry Walden, located at NCSA.

9. Shirts, *Hamilton County to the Civil War*, 27–28, 42–44; Newby, *Reminiscences*, 2–4 and passim; U.S. agricultural census manuscripts, 1850, Rush and Hamilton counties, Indiana, located on microfilm at Indiana State Archives. The amounts of land cleared and uncleared are from agricultural census reports. Owing to a number of factors—enumerators' oversights, management of fields by someone other than the owner, and so forth—not all farmowners were counted in the report of 1850; the farms of nine Beech landowners with 429 acres, and three Roberts landowners with 200 acres are absent.

10. Shirts, *Hamilton County to the Civil War*, 155–56; Newby, notes; Abraham Lincoln Gary and E. B. Thomas, ed., *Centennial History*, 1: 93; *History of Rush County, Indiana from the Earliest Time to the Present* (1888; reprint ed., Knightstown, Ind.: Eastern Publishing, 1966), 309–10. Local residents typically petitioned county commissioners for roads to be laid out through their neighborhoods and the commissioners complied with these wishes. It is difficult to determine when the first roads were laid out through Beech and Roberts because many petitioners described their proposed roads largely if not entirely in terms of the property holders at each turn (e.g. "south to the southwest corner of Farmer X's field, then east to Y's Mill, then southeast along Farmer Z's west boundary" etc.).

Local historian Sarah Newby, fortunately, abstracted Ripley Township proposals from the minutes of the Rush County commissioners' meetings. A brief survey of these abstracts indicates that roads crossing Beech Settlement holdings were laid out in 1840 and 1846; the latter provided direct access to the village of Carthage. Few if any county roads connected Beech families to the outside world before that time.

Roberts Settlement land was located near an Indian path connecting Strawtown, in northeastern Hamilton County, with Lafayette, in Tippecanoe County; the path was converted into a state road about 1830.

11. Sarah Newby, notes; Thomas T. Newby, *Reminiscences*, 17, 21, 25; Shirts, *Hamilton County to the Civil War*, 155–56; Conkling, "Roberts Settlement," 54–55. Conditions in Hamilton County lagged behind those in Rush County, which had been settled roughly a decade earlier. Shirts emphatically states that virtually no grain was exported by Hamilton County farmers before the arrival of railroads in the early 1850s.

12. Rodney C. Loehr, "Self-Sufficiency on the Farm," *Agricultural History* 26 (1952): 37–41; Newby, notes; Newby, *Reminiscences*, 25, 31; Shirts, *Hamilton County to the Civil War*, 370; agricultural census, 1850, Rush and Hamilton counties.

13. Newby's *Reminiscences* provides several sketches of the local activities of Ripley Township farmers, merchants, and craftsmen during the pioneer period. Perhaps the best evidence of the broad range of financial ties among early settlers at and near Beech and Roberts settlements is found in receipts included in the estate papers of pioneers from Rush County who died during this era. Similar records for Hamilton County apparently have been destroyed.

14. Economic discrimination was one of the most pressing problems confronting free blacks throughout America. For the difficulties faced in urban settings, see Curry, *Free Black in Urban America*, chap. 2 and sources cited below in n. 73.

15. Estate papers of David Watkins (died 1840), Bryant Walden (1844), Benjamin Roberts (1846), Willis Roberts (1846), James D. Roberts (1849), Daniel Wat-

kins (1852), located at Clerk's Office, Rush County Courthouse; estate papers of Elijah Roberts (1848), located at Clerk's Office, Hamilton County Courthouse; Elijah Roberts Collection, Indiana Historical Society Library, Indianapolis; financial account shared by Willis Roberts and Stephen Roberts, Jonathan Roberts Collection.

16. Ibid.; estate papers of John Winslow, Rush County Clerk's Office; minutes of Committee on the Concerns of People of Color (CCPC), Spiceland Quarterly Meeting of Friends, March 1840, June 1840, and passim, located in Quaker Collection, Earlham College, Richmond, Indiana. The membership of the Spiceland CCPC included prominent farmers as well as merchants and other businessmen. Among its more notable members from Ripley Township: Tristam Coggeshall (tanner), Henry Henley (merchant), John Winslow (miller), John Clark (miller), Verlin Kersey (doctor), Henry Newby (farmer), Joseph Hill (farmer), and Henry Macy (farmer).

James Oliver Horton has noted the importance of skin color and appearance as a factor in antebellum Cincinnati whites' economic relations with mulattoes and darker-skinned African Americans, with mulattoes benefiting from their lighter complexions; see Horton, "Shades of Color," 37–59, esp. 51–52, 54–56.

17. Newby, *Reminiscences,* 16–18; Carter, notebooks, I: 5, 91–92, and passim; census, 1850, Rush County; estate papers of David Watkins, Willis Roberts, Daniel Watkins, Rush County; mortgage deed, Elias Roberts to Dennison and Parthenia White, 2 March 1850, located in Hamilton County Deed Books, A: 496, Recorder's Office; mortgage deed, Henry Brown to Reddick Brooks, 1 February 1847, located in Rush County Mortgage Deed Books, P: 518, Recorder's Office.

18. Estate papers of David Watkins, Benjamin Roberts, James D. Roberts, Willis Roberts, Daniel Watkins, Rush County Clerk's Office.

19. Estate papers of Daniel Watkins, Bryant Walden, Daniel Watkins, Rush County Clerk's Office; mortgage deeds, John Walker to Turner Newsom, 9 March 1841, 1 January 1851, 10 October 1857, mortgage deed books L: 392, 1: 441, 2: 415.

20. David E. Schob, *Hired Hands and Plowboys: Farm Labor in the Midwest, 1815–60* (Urbana: University of Illinois Press, 1975); Thornbrough, *Negro in Indiana,* 134–35, 138; Clarence Danhof, *Change in Agriculture: The Northern United States, 1820–1870* (Cambridge, Mass.: Harvard University Press, 1969), 90–92.

21. Newby, *Reminiscences,* 16–18; deed, N: 400, Rush County land deeds.

22. Newby, *Reminiscences,* 18; agricultural census, 1850, Rush and Hamilton counties. Mortgagors arranging chattel mortgages frequently used crops grown on leased land as collateral, hence providing descriptions of leasing agreements. For examples of such mortgages involving Beech residents, see Rush County mortgage deeds, P: 518, 2: 661, 3: 28, 3: 98, 3: 259, 3: 324, 4: 343; for examples involving Roberts residents, see E: 452, F: 489, K: 122.

Farm tenants are not identified as such on agricultural census manuscripts from 1850 to 1870, but their identity can be inferred by comparing the agricultural census manuscripts with population census manuscripts, land deeds, and other records. Unfortunately, all of the inferential methods have their drawbacks. For a summary of methods and problems, see John T. Houdek and Charles F. Heller, "Searching for Nineteenth-Century Farm Tenants: An Evaluation of Methods," *Historical Methods* 19 (1986): 55–61.

23. Scattered studies of other frontier locations point to broadly similar patterns. See Merle Curti, *The Making of an American Community: A Case Study of Democracy in a Frontier County* (1959; reprint ed., Stanford: Stanford University Press, 1969); Allan G. Bogue, *From Prairie to Cornbelt: Farming on the Illinois and Iowa Prairies in the*

Nineteenth Century (Chicago: University of Chicago Press, 1963); John L. Shover, *First Majority—Last Minority: The Transforming of Rural Life in America* (DeKalb: Northern Illinois University Press, 1976); Herbert J. Mays, "A Place to Stand: Families, Land and Permanence in Toronto Gore Township 1820–1890," in *Canadian Historical Papers,* 1980 (Toronto: Canadian Historical Association, 1981), 185–211. May's study of Toronto Gore provides an especially insightful discussion about the role played by the core landholders in shaping an area's character over subsequent generations.

24. Land deeds, Rush County; census manuscripts, 1850, Rush County.

25. Land deeds, Rush County; Newby, *Reminiscences,* 16–17.

26. Land deeds, Rush County; agricultural census manuscripts, 1850, Rush County; Newby, *Reminiscences,* 16–18; mortgage deed, 2: 30, Rush County.

27. Land deeds, Rush County; census manuscripts, 1850, Rush County; Nathan Hill, "Beech Settlement," *Indiana Negro History Society Bulletin* (May 1943): 2.

28. Land deeds, Rush County, U.S. census manuscripts, 1850, Vigo, Hancock and Hamilton counties, Indiana and Van Buren County, Michigan, available on microfilm at Indiana State Library; letter of Willis Roberts Jr. to Elias and Stephen Roberts, 25 August 1852, Jonathan Roberts Collection; tax receipts in estate file of Humphrey Bobson, available on microfiche in Clerk's Office, Hancock County Courthouse, Greenfield, Indiana.

29. U.S. census manuscripts, 1840, Rush County, and 1850, Rush, Hamilton, and Marion counties, Indiana, available on microfilm at Indiana State Library.

30. James Oliver Horton found extraordinarily high rates of population turnover (92%–95%) among free people of color in Boston, Buffalo, and Cincinnati, 1850–1860. Few additional studies of persistence among urban free blacks have been attempted. Most studies of urban persistence have found turnover rates of roughly three-fifths to two-thirds per decade during the late antebellum era. Given the tremendous job discrimination facing free blacks, one would expect higher levels of transiency, although Horton's findings may also reflect shortcomings with the censuses themselves. See James Oliver Horton, *Free People of Color: Inside the African American Community* (Washington, D.C.: Smithsonian, 1993), 127, 219.

31. Land deeds, Rush County; census, 1840 and 1850, Rush County.

32. Land deeds, Hamilton County; census, 1840, Hamilton and Rush counties, and 1850, Hamilton County.

33. Land deeds, Hamilton County; estate papers of Bryant Walden, Rush County; land deed, N: 319, Rush County.

34. Land deeds, Hamilton County. Williams sold Roads a portion of his farm in 1839, two years after Roads' arrival as a runaway slave. In 1845 Williams was in the fore of legal efforts to establish Roads' right to freedom when his former owner tried to reclaim him.

35. Land deeds, Hamilton County; census manuscripts, 1850, Hamilton County; claim of Alfred Weaver (10886), Eastern Cherokee Indian Claims, Record Group 54, National Archives and Records Service, Washington, D.C. Anthony Roberts purchased another 59 acres at Roberts Settlement in 1858. William and Edward were listed as farm operators in the agricultural censuses of 1860 and 1870, although they themselves held no title to land. At least three of Anthony's other children lived at Roberts Settlement at one time or another. A daughter, Nancy, was the wife of Micajah Walden and among the area's earliest pioneers. Anthony transferred ownership

of his holdings to his children and his children's survivors only in the early 1880s, after he had reached the age of 90.

36. Census manuscripts, 1840, Rush County, and 1850, Hamilton County; land deeds, Hamilton County. James L. Roberts was the brother of Elijah Roberts and the cousin of Hansel Roberts.

37. Land deeds, Hamilton County; census manuscripts, 1840 and 1850, Hamilton County.

38. For a concise overview of the contrasting opportunities available to free people of color in the North relative to those in the South, see Ira Berlin, "The Structure of the Free Negro Caste in the Antebellum United States," *Journal of Social History* 9 (1975–1976): esp. 302–303, 313.

39. Robert H. Wiebe, *The Opening of American Society: From the Adoption of the Constitution to the Eve of Disunion* (New York: Alfred A. Knopf, 1984), 337–39; Alexis de Tocqueville, *Democracy in America*, ed. Phillips Bradley, 2 vols. (New York: Vintage, 1945), I: 373–74; Berwanger, *Frontier against Slavery*, 30–38.

40. Leon F. Litwack, *North of Slavery: The Negro in the Free States, 1790–1860* (Chicago: University of Chicago Press, 1961), 73, 74, 100; Thornbrough, *Negro in Indiana*, 128–30, 157; Richard Wade, "The Negro in Cincinnati," *Journal of Negro History* 25 (1940): 43–57; Frederick Douglass, *Life and Times of Frederick Douglass* (1892; reprint ed., New York: Collier, 1962), 230–31. Douglass almost met a similar fate when he attempted to speak in Noblesville, the county seat of Hamilton County. After being apprised that a mob would attempt to disrupt his appearance, presumably using violent means, supporters spirited him out of town. See Haines, *History of Hamilton County, Indiana, Her People . . .* (Indianapolis: Bowen, 1915), 494.

41. No comprehensive history of Indiana Quakerism has been written. Consequently, the best source on the Friends' attitudes are the minutes of the groups' monthly, quarterly, and yearly meetings. The published yearly meeting minutes for the pioneer period are available at the Indiana University Library, Bloomington, and the Quaker Collection, Earlham College Library, Richmond, Indiana. Also helpful are the unpublished quarterly reports of the Committee on the Concerns of People of Color located at the Quaker Collection, Earlham College. On the persistence of negative racial stereotypes, see also William Tallack's observations on Richmond, Indiana Friends' relations with free people of color in his *Friendly Sketches in America* (London: A. W. Bennett, 1861), 52–53, 231–32.

Helpful secondary sources on western Friends include Thomas D. Hamm, *The Transformation of American Quakerism: Orthodox Friends, 1800–1907* (Bloomington: Indiana University Press, 1988); Thomas D. Hamm et al., "Moral Choices: Two Indiana Quaker Communities and the Abolitionist Movement," *Indiana Magazine of History* 87 (1991): 117–54; Thornbrough, *Negro in Indiana*, passim.

42. *Vaughan v. Williams*, United States Circuit Court, Indiana District, May Term 1845, reported as Case No. 16,903 in Vol. 28 *Federal Cases*, 1116; Helen Catterall, *Judicial Cases Concerning American Slavery and the Negro*, 5 vols. (Washington, D.C.; 1926), 5: 33–34; Julia Conklin, "The Underground Railroad in Indiana," *Indiana Magazine of History* 6 (1910): 70–72; *New Garden, Ind., Free Labor Advocate*, 17 May 1844, 25 May 1844, 5 July 1844.

43. *Federal Cases*, 1115–18; Catterall, *Cases Concerning American Slavery*, 5: 33–34; Conklin, "Underground Railroad," 72–73; *Free Labor Advocate*, 17 May 1844, 25 May 1844, 5 July 1844.

44. Haines, *History of Hamilton County,* 490–91; *Portrait and Biographical Record of Madison and Hamilton Counties, Indiana, Containing Biographical Sketches of Prominent and Representative Citizens* (1893; reprint ed., Evansville: Unigraphic, 1973), 263–64; Conklin, "Underground Railroad," 66–74; *History of Westfield,* 13–18; Newby, *Reminiscences,* 19–21; Sarah Newby, "Underground Railroad," unpublished manuscript on microfilm at Rushville (Ind.) Public Library, 1–3; "History of Carthage Friends," unpublished manuscript on microfilm at Rushville (Ind.) Public Library, 6–7; untitled biographical sketch of Henry Newby, unpublished manuscript on microfilm at Rushville (Ind.) Public Library; Larry Gara, *The Liberty Line: The Legend of the Underground Railroad* (Lexington: University of Kentucky Press, 1961); Benjamin Quarles, *Black Abolitionists* (New York: Oxford University Press, 1969), 143–67.

The escape of Ellen Taylor, who briefly stopped south of Roberts Settlement in Westfield in 1853 en route to Windsor, Canada, is recounted in *Syracuse True Wesleyan,* 31 January 1855.

45. The Friends' efforts to aid kidnapped and similarly endangered free people of color are reported in the published minutes of the Indiana Yearly Meeting of Friends and partly recounted in Thornbrough, *Negro in Indiana,* 100–102.

46. Conkling, "Roberts Settlement," 27; estate papers, Hamilton and Rush counties. Those with white administrators included Benjamin Roberts (Beech), James D. Roberts (Beech), and Bryant Walden (Beech); whites witnessed the wills of Elijah Roberts (Roberts) and Wade Roberts (Roberts), while another became the executor of Willis Roberts' will when Willis' wife relinquished the role of executrix.

47. Friends' attitudes and actions are described in the quarterly and annual minutes of the Committee on the Concerns of Colored People, a committee which monitored the progress of free blacks in Indiana. The annual minutes are printed in the *Minutes of the Indiana Yearly Meeting of Friends,* published annually from 1821.

48. Berlin, *Slaves without Masters,* 273–79; David Gerber, *Black Ohio and the Color Line* (1976), 128–29; E. Franklin Frazier, *The Negro Family in the United States* (Chicago: University of Chicago Press, 1940), 215–45; Willard B. Gatewood, *Aristocrats of Color: The Black Elite, 1880–1920* (Bloomington: Indiana University Press), 10–15; Lawrence Carter, Notebooks, I: 65, 117, 135; Conkling, "Roberts Settlement," 30–31.

By combining information from census manuscripts and marriage records, it is possible to identify in a crude way the skin colors of 41 couples from Beech and Roberts who were married between 1830 and 1849, using the census designations of "black" and "mulatto" to distinguish between those who were dark and light skinned. In thirty cases mulattoes married mulattoes; in six instances blacks married blacks; and in five cases blacks married mulattoes. The accuracy of the census designations, however, is open to question.

Color and/or group consciousness may have been especially acute at Roberts Settlement. The only early dark-skinned landowners in the neighborhood were John Roads and Edmund Hurley. Both were natives of Kentucky. None of their children intermarried with lighter skinned members of the Roberts neighborhood, the families' landholding status notwithstanding. Unsurprisingly, their children all emigrated from the Roberts area after they came of age.

49. Marriage records, Rush County, Clerk's Office, Rush County Courthouse; marriage records, Hamilton County, Clerk's Office, Hamilton County Courthouse.

50. Adams and Kasakoff, "Endogamous Group Size," "Migration and the Fam-

NOTES TO PAGES 70-72

ily," 28–29; census manuscripts, 1850, Rush and Hamilton counties. Census manuscripts in 1850 list the names and ages of all individuals, but do not indicate individu-
als' marital status or status within a specific household; a satisfactory method for in-
ferring such relationships, however, has been developed by Buffington Clay Miller.
For a brief discussion of Miller's work and a summary of his rules, see Theodore
Hershberg, "A Method for Computerized Study of Family and Household Structure
Using the Manuscript Schedules of the U.S. Census of Population, 1850–1880," *The
Family in Historical Perspective* 1 (1973): 6–20.

Using these methods to separate married household heads and married couples
within households from other household members, it appears that fifty-eight blacks
in Ripley Township in 1850 were between 15 and 45 years of age and unmarried, and
that another thirty-one blacks in Jackson and Adams townships fit these criteria. Eligible men outnumbered women by a 17 to 14 count at Roberts Settlement. These
figures, it should be emphasized, are only close approximations. The actual numbers
may have varied slightly.

51. Marriage records, Rush and Hamilton counties.

52. Edmund Cary often spoke in Quaker meetings. Anthony Roberts steadfastly
refused to have anything to do with religion.

53. Founding agreement, [Mount Pleasant] Methodist Church, 18 July 1832, in
Jonathan Roberts Collection; Carter, Notebooks, I: 66, 128; Henry Woods, "Indiana's
A.M.E. Birthplace," *Indianapolis Star Magazine,* 17 May 1970, 24; Thornbrough,
Negro in Indiana, 151–56. Carter states that the Mount Pleasant congregation's affiliation with the A.M.E. faith can be traced to a meeting of church members on June
16, 1832. The founding agreement for the congregation, however, is dated July 18,
1832 and describes the founders' intention to form a Methodist Episcopal denomination.

54. Nathan O. Hatch, *The Democratization of American Christianity* (New Haven: Yale University Press, 1989), 81–91; Daniel Alexander Payne, *History of the African Methodist Episcopal Church* (Nashville, 1891; reprint ed., New York: Arno Press,
1969); Harry V. Richardson, *Dark Salvation: The Story of Methodism As It Developed
among Blacks in America* (Garden City, N.J.: Doubleday, 1976), 84–88, 97–99, 111–
13; Carter, notebooks.

55. Payne, *History of the A.M.E.;* Richardson, *Black Salvation,* 108–11; Monroe
Fordham, *Major Themes in Northern Black Religious Thought, 1800–1860* (Hicksville,
N.Y.: Exposition Press, 1975), 33–56; Newby, *Reminiscences,* 16; minutes of Committee on the Concerns of People of Color, Spiceland Quarterly Meeting, 1854, located
in Quaker Collection, Earlham College. Quote is from Payne, 98.

56. Fordham, *Major Themes;* Richardson, *Black Salvation,* 99–113.

57. Carter, Notebooks, I: 29, 47; land deed, U:311, Rush County.

58. Conkling, "Roberts Settlement," 27–29; John F. Haines, *History of Hamilton
County, Indiana* (Indianapolis: Bowen, 1915), 304–305; Thomas B. Helms, ed., *History of Hamilton County, Indiana, with Illustrations and Biographical Sketches....* (Chicago, 1880; reprint ed., Evansville: Unigraphic, 1973), 122; Shirts, *Hamilton County to
the Civil War,* 153; land deed, L: 436, Hamilton County. Edgar Conkling has asserted
that the first meetinghouse was built in 1841 on Jesse Newsom's farm, more that a
mile west of the current Roberts church. Few if any black pioneers, however, lived
near the Newsom farm in the early 1840s. Cyrus W. Roberts, who was born at Roberts Settlement in 1848, notes in his "Autobiography" that he attended school in a log
cabin, "the first built in the community for both church and school purposes." Since

Roberts went to school after Elias and Mariah Roberts had donated the permanent meetinghouse property, he apparently is referring to that building. "Autobiography of Rev. C. W. Roberts," *Noblesville [Ind.] Daily Ledger,* 2 July 1925, 2.

59. Lee M. Haines, "Radical Reform and Living Piety: The Story of Earlier Wesleyan Methodism, 1843–1848," in Wayne E. Caldwell, ed., *Reformers and Revivalists: The History of the Wesleyan Church* (Indianapolis: Wesley Press, 1992), 40–42; *Syracuse True Wesleyan,* 10 February 1844, 8 February 1845, 25 October 1845, 13 May 1848, 11 January 1851; Lee Mark Haines, "The History of Wesleyan Methodism in Indiana, 1843–1876" (B.D. research paper, Christian Theological Seminary, 1959; copy in Wesleyan Church Archives, Indianapolis), 90–96.

60. Lee M. Haines, "Radical Reform and Living," 31–32, 40–67; Ira Ford McLeister and Roy Stephen Nicholson, *Conscience and Commitment: The History of the Wesleyan Methodist Church of America* (Marion, Ind.: Wesley Press, 1976), 26–38; John R. McKivigan, *The War against Proslavery Religion: Abolitionism and the Northern Churches, 1830–1865* (Ithaca: Cornell University Press, 1984), 84–86, 93–99. Quote on race as a physical peculiarity is from *True Wesleyan,* 12 April 1845; quote from 1849 conference is from *True Wesleyan,* 27 October 1849. The reform aspect of Indiana Wesleyanism is seen in reports of the Indiana Conference's annual meetings, found in *True Wesleyan,* 27 October 1849, 5 October 1850, 11 October 1851, 20 October 1853, 5 October 1854, 10 October 1855.

61. On the appeal of Wesleyanism among free people of color, and the tensions between black and white Wesleyans that sometimes resulted, see *True Wesleyan,* 12 April 1845, 20 September 1845, 15 November 1845, 22 February 1848, 19 May 1848. All-black Wesleyan congregations were formed in New York, Massachusetts, Ohio, Indiana, and Ontario, while an interracial congregation was active in Pittsburgh.

Explicit or implicit references to interactions between the Roberts congregation and other nearby Wesleyans can be found in *True Wesleyan,* 3 January 1851, 3 January 1852, 20 March 1852, 10 February 1853, 30 November 1854, 1 August 1855. Also revealing are the obituary and tributes to Wade Roberts in *True Wesleyan,* 1 August 1855 and 12 September 1855.

62. Wayne E. Fuller, *The Old Country School: The Story of Rural Education in the Middle West* (Chicago: University of Chicago Press, 1982), 25–34; Payne, *History of the A.M.E.,* 98, 118, 180, 184, 393–401; V. P. Franklin, *Black Self-Determination,* 161–65; Litwack, *North of Slavery,* 113. Quote is from *Minutes and Proceedings of the Second Annual Convention, for the Improvement of the Free People of Color in these United States* (Philadelphia, 1832), as cited in Litwack.

63. Census manuscripts, 1850, Hamilton and Rush counties; Barnhart and Carmony, *Indiana from Frontier to Industrial Commonwealth,* II: 112.

64. Barnhart and Carmony, *Indiana from Frontier to Commonwealth,* I: 256–65, II: 112–14; Thornbrough, *Negro in Indiana,* 160–66; Fuller, *Old Country School,* 34–41; Herbert Lynn Heller, "Negro Education in Indiana from 1816 to 1869" (Ph.D. dissertation, Indiana University, 1951).

65. *History of Rush County,* 805–806; autobiography of O. W. Coggeshall, in Sarah Newby papers; Newby, *Reminiscences,* 16; receipts of Willis Roberts, 3 March 1835, 21 April 1836, 22 March 1838, Jonathan Roberts Collection. Coggeshall, a Quaker who was born in 1834, noted in the early twentieth century that: "Among the pupils who attended my first school were some colored boys and girls, which fact was looked upon as a matter of course, where no 'color line' was thought of." Newby, another Quaker who was born a few years later, also noted in the early twentieth century

that in Carthage "there were not many terms but that there were some and often several colored children in attendance. The tuition when not paid by the parents was by benevolent persons."

66. *History of Rush County*, 805–806; Newby, *Reminiscences,* 16; receipts of Willis Roberts, 3 March 1835, 21 April 1836, 22 March 1838, Jonathan Roberts Collection; guardianship papers of Peter Davis et al., and probate papers of Daniel Watkins, Clerk's Office, Rush County. Free black instructors at the Beech before the Civil War included James D. Roberts (1835); Henry Byrd (1836); Anthony Roberts (1838–39); Sarah Jeffries (1852–54); Alex McCowan (1851–52); Frances Roberts (1852); William Trail (1853, 1858); Jesse H. Keen (1854); Joshua Keen (ca. 1855); Clark Vaughn (1856); Wright Jeffries (1857); Allas H. Evans (1859); Clarissa Brown (1859); Benjamin Trail (1860); William Roberts (?); and Pleasant Keen (?). Friends teaching at the Beech included Alfred Gordon, Rebecca Gordon, John Young, and John Street. Two others who taught, probably Friends, were Jordan Hays and Hezekiah Clark. These lists are clearly incomplete.

67. Mount Pleasant Library Collection, Indiana Historical Society Library, Indianapolis; *Minutes of the Indiana Yearly Meeting of Friends . . . 1841* (Richmond, 1841), 19; *Minutes of the Indiana Yearly Meeting of Friends . . . 1843* (Richmond, 1843), 23. The Quaker ties to the Mount Pleasant Library are difficult to assess in any detailed fashion. At least five of the fifty-six charter members of the Mount Pleasant Library in 1842 were Friends; one, Henry Henley, served as a trustee in 1842, although no mention is found of Quaker involvement thereafter. The minutes of the Indiana Yearly Meeting of Friends, in apparent references to the Mount Pleasant Library, noted in 1841 that "friends have assisted [local blacks] in raising means for the establishment of a library for their use." In 1843, the Meeting noted in a second apparent reference that the library "has been a valuable auxiliary in promoting the intellectual elevation of those within its reach."

Officials of the Mount Pleasant Library—trustees, secretaries, and librarians—during its first ten years included: Henry Henley (Quaker), John Brooks, Macklin Jeffries, Walker Jeffries, Wright Jeffries, Anthony Roberts, Benjamin Roberts, James D. Roberts, William Roberts, William Sweat, Daniel Watkins, John Watkins, John Winburn, Lewis Winburn. Nine of the thirteen Beech men were landowners.

68. Census manuscripts, 1850, Rush County; Barnhart and Carmony, *Indiana from Frontier to Commonwealth*, II: 112, 114. Caleb Mills, the leading advocate of an improved public school system in Indiana, estimated that in 1850, 56 percent of school-age children attended classes.

The actual proportion of Beech children who would be educated before reaching adulthood was much higher than the census might suggest. Most children attended class only a few years while growing up. Many who were five to twenty years of age in 1850 went to classes at the Beech before or after that year, but were simply not in attendance during the months immediately prior to the census. Friends in the mid-1850s estimated that virtually all Beech children were exposed to schooling.

69. Conkling, "Roberts Settlement," 27–29; Shirts, *Hamilton County to the Civil War*, 153; land deed, L: 436, Hamilton County.

70. Land deed, L: 436, Hamilton County; Thornbrough, *Negro in Indiana*, 160–66; Roberts, "History of Roberts Settlement," 2; Roberts, "Autobiography," 1–2.

71. Census manuscripts, 1850 and 1860, Hamilton County.

72. U.S. Bureau of the Census, *Statistical View of the United States . . . a Compendium of the Seventh Census* (1854; reprint ed., New York: Gordon and Breach Science

Publishers, 1970), 72, 144; Litwack, *North of Slavery*, 113–35; David A. Gerber, *Black Ohio and the Color Line 1860–1915* (Urbana: University of Illinois Press, 1976), 4–5; Thornbrough, *Negro in Indiana*, 160–73; Robert L. McCaul, *The Black Struggle for Public Schooling in Nineteenth Century Illinois* (Carbondale: Southern Illinois University Press, 1987), 1–54; Arnie Cooper, "A Stony Road: Black Education in Iowa, 1838–1860," *Annals of Iowa* 48 (1986): 113–34.

In analyzing 1850 census data, census officials devised a crude measure of school attendance rates by dividing the total number of all children in school by the number of children ages five to fifteen. When this method is applied to the northern free black population, it yields the following attendance rates: Beech and Roberts settlements, 62 percent; Old Northwest, 33 percent; Middle Atlantic (New York, Pennsylvania, New Jersey), 49 percent; and New England, 78 percent.

73. For important analyses of northern free black community life see Horton, *Free People of Color*, and Nash, *Forging Freedom*. Nash's metaphor refers specifically to Philadelphia's free black community; see *Forging Freedom*, 6–7.

4. FROM FRONTIER TO MATURE FARM SETTLEMENTS, 1850–1870

1. Junius B. Roberts to Stephen Roberts, 19 September 1865, Jonathan Roberts Collection, Library of Congress, Washington, D.C. Neither Junius Roberts nor Joe Winburn acquired portions of the Roads estate when they returned to Roberts Settlement. Hamilton County land records indicate that Junius did, however, buy 20 acres near the Roads place in February 1866; two years later he sold the land and purchased a 40-acre parcel, only to sell it as well the following year. Shortly thereafter Junius left Roberts Settlement and became an A.M.E. minister, traveling extensively throughout the United States and Canada during the decades that followed.

2. Victor Bogle, "Railroad Building in Indiana, 1850–1855," *Indiana Magazine of History* 58 (1962): 212–20, 227; Emma Lou Thornbrough, *Indiana in the Civil War Era, 1850–1880,* History of Indiana series, vol. 3 (Indianapolis: Indiana Historical Bureau and Indiana Historical Society, 1965), 322–36; Paul L. Farris and R. S. Euler, comp., *Prices of Indiana Farm Products, 1841–1955,* Agricultural Experiment Station series, Bulletin 644 (Lafayette, Ind.: Purdue University, 1957), 26–28, 36, 39, 45.

3. Bogle, "Railroad Building," 212, 218; *History of Rush County,* 658; Newby, *Reminiscences* [22–24].

4. Impressionistic evidence of the changing living standards of Beech residents, along with their shifting patterns of trade, can be found in the receipts and inventories included among the estate records of Daniel Watkins, who died in 1852; Richard Roberts (1858); Turner Newsom (1860); William Sweat (1860); and Allen Brown (1870). Located in Clerk's Office, Rush County Courthouse, Rushville, Indiana. Many of the changes in rural life that occurred after 1850 in Ripley Township are discussed in the notebooks of Sarah Newby, available on microfilm at Rushville [Ind.] Public Library.

On the general rise of commercial agriculture in the North and its uneven impact on farmers of differing statuses, see Barbara J. Steinson, "Rural Life in Indiana, 1800–1950," *Indiana Magazine of History* 90 (September 1994): 210–14; Hal S. Barron, "Listening to the Silent Majority: Change and Continuity in the Nineteenth-Century Rural North," in Lou Ferleger, ed., *Agriculture and National Development: Views on the Nineteenth Century* (Ames: Iowa State University Press, 1990), 4–8; Jeremy Atack and Fred Bateman, "Yeoman Farming: Antebellum America's Other 'Peculiar' Institution," in Ferleger, *Agriculture and National Development*, 37–47; Jeremy Atack and Fred Bateman, *To Their Own Soil: Agriculture in the Antebellum North* (Ames: Iowa State University Press, 1987), esp. chaps. 12–15; and Danhof, *Change in Agriculture*, esp. chap. 1.

5. Carter, notebooks, I: 198, 209.

6. Estate papers of William Sweat and Richard Roberts; United States agricultural census manuscripts, 1850–1870, Rush County, Indiana, available on microfilm at Indiana State Archives, Indianapolis; mortgage deed books, Rush County, Indiana, located in Recorder's Office, Rush County Courthouse, Rushville, Indiana.

7. Estate papers of Daniel Watkins, Turner Newsom, William Sweat, Richard Roberts, Allen Brown; mortgage deeds, Rush County. Historians have found similar patterns of continuity amidst the transformations brought by commercial farming elsewhere in the North; see Hal S. Barron, "Listening to the Silent Majority," 7–9.

8. Thomas J. Pressly and William H. Scofield, eds., *Farm Real Estate Values in the United States by Counties, 1850–1959* (Seattle: University of Washington Press, 1966), 28–29; Atack and Bateman, "Yeoman Farming," 31–33.

9. U.S. agricultural census, 1850–1870, Rush County; land deed books, Rush County, Indiana, located in Recorder's Office, Rush County Courthouse, Rushville, Indiana.

The following table, drawn from Rush County land deeds, indicates the price of land purchased and sold by blacks in rural Ripley Twp. from 1830 to 1869:

Date	Number of Transactions	Price per Acre
1830–1834	29	$1.36
1835–1839	5	5.18
1840–1844	8	4.96
1845–1849	15	7.67
1850–1854	14	17.92
1855–1859	11	28.14
1860–1864	14	32.32
1865–1869	10	47.04

Note: Excluded are transactions involving parcels of less than five acres and inheritance partitions.

10. Land deeds, Rush County; U.S. census manuscripts, 1850–1870, Rush County, Indiana, available on microfilm, Indiana State Library, Indianapolis. The ongoing dominance of early landowning families in areas settled at roughly the same time in Ontario and Illinois, respectively, are noted in Mays, "A Place to Stand," 185–211; and Faragher, *Sugar Creek*, 145. High persistence rates among landowners in Vermont are discussed in Hal Barron, *Those Who Stayed Behind: Rural Society in Nineteenth-Century New England* (New York: Cambridge University Press, 1984), chap. 5.

11. Land deeds, Rush County. Large farmers' general ability to move ahead more readily than their less well-positioned neighbors is described in Faragher, *Sugar Creek*, 202, and, especially, Atack and Batemen, "Yeoman Farming," 43–45, and *To Their Own Soil*, 256–59.

12. United States agricultural census, 1850–1870, Rush County. Estimates of

marketable farm surpluses for several locations in the Old Northwest in 1859 and 1860 indicate that large farmers enjoyed substantial advantages over their less fortunate neighbors. See Jeremy Atack and Fred Bateman, "Marketable Farm Surpluses: Northeastern and Midwestern United States, 1859 and 1860," *Social Science History* 8 (1984): 382; and Atack and Bateman, "Yeoman Farming," 41–45.

The shift toward wheat production is apparent from aggregate census data for Indiana counties, 1850–1870. See *Seventh Census of the United States: 1850* (Washington, 1853), 790–91; *Agriculture of the United States in 1860; Compiled from . . . the Eighth Census* (Washington: Government Printing Office, 1864), 38, 42; *Statistics of the Wealth and Industry of the United States . . .* (Washington, 1872), 138, 142.

In 1870 Macklin and Walker Jeffries, the two largest farmers at the Beech, owned farm machinery valued at $400 and $300, respectively, according to agricultural census records; four other Beech farmers owned machinery valued at $200. In contrast, the average value was $196 for all Rush County farmers and $151 for all Beech farmers.

13. Land deeds, Rush County; Atack and Bateman, "Marketable Farm Surpluses," 382; Atack and Bateman, "Yeoman Farming," 44–45; *Prices of Indiana Farm Products,* 36, 39, 45.

Average decadal prices for Beech Settlement land and the three principal market commodities:

	Land/Acre	Corn/Bu.	Wheat/Bu.	Hogs/Cwt.
1840s	$6.83	$.21	$.57	NA
1850s	23.19 (+240%)	.40 (+90%)	.88 (+54%)	$4.57
1860s	36.08 (+56%)	.52 (+30%)	1.37 (+56%)	6.00 (+31%)

14. Land deeds, Rush County; land deed, V: 504, located in Hamilton County Recorder's Office, Noblesville, Indiana; U.S. census manuscripts, 1870, Van Buren County, Michigan, available on microfilm at Indiana State Library, Indianapolis.

The Lassiters had purchased 32 acres in 1845 and an additional 50 acres in 1850. They sold their holdings in the fall and winter of 1853–1854, but remained in the Beech neighborhood for several years thereafter; in 1865 they moved to Grant County, Indiana.

15. Guardianship papers of Lucy, Jemima, Martha, Benjamin, Peter, Lavina, and Celia Ann Davis, located in Clerk's Office, Rush County Courthouse; census manuscripts, 1850–1870, Rush County.

For evidence concerning lower land prices to the north and west, see Pressly and Scofield, *Farm Real Estate Values;* for evidence concerning the overall lower farm costs in states to the north and west, see Atack and Bateman, "Yeoman Farming," 31–33.

16. Land deeds, Rush County. Free papers of James Watkins, filled out in Greensville County, Virginia in 1833, describe him as the son of Clara Watkins and the indentured servant of Daniel Watkins; see deed, L: 656, Rush County land deeds.

17. Census manuscripts, 1870, Van Buren County; census manuscripts, 1870, Hamilton County, Indiana, available on microfilm, Indiana State Library; deed, Y: 407, Hamilton County land deeds; Lawrence Carter, unpublished notebooks on history of Beech Settlement (4 vols.), I: 25–28; deeds, 5: 257 and 5: 283, Rush County land deeds; deed, NN: 94, located in Hancock County Recorder's Office, Greenfield, Indiana.

18. Estate papers, Daniel Watkins and Turner Newsom; Court of Common Pleas Order Books, 4: 204–205, 446–49, located in Rush County Clerk's Office.

19. Land deeds, Rush County; census manuscripts, 1870, Rush County.

20. Land deeds, Rush County; census manuscripts, 1870, Van Buren County. Few studies have explored the fate of the landless in maturing farm regions of the North, as Hal Barron notes in "Listening to the Silent Majority," 12–14; an exception is John Faragher's *Sugar Creek,* which found conditions similar to that of the Beech on the Illinois prairie of the 1840s and 1850s. See Faragher, *Sugar Creek,* 184–87.

21. Agricultural census manuscripts, 1850–1870, Rush County; mortgage deeds, Rush County. Agricultural census manuscripts from 1850 to 1870 listed all farmers together, without reference to their tenure status; thus farm owners and farm renters are not differentiated. Beech Settlement farm owners and farm renters can nonetheless be distinguished from one another since land deeds identify those who owned their farms.

In other regions the size of rented farms tended to increase, rather than diminish, as the farm economy matured in the late nineteenth century; see Donald L. Winters, *Farmers without Farms: Agricultural Tenancy in Nineteenth Century Iowa* (Westport, Conn.: Greenwood Press, 1978), 20–26.

22. Census manuscripts, 1850–1870, Rush County. The number of laborers on the Illinois prairie also increased as farming matured; see Faragher, *Sugar Creek,* 187.

23. Ibid.

24. Census manuscripts, 1870, Rush County; Thornbrough, *Negro in Indiana,* 141–42; Gerber, *Black Ohio,* 15, 60–92.

25. Census manuscripts, 1850–1870, Rush County; land deeds, Rush County.

26. Ibid. Twenty-five of the fifty-one black householders in rural Ripley Township in 1870 (49 percent) owned 10 acres or more; two others owned smaller acreages. Another twelve householders (24 percent) were kin of landowners with 10 acres or more; that is, they either shared the surname of an owner or had married a child of an owner.

Decadal persistence rates for black householders in rural Ripley Township rose as follows: 1840–1850, 41 percent; 1850–1860, 53 percent; 1860–1870, 50 percent.

27. Land deeds, Rush County.

28. Ibid.; census manuscripts, 1870, Rush County; estate papers of Allen Brown.

29. Bogle, "Railroad Building," 218–19, 224; Shirts, *Hamilton County to the Civil War,* 92, 370; U.S. agricultural census manuscripts, 1850, Hamilton County, Indiana, available on microfilm at Indiana State Archives, Indianapolis. Thirty-two percent of the land credited to Roberts farmers in the agricultural census of 1850 (822 acres total) had been cleared. A similar proportion, 34 percent, had been cleared in Jackson and Adams townships overall.

Edgar Conkling has noted that the increased marketing demands occasioned by the Civil War "first made commercial farming profitable for the Roberts Settlement folk." See Edgar C. Conkling, "Roberts Settlement: A Mixed-Blood Agricultural Community in Indiana" (M.A. thesis, University of Chicago, 1957), 54–55. While Civil War demands undoubtedly increased efforts to produce for commercial markets, the origins of the market orientation can more properly be traced to the arrival of the Peru and Indianapolis Railroad.

30. U.S. agricultural census manuscripts, 1870, Hamilton County, Indiana, available on microfilm, Indiana State Library, Indianapolis; land deeds, Hamilton County. Sixty-two percent of the land credited to Roberts farmers in the agricultural census of

1870 (1,267 acres total) had been cleared. A slightly larger proportion, 67 percent, had been cleared in Jackson and Adams townships overall.

The following table, drawn from Hamilton County land deeds, indicates the price of land purchased and sold by blacks in rural Jackson and Adams Twps. from 1835 to 1869:

Date	Number of Transactions	Price per Acre
1835–1839	18	$1.29
1840–1844	2	3.56
1845–1849	4	4.38
1850–1854	12	6.96
1855–1859	14	12.15
1860–1864	10	17.91
1865–1869	16	25.31

Note: Excluded are transactions involving parcels of less than five acres and inheritance partitions.

31. U.S. census manuscripts, 1850–1870, Hamilton County, Indiana, available on microfilm at Indiana State Library, Indianapolis; land deeds, Hamilton County.

32. Land deeds, Hamilton County. In 1862 Stephen and Elias Roberts jointly received $4,467 in the final settlement of Jonathan's estate; see estate papers, Jonathan Roberts, located in Clerk's Office, Hamilton County Courthouse.

33. Estate papers of Elijah Roberts, Wade Roberts, John Roads, Axsum Sweat, and Stephen Roberts, Hamilton County Clerk's Office.

34. Annie B. W. Effland, Denise M. Rogers, and Valerie Grim, "Women as Agricultural Landowners: What Do We Know about Them?" *Agricultural History* 67 (1993): 235–61; Elizabeth Fox-Genovese, "Women in Agriculture during the Nineteenth Century," in Ferleger, *Agriculture and National Development*, 267–301.

35. Land deeds, Hamilton County; census manuscripts, Rush County, 1850–1860.

36. Land deeds, Hamilton County.

37. Ibid., census manuscripts, 1860–1870, Hamilton County.

38. Agricultural census manuscripts, 1850–1870, Hamilton County.

39. Census manuscripts, 1870, Hamilton County, Indiana and Vernon County, Wisconsin, available on microfilm at Indiana State Library, Indianapolis.

40. Litwack, *North of Slavery*, 59–63, 246–52, 263–64; Thornbrough, *Negro in Indiana*, 114–18; Horton, *Free People of Color*, 58, 93.

41. Berwanger, *Frontier against Slavery*, 3–6, 38–59; Thornbrough, *Negro in Indiana*, 63–69, 82–85, 123, 130–33, 138–39.

42. Litwack, *North of Slavery*, 249, 257–62, 264–67; Quarles, *Black Abolitionists* (New York: Oxford University Press, 1969), 197–222, 228–49; Stanley W. Campbell, *The Slave Catchers: Enforcement of the Fugitive Slave Law, 1850–1860* (Chapel Hill: University of North Carolina Press, 1968), 62–63; Thornbrough, *Negro in Indiana*, 53–54, 88–89, 144–47; Horton, *Free People of Color*, 28, 50–51, 58, 91–92.

43. Thornbrough, *Negro in Indiana*, 145–146; Rush County Court records, entries of 15 October 1851, 11 January 1854 and n.d. [Fall term 1854], Clerk's Office.

44. Thornbrough, *Negro in Indiana*, 53–54; census manuscripts, 1860, Hamilton County.

45. *Syracuse True Wesleyan*, 11 October 1851, 1 August 1855, 12 September 1855. Annual meetings of the Indiana Conference of the Wesleyan Connection consistently attacked slavery throughout the 1850s as well; see, for example, reports in the *True Wesleyan*, 5 October 1850, 20 October 1853, 30 November 1854, 10 October 1855, 27 October 1858, 5 October 1859. Among the other items in the *True Wesleyan* shedding light on black–white relations near Roberts Settlement in the 1850s: an account of an anti-slavery sermon delivered by a Wesleyan minister to a Methodist Episcopal congregation in Boxley (26 May 1853); a letter from a Roberts area abolitionist, Aaron Lindley, on recent anti-black laws in Indiana and Illinois (26 May 1853); and reports of meetings at the Roberts Settlement meetinghouse (3 January 1851, 30 November 1854, 1 August 1855, 9 July 1856, 30 December 1857).

46. Whitewater Quarterly Meeting of Friends, Minutes, 1826–1840, and Spiceland Quarterly Meeting of Friends, Minutes, 1840–1860, located in archives of Indiana Yearly Meeting of Friends, Earlham College, Richmond, Indiana; Union Quarterly Meeting of Friends, 1849–1860, located in archives at Western Yearly Meeting of Friends, Plainfield, Indiana.

47. Thornbrough, *Negro in Indiana*, 184–92; Benjamin Quarles, *The Negro in the Civil War* (Boston, 1953; reprint ed., New York: Da Capo Press, 1989), 235–44; V. Jacque Voegeli, *Free but Not Equal: The Midwest and the Negro during the Civil War* (Chicago: University of Chicago Press, 1967), 4–9, 34–35, 88–90.

48. *History of Rush County*, 448–59, 467; M. Howard Winslow, "A History of Walnut Ridge Quarterly Meeting," unpublished manuscript available on microfilm at Rushville [Ind.] Public Library, 23–24; George Levi Knox, *Slave and Freeman; the Autobiography of George L. Knox* (Lexington: University of Kentucky Press, 1979), 74.

49. Ira Berlin et al., *Slaves No More: Three Essays on Emancipation and the Civil War* (New York: Cambridge University Press, 1992), 194–95, 199–200, 203, 207; Thornbrough, *Negro in Indiana*, 183–84, 192–96; Joseph T. Glatthaar, *Forged in Battle: The Civil War Alliance of Black Soldiers and White Officers* (New York: Meridian, 1991), 3, 71–72.

50. Glatthaar, *Forged in Battle*, 71–72; Berlin, *Slaves No More*, 203, 207; Thornbrough, *Negro in Indiana*, 192–97; W. H. H. Terrell, *Report of the Adjutant General of the State of Indiana* (8 vols., Indianapolis, 1869), 3: 382; muster rolls, 28th United States Colored Troops, Indiana State Archives; Carter, Notebooks, I: 163; Conkling, "Roberts Settlement," 30.

While the muster rolls for the 28th have survived, it is difficult to determine precisely how many men from Beech and Roberts settlements served in its ranks. The rolls provide only limited information for each soldier, including a brief physical description along with the soldier's age, birthplace, occupation, and place of enlistment (not residence). As Beech and Roberts surnames were often shared with blacks from other communities, it is often difficult to tell where a particular soldier lived prior to his enlistment. A Joe Roberts enlisting in Indianapolis may have been from Roberts Settlement, Indianapolis, or some other community. Nonetheless a close estimate is possible with the help of local histories, census manuscripts, obituaries, and other primary sources.

Based on this estimate, those serving in the 28th from Beech Settlement included Alfred Means, Benjamin Trail, Gooding Newsom, George Jones, William Bass, James Keemer, Charles A. Roberts, and John J. Roberts; those from Roberts

Settlement included Lorenzo Brooks, Calvin Brooks, Thomas Lawrence, Junius B. Roberts, Joseph Winburn, George Dempsey, George Sweat, William Hurley, Nelson Locklear, John H. Roberts, and Richard Roberts.

Local histories provide the names of at least eight men who served in the Union Army, but whose records are not immediately found among those of the 28th. Many may have served in the troops of other northern states that recruited black soldiers in Indiana. At least one Beech Settlement resident, Alex Moss, appears to have enlisted in the Massachusetts 54th Regiment in 1863; see Terrell, *Report of the Adjutant General,* 7: 692.

51. William Robert Forstchen, "The 28th United States Colored Troops: Indiana's African Americans Go to War, 1863–1865" (Ph.D. diss., Purdue University, 1994); Terrell, *Report of the Adjutant General,* 3: 382–83; muster rolls; *War of the Rebellion . . . Official Records of the Union and Confederate Armies,* 128 vols. (Washington, D.C.: Government Printing Office, 1880–1901), vols. 36, 40, 42 passim.

52. Terrell; muster rolls; *Official Records,* vol. 46 passim; Glatthaar, *Forged in Battle,* 218–21.

53. Muster rolls; letters of Junius B. Roberts, Jonathan Roberts Collection, Library of Congress.

54. Thornbrough, *Negro in Indiana,* 231–48; Voegeli, *Free but Not Equal,* 125, 160–81.

55. Whitewater Quarterly Meeting of Friends, Minutes, 1826–1840; Spiceland Quarterly Meeting of Friends, Minutes, 1840–1860; Union Quarterly Meeting of Friends, 1849–1860. Spiceland Quarterly Meeting allocated $367.51 to aid free blacks between 1828 and 1870, an average of less than $9 per year; most was spent for the educational needs of Beech residents. In contrast, $10,454.50 was raised for southern freedmen between 1863 and 1867.

56. Conkling, "Roberts Settlement," 104, 107, 110; muster rolls, 28th Regiment.

57. Thornbrough, *Negro in Indiana,* 206–208, 211; census manuscripts, Rush and Hamilton counties, 1860 and 1870. In 1860 there were a total of thirty-eight African-American households in Rush and Hamilton counties, exclusive of the Beech and Roberts neighborhoods; ten years later sixty-eight African-American households were counted in the same areas.

58. Berlin, *Slaves without Masters,* 386–95; Eric Foner, *Reconstruction: America's Unfinished Revolution, 1863–1877* (New York: Oxford University Press, 1988), 100–102; Williamson, *New People,* 2–3, 62–63, 75–91; Gatewood, *Aristocrats of Color,* 13–14; Wilson, *Rural Black Heritage,* 83–89.

59. Carter, notebooks, I: 167–69; Conkling, "Roberts Settlement," 30–31, 72; Meade Vestal, "Men of Yesterday," unpublished manuscript in Noblesville [Ind.] Public Library, 64.

At his death in 1892, Rice owned 242 acres; his first purchase of land in 1869 was made possible with a mortgage from his wife's uncle, Hansel Roberts; see Mortgage Records, F: 412.

60. Carter, notebooks, passim; obituary, Marian Bundy Roberts, in *Noblesville [Ind.] Daily Ledger,* 26 January 1904; published minutes of the Annual Conference, Indiana District, African Methodist Episcopal Church, 1858, 1862, 1867, 1868, 1871–1881, available at Wilberforce University, Wilberforce, Ohio; Lori B. Jacobi, "More Than a Church: The Educational Role of the African Methodist Episcopal Church in Indiana, 1844–1861," in Gibbs, ed., *Indiana's African-American Heritage,* 3–17.

61. Minutes of the Annual Conference, Indiana District, African Methodist Episcopal Church, 1858, 1862, 1867, 1868, 1871–1881, available at Wilberforce University, Wilberforce, Ohio; Carter, notebooks, passim. Other preachers from the second generation included James McDuffey, John Brooks, Benjamin Roberts, and Dolphin Roberts.

62. Haines, "Radical Reform and Living Piety," 90–103; Lee M. Haines, "The Grander, Nobler Work: Wesleyan Methodism's Transition, 1867–1901," in Caldwell, *Reformers and Revivalists*, 118–51.

63. Roberts, "Autobiography"; *Minutes of Western Yearly Meeting of Friends . . . 1858*, report of Committee on the Concerns of People of Color, Union Quarterly; *True Wesleyan*, 28 December 1870; 19 May 1869; Conkling, "Roberts Settlement," 107–109. Edgar Conkling's study of Roberts Settlement incorrectly notes that the community's frame church was built in 1861; see Conkling, "Roberts Settlement," 32.

64. Deed, Edmund Hurley to Nathaniel Rice (selling Second Cicero Baptist Church property), 7 June 1871, 16: 258; Moses Broyles, *History of the Second Baptist Church of Indianapolis* (Indianapolis, 1876), 61; William T. Stott, *Indiana Baptist History 1789–1908* (Franklin, Ind., 1908), 264. Hurley had joined the Second Baptist Church by 1876, according to Broyles.

65. Thornbrough, *Negro in Indiana*, 147; Gerber, *Black Ohio*, 21, 159–60; Carter, Notebooks, I: 221; obituary of Hansel Roberts, *True Wesleyan*, 28 December 1870; *Hamilton County Register*, 25 February 1869.

66. William A. Muraskin, *Middle-Class Blacks in a White Society: Prince Hall Freemasonry in America* (Berkeley: University of California Press, 1975), esp. chap. 1; Thornbrough, *Negro in Indiana*, 147–48; Gerber, *Black Ohio*, 158–65; Horton, *Free People of Color*, 111, 153; Litwack, *North of Slavery*, 231–32.

67. Carter, notebooks, I: 188, 212.

68. *Hamilton County Register*, 10 June 1869, 24 June 1869, 5 August 1869; Carter, Notebooks, I: 212; Thornbrough, *Negro in Indiana*, 147–48, 376n.

69. Haines, "Grander, Nobler Work," 120–26; Richard R. Wright, Jr., *Centennial Encyclopedia of the African Methodist Episcopal Church, 1816–1916* (Philadelphia: A.M.E. Church Book Concern, 1916), 317.

70. Obituary of Hansel Roberts, *True Wesleyan*, 28 December 1870; news report from "Roberts Cross-roads," *Hamilton County Register*, 16 November 1870; *Hamilton County Register*, 6 November 1874. See also a direct criticism of Wesleyan opposition to Masonry in news report from "Roberts Cross Roads," in *Hamilton County Register*, 20 July 1870; a report on the decline in influence of secret societies near Roberts Settlement by the Rev. J. W. Hiatt, in *True Wesleyan*, 17 May 1871; and a report of the ongoing concern about the "evils" of Masonry expressed in a lecture in nearby Boxley, in *True Wesleyan*, 16 January 1878.

71. Thornbrough, *Negro in Indiana*, 166, 323; minutes, Spiceland Quarterly Meeting, 1858–68; minutes, Union Quarterly Meeting, 1860–68.

72. Roberts, "Autobiography"; census manuscripts, 1870, Rush and Hamilton counties.

73. Census manuscripts, 1870, Rush and Hamilton counties.

74. Litwack, *North of Slavery*, 113–52 passim; McCaul, *Black Struggle for Public Schooling*; Thornbrough, *Negro in Indiana*, 160–82; Gerber, *Black Ohio*, 4–5, 190–99; Charles Warren, "Illiteracy in the United States in 1870 and 1880," published as *Circulars of Education of the Bureau of Education, No. 3-1884* (Washington, D.C.: Government Printing Office, 1884), 72, 86.

5. SETTLEMENTS IN DECLINE, 1870–1900

1. Carter, notebooks, I: 203–204; land deed, 26: 10, Rush County, Indiana, located in Recorder's Office, Rush County Courthouse, Rushville, Indiana.

2. Thornbrough, *Indiana in the Civil War Era*, 274–77, 389–94; Clifton J. Philips, *Indiana in Transition: The Emergence of an Industrial Commonwealth, 1880–1920* (Indianapolis: Indiana Historical Bureau & Indiana Historical Society, 1968), 30–31; Farris and Euler, *Prices*, 26–28, 36, 39, 45; Donald L. Winters, "The Economics of Midwestern Agriculture, 1865–1900," in Ferleger, *Agriculture and National Development*, 86–87; Anne Mayhew, "A Reappraisal of the Causes of Farm Protest in the United States, 1870–1900," *Journal of Economic History* 32 (1972): 464–75. Corn prices are the ten-year averages derived from annual prices reported in Farris and Euler, *Prices*, 36.

3. Thornbrough, *Indiana in the Civil War Era*, 375–82; Philips, *Indiana in Transition*, 136–39; Steinson, "Rural Life in Indiana," 214–17; Winters, "Economics of Midwestern Agriculture," 80–86; R. Douglas Hurt, *American Agriculture: A Brief History* (Ames: Iowa State University Press, 1994), 172–73, 195–202.

4. Thornbrough, *Indiana in the Civil War Era*, 369; Phillips, *Indiana in Transition*, 133–36, 364–66. For discussions of late nineteenth century population pressures and out-migration in other midwestern communities, see Bieder, "Kinship in Migration," 429–39; and Jon Gjerde, "The Effect of Community on Migration: Three Minnesota Townships, 1885–1905," *Journal of Historical Geography* 5 (1979): 403–22.

5. Steinson, "Rural Life in Indiana," 215, 217; Winters, "Economics of Midwestern Agriculture, 1865–1900," 87–88.

6. Land deeds, Rush County; Pressly and Scofield, eds., *Farm Real Estate Values*, 27–29; U.S. Bureau of the Census, *The Statistics of the Population of the United States . . . of the Ninth Census* (Washington, D.C., 1872), 129; U.S. Bureau of the Census, *Twelfth Census of the United States . . . 1900*, 10 vols. (Washington, D.C.: Government Printing House, 1901–1902), II: 142.

7. Land and mortgage deeds, Rush County, available in Recorder's Office, Rush County Courthouse; estate records, Rush County, available in Clerk's Office, Rush County Courthouse.

8. Land and estate records, Rush County.

9. Ibid.; will of John Watkins, Clerk's Office, Henry County Courthouse, New Castle, Indiana.

10. Mark Friedberger, "The Farm Family and the Inheritance Process: Evidence from the Corn Belt, 1870–1950," *Agricultural History* 57 (1983): 1–13; land deeds, Rush County.

11. Land deeds, Rush County.

12. Ibid.

13. Land deeds and estate records, Rush County; land deeds, Hamilton County, Indiana, located in Recorder's Office, Hamilton County Courthouse, Noblesville, Indiana. Brown's strategy is inferred from the fact that he sold his holdings and contracted to have a house built in the nearby village of Charlottesville shortly before his death in 1870. Hunt's actions are suggested partly by the fact that he sold his holdings and moved to adjacent Henry County in the early 1870s when he was in his seventies. In the 1870 census Hunt was living in the household of his daughter and son-in-law and was listed without an occupation, an indication that he apparently had already retired from farming by that time.

Roberts divided his combined holdings of 80 acres at the Beech and 100 acres at Roberts Settlement among his surviving children and the heirs of his deceased children in the spring of 1883. He died in 1886, when he was in his mid-nineties. In distributing his land Anthony showed little partiality; seven children (or their surviving heirs) received 20 acres each, while one received a double portion of 40 acres.

14. U.S. census manuscripts, 1870–1900, Rush County, Indiana, available on microfilm at Indiana State Library, Indianapolis.

15. Ibid.

16. Land deeds, Rush County.

17. Pressly and Scofield, *Farm Real Estate Values*, 27–29; land deeds, Hamilton County.

18. Land deeds, Hamilton County; estate records, Hamilton County, Clerk's Office, Hamilton County Courthouse.

19. Ibid.

20. Ibid.

21. U.S. census manuscripts, 1870–1900, Hamilton County, Indiana, available on microfilm at Indiana State Library, Indianapolis; obituaries, Sarah Davis, *Noblesville Daily Ledger*, 7 January 1930, and William A. Mathews, *Noblesville Daily Ledger*, 3 January 1922; U.S. census manuscripts, 1870, Cass County, Michigan; census manuscripts, 1870, Rush County. In 1870 Samuel and Jacob Mathews resided in Calvin Twp., Cass County, Michigan, near others originally from Beech and Roberts settlements; the William and Mary Mathews family lived in Noble Twp., Rush County, several miles from the Beech.

22. Census manuscripts, 1870–1900, Hamilton County.

23. Land deeds, Hamilton County.

24. Leslie Fishel, Jr., "Repercussions of Reconstruction: The Northern Negro, 1870–1883," *Civil War History* 14 (December 1968): 327–45; Thornbrough, *Negro in Indiana*, 231–366; Gerber, *Black Ohio*.

25. Carter, notebooks, I: 193–94; J. H. Binford, *History of Hancock County*, 168.

26. Carter, notebooks, I: 193–94; Binford, *Hancock County*, 168–70.

27. Thornbrough, *Negro in Indiana*, 276–87; Gerber, *Black Ohio*, 249–54.

28. Conkling, "Roberts Settlement," 33–34; Gary and Thomas, *Centennial History of Rush County*, I: 96–99, 107; *History of Rush County*, 248; Thornbrough, *Indiana in Civil War Era*, 337–61 passim; Phillips, *Indiana in Transition*, 224–52 passim; "The History of Roberts Settlement," in *A History of Arcadia, Indiana* (Arcadia Study Club, 1972), 53.

29. Interview with Jeanetta Duvall, 9 July 1986; census manuscripts, 1900, Hamilton County; Conkling, "Roberts Settlement," 34. Conkling interviewed Roberts residents and ex-residents in the early 1950s concerning race relations in the late nineteenth century; his subjects recalled that prejudice was encountered only when they traveled to locations beyond their surrounding neighborhood.

30. Interview with Jeanetta Duvall; Sarah Newby, untitled notes on history of Ripley Township, Rush County, available on microfilm at Rushville (Ind.) Public Library; census manuscripts, 1870–1900, Hamilton and Rush counties. Quote is from Newby.

31. Fishel, "Repercussions of Reconstruction," 328–30; Foner, *Reconstruction*, 527–28.

32. Minutes of Union Quarterly Meeting of Friends, 1865–1879, and Western Yearly Meeting, 1870–1876, located at archives of Western Yearly Meeting of

Friends, Plainfield, Indiana; minutes of Spiceland Quarterly Meeting, 1865–1867, Walnut Ridge Quarterly Meeting, 1867–1875, Walnut Ridge Monthly Meeting, 1865–1900, and Carthage Monthly Meeting, 1866–1900, located in Quaker Archives, Lilly Library, Earlham College, Richmond, Indiana. The actions of individual Committees on the Concerns of Colored People (CCPC) varied from one monthly meeting to the next. Minutes of monthly and quarterly meetings nonetheless indicate a clear shift away from local benevolent activities during the Civil War, and the virtual abandonment of such activities after 1870–1871. The Carthage Monthly Meeting formally disbanded in August 1871 "not seeing a necessity for continuing. . . ." In other instances reports by local CCPCs cease after 1870–1871, although the actual date of the committees' demise is not indicated.

33. *Syracuse American Wesleyan*, 1865–1881, available on microfilm at Archives and Historical Library of the Wesleyan Church, Indianapolis, Indiana; Ira F. McLeister and Roy S. Nicholson, *Conscience and Commitment*, 586–87; Lee Mark Haines, "A History of the Indiana Conference of the Wesleyan Methodist Church, 1867–1971" (M.A. thesis, Christian Theological Seminary, 1973), 1–18. The shift in the focus of Wesleyan Methodism is best seen in the group's weekly newspaper, the *American Wesleyan*.

34. *American Wesleyan*, 7 April 1880; Roberts, "Autobiography," 1–2.

35. *American Wesleyan*, 4 May 1870, 2 February 1876; Conkling, "Roberts Settlement," 43, 44, 59–66; Haines, History of the Indiana Conference, 137.

36. Conkling, "Roberts Settlement," 34, 59–66; Newby, notes.

37. Scattered references to Roberts voters, their involvement in Republican campaigns, and their participation in party conventions can be found in the *Hamilton County Register* and *Noblesville Ledger*; similar references for the Beech can be found in the *Rushville Republican* and *Carthage Record*. Quote is from *Hamilton County Register*, 20 July 1870.

38. *Noblesville Ledger*, 23 October 1874; *Rushville Republican*, 11 April 1878, 6 April 1882; Conkling, "Roberts Settlement," 103–104; Carter, notebooks, I: 104, 172, 205; Edwin A. Davis, comp., *The Statutes of the State of Indiana . . . 1870*, 2 vols. (Indianapolis, 1870), 2: 576–83, 617–23; Thornbrough, *Negro in Indiana*, 288–316.

39. *Noblesville Ledger*, 2 April 1880.

40. *Indianapolis World* article reprinted in *Noblesville Independent*, 1 October 1886; *Hamilton County Register*, 5 April 1878, 20 September 1878; *Noblesville Ledger*, 7 April 1882, 23 April 1886.

41. David Gerber, "A Politics of Limited Options: Northern Black Politics and the Problem of Change and Continuity in Race Relations Historiography," *Journal of Social History* 14 (1980): 235–55; Gerber, *Black Ohio*, 209–44, 331–70; Thornbrough, *Negro in Indiana*, 288–316; Fishel, "Repercussions of Reconstruction," 328–30.

42. Conkling, "Roberts Settlement," 91–95. Conkling notes that Roberts community leaders worked strenuously to encourage younger residents to remain in the countryside and maintain the settlement's heritage.

43. Pauline Wallace Baltimore, "Pearls of Pauline: Recollections of Life in Roberts Settlement Long Ago," in Wallace Baltimore, Milton Baltimore, et al., "A Children's History of Roberts Settlement" (unpublished manuscript, 1985, in possession of author), 17–20, 22–23; U.S. agricultural census manuscripts, 1860–1880, Hamilton and Rush counties, available on microfilm at Archives Division, Indiana State Library, Indianapolis; estate records, Hamilton and Rush counties; Conkling, "Roberts Settlement," 33–34.

44. Carter, notebooks, I: 39–41, 155; Conkling, "Roberts Settlement," 56–58; estate records of Eaton McDuffey, Rush County Clerk's office; estate records of Eaton and James Roberts, Hamilton County Clerk's office.

45. A positive assessment of the economic independence present at Roberts Settlement in the late nineteenth and early twentieth centuries is provided in Baltimore, "Recollections," 24–25.

46. Conkling, "Roberts Settlement," 66–75; Elizabeth Pleck, *Black Migration and Poverty: Boston 1865–1900* (New York: Academic Press, 1979), 122–60; Gerber, *Black Ohio*, 60–92; Thornbrough, *Negro in Indiana*, 347–66; Darrel E. Bigham, *We Ask Only a Fair Trial: A History of the Black Community of Evansville, Indiana* (Bloomington: Indiana University Press, 1987), 53–69.

47. Conkling, "Roberts Settlement," 72. The changing demographics of Indiana's black population during the late nineteenth century is discussed in Thornbrough, *Negro in Indiana*, 206–207, 224, 228–30.

48. Baltimore, "Recollections," 20–22; Carter, notebooks, passim; *American Wesleyan*, 4 May 1870, 2 February 1876, 2 April 1879, 25 February 1880; minutes of Walnut Ridge Monthly Meeting of Friends, January 1882.

49. Census manuscripts, 1870–1900, Rush and Hamilton counties; Conkling, "Roberts Settlement," 47–48; Carter, notebooks, I: 121, 169, and passim. Conkling notes that white children from surrounding farms occasionally attended the Roberts school, one indication of the high esteem in which the school was held. Carter indicates that Beech instructors participated in local teacher's institutes, state-mandated monthly meetings designed to improve the quality of elementary education. The changing nature of educational opportunities for blacks in Indiana during the late nineteenth century is discussed in Thornbrough, *Negro in Indiana*, 323–46.

50. Information on the subsequent careers of Beech and Roberts teachers is drawn from a variety of sources, including Conkling, "Roberts Settlement;" Carter, notebooks; census manuscripts; "History of Roberts Settlement," 54; Roberts, "History of Roberts Settlement"; and Hill, "Beech Settlement," 3.

51. Information on high school and college graduates is drawn from a large number of sources, including Conkling, "Roberts Settlement;" Carter, notebooks; Roberts, "History of Roberts Settlement"; Roberts, "Autobiography"; Thornbrough, *Negro in Indiana*, 345n; "History of Roberts Settlement," 53.

52. Philips, *Indiana in Transition*, 296–305, 363–67; census manuscripts, 1870–1900, Rush and Hamilton counties; *Ninth Census*, 124, 125, 129; *Twelfth Census*, I: 137, 138, 142.
Population statistics for 1870 and 1900, shown below, provide one measure of the growth of nearby towns and villages.

	1870	1900
Carthage	481	1,028
Knightstown	1,528	1,942
Rushville	1,696	4,541
Arcadia	312	1,413
Westfield	NA	670
Noblesville	1,435	4,792

53. Thornbrough, *Negro in Indiana,* 229–30 and 367–90 passim.

54. Ibid., 228–30.

55. Conkling, "Roberts Settlement," 77, 78.

56. Out-migration discussion in this and following paragraphs is based on information from a large number of sources, hereafter referred to as "out-migration sources." The most important of these include: Conkling, "Roberts Settlement"; Carter, notebooks; U.S. census manuscripts, 1870–1900, and U.S. census Soundex indexes, 1880 and 1900; obituaries from *Noblesville [Ind.] Daily Ledger;* probate and estate records, Rush and Hamilton counties; land deeds, Rush and Hamilton counties; Eastern Cherokee claims. Soundex indexes, a valuable source for tracing migration in 1880 and 1900, are available on microfilm from the National Archives. Eastern Cherokee claims are located at the National Archives as well.

To trace out-migrants, a list was compiled of Beech and Roberts residents who were reported at the settlements in either 1870 or 1880 censuses but were not reported at the communities in the census that followed—in other words, those who were present in 1870 but not 1880 and those who were present in 1880 but not 1900. Excluded from the lists were those known to have died at the settlements during the interim between censuses. The final list of "non-persisters" includes 564 residents.

Altogether, out-migration site(s) for 192 residents (34 percent) were found. Two factors suggest that the actual proportion of those traced is somewhat higher. First, cemetery records for the settlements apparently are not exhaustive; a number of individuals not traced, especially children, may therefore have died at the communities and not moved on. Second, a number of other "non-persisters" may have remained at the settlements but were simply overlooked by census enumerators; a small proportion of Beech and Roberts residents tended to go unreported in census manuscripts from one census to the next. (Less affluent Americans generally, and African-Americans especially, have often been missed by United States census takers. For a discussion of the problems related to census reports concerning blacks in Boston in the late nineteenth century, see Pleck, *Black Migration,* 214–19.)

57. Out-migration sources.

58. Jane Pederson, "The Country Visitor: Patterns of Hospitality in Rural Wisconsin, 1880–1925," *Agricultural History* 58 (1984): 347–64.

59. Census manuscripts, 1870–1900. At least 8 Beech and Roberts residents in 1870 were listed in census returns a decade later as "farm laborers" at other locations in Indiana and Michigan; an additional 7 other former residents were listed as "farmers." In 1900, 5 individuals who been residents at the settlements in 1880 were listed as farm laborers in Hamilton and Rush counties; an additional 5 others were reportedly farmers.

60. Conkling, "Roberts Settlement," 108–109; Thornbrough, *Negro in Indiana,* 306; Wright, *Centennial Encyclopedia,* 188–89.

61. Out-migration sources; Bigham, *Fair Trial,* 54–55; Gerber, *Black Ohio,* 91; Pleck, *Black Migration,* 125; Thornbrough, *Negro in Indiana,* 363–66.

62. For a discussion of the middle-class values and aspirations of African Americans in another midwestern state, see Gerber, *Black Ohio,* 111–16. Noted black sociologist E. Franklin Frazier has commented on the exceptional strength of middle-class values at "cultural islands" organized by African Africans of "mixed blood" including those at Roberts Settlement. After discussing the drive and determination characteristic of these communities' founders, he observes that "the children in such

families generally exhibit the restraint and self-discipline which have distinguished their forebears. . . ." See Edward Franklin Frazier, *The Negro Family in the United States* (Chicago: University of Chicago Press, 1940), 215–45; quote, 245.

63. Thornbrough, *Negro in Indiana*, 347–66; Gerber, *Black Ohio*, 297–319; Conkling, "Roberts Settlement," 104–105, 110–16.

64. *Noblesville Daily Ledger*, 8 April 1915; Carter, notebooks, I: 156.

65. Out-migration sources. The careers of successful teachers and ministers from the settlements are discussed in many sources, including obituary of Willard Gilliam, *Noblesville Daily Ledger*, 29 November 1935; obituary of Frank Roberts, *Noblesville Daily Ledger*, 11 July 1921; Roberts, "Autobiography"; "On the Ball Community Leaders of Yesterday," in Baltimore, "Children's History"; Wright, *Centennial Encyclopedia*, 188–89; Hill, "Beech Settlement," 3.

66. Census manuscripts, 1870–1900, Hamilton and Rush counties; Carter, notebooks, I: 76.

67. Out-migration sources.

68. Census manuscripts, 1870–1900, Rush and Hamilton counties.

69. Census manuscripts, 1870–1900, Rush and Hamilton counties; Bigham, *Fair Trial*, 68–69.

70. Out-migration sources; Carter, notebooks, I: 125, 149–50; "On the Ball Community Leaders"; Thornbrough, *Negro in Indiana*, 345n; Irvin Armstrong, "Negro Pioneers: First Settlers Came into Indiana in 1820," *Indianapolis Recorder* 7 July 1945.

71. Williamson, *New People*, 100–103; Gatewood, *Aristocrats of Color*, 175–76; Gerber, *Black Ohio*, 326–27; F. James Davis, *Who Is Black? One Nation's Definition* (University Park: Pennsylvania State University Press, 1991), 56–57; Gary B. Mills, "Miscegenation and the Free Negro in Antebellum 'Anglo' Alabama: A Reexamination of Southern Race Relations," *Journal of American History* 68 (1981): 16–34.

72. Williamson, *New People*, 100–103; Gatewood, *Aristocrats of Color*, 75–76; Gerber, *Black Ohio*, 326–27; Davis, *Who Is Black*, 56.

73. E. Franklin Frazier, *The Negro Family in the United States* (Chicago: University of Chicago Press, 1940), 520–21; Conkling, "Roberts Settlement," 108–109; Carter, notebooks, I: 47, 51, 52, 54–55. Much of the discussion on passing is based on private conversations between the author and Beech and Roberts descendants.

74. Frazier, *Negro Family*, 520–21; Carter, notebooks, I: 47, 51, 52, 54–55; George L. Richman, *History of Hancock County, Indiana: Its People, Industries and Institutions* (Indianapolis: Federal Publishing, 1916), 894–95, 1114–17.

75. DuBois, "Long in Darke," 553–55; James E. DeVries, *Race and Kinship in a Midwestern Town: The Black Experience in Monroe, Michigan, 1900–1915* (Urbana: University of Illinois Press, 1984), Conclusion.

76. DuBois, "Long in Darke," 555.

CONCLUSION

1. Conkling, "Roberts Settlement," 110–16; Joseph J. Boris, ed., *Who's Who in Colored America 1929* (New York: Who's Who in Colored America Corp., 1929), 310; obituary of Carl Roberts, *Journal of the National Medical Association* 42 (1950): 109.

2. Oral history interviews, Virginia Hampton and Mildred Varnado, 28 June 1994, Jeanetta Duvall, 30 June 1994, Herbert Rice, 30 June 1994, Ronald Tuttle, 3 July 1994; Lawrence Carter, unpublished notebooks on history of Beech Settlement

(4 vols.), available on microfilm, Indiana Historical Society Library, Indianapolis; Conkling, "Roberts Settlement," 90–95; United States Census manuscripts for Rush and Hamilton counties, Indiana, 1910, available on microfilm at Indiana State Library, Indianapolis.

3. Carter, notebooks; interviews, Ronald Tuttle, Virginia Hampton, Mildred Varnado.

4. Conkling, "Roberts Settlement," 91–95; interviews, Jeanetta Duvall, Herbert Rice; *History of Arcadia,* 53.

5. Interviews, Jeanetta Duvall, Herbert Rice, Ronald Tuttle, Virginia Hampton, Mildred Varnado. Visiting patterns in the early twentieth century are also apparent from neighborhood reports in local newspapers; see *Carthage Record* (later *Citizen),* available at the Henry Henley (Carthage Public) Library and Recorder's Office, Rush County Courthouse, Rushville, and *Noblesville Daily Ledger,* available on microfilm at the Noblesville Public Library.

6. Carter, notebooks, I: 213; Henry Woods, "Indiana's A.M.E. Birthplace," *Indianapolis Star Magazine,* 17 May 1970, 27; interview, Jeanetta Duvall; Conkling, "Roberts Settlement," 94–95; E. Franklin Frazier, *The Free Negro Family* (1932; reprint ed., New York: Arno Press, 1968), 67.

7. Interviews, Jeanetta Duvall, Herbert Rice, Ronald Tuttle, Virginia Hampton, Mildred Varnado; Conkling, "Roberts Settlement," 94–95; Frazier, *Free Negro Family,* 67; "The Roberts Settlement: Unique Community Dates Back 200 Years, Has Amazing Record of Family Achievement," *Ebony,* November 1951, 40–44ff. Carl Roberts estimated that the early Roberts homecoming at its peak attracted "eight or nine hundred people." *Ebony* placed attendance at the same gathering in the early 1950s at around 400.

8. Interviews, Jeanetta Duvall, Herbert Rice, Ronald Tuttle, Virginia Hampton, Mildred Varnado.

9. Robert M. Taylor, Jr., "Summoning the Wandering Tribes: Genealogy and Family Reunions in American History," *Journal of Social History* 16 (1982): 21–37; Michael Kammen, *Mystic Chords of Memory: The Transformation of Tradition in American Culture* (New York: Alfred A. Knopf, 1991), 215–23.

10. Frazier, *Free Negro Family,* 66–67; idem, *The Negro Family in Chicago* (Chicago: University of Chicago, 1932), 131–32; idem, *The Negro Family in the United States* (Chicago: University of Chicago, 1940), 519–24.

11. Roberts, "History of Roberts Settlement."

12. Ibid.

13. Ibid.

14. Ibid.

15. Jonathan Roberts Collection, Library of Congress; "Roberts Settlement," *Ebony,* 44. Quote is from [Carl G. Roberts], "Explanatory Notes," unpublished manuscript in Jonathan Roberts Collection, 2.

16. Nathan Hill, "Beech Settlement," *Indiana Negro History Society Bulletin,* May 1943, 2–3; Lawrence Carter Collection; Woods, "Indiana's A.M.E. Birthplace."

17. Woods, "Indiana's A.M.E. Birthplace."

18. Taylor, "Wandering Tribes," 30–31; Kammen, *Mystic Chords,* 640–45.

19. Interviews, Jeanetta Duvall, Herbert Rice, Ronald Tuttle, Virginia Hampton, Mildred Varnado.

20. Ibid. Quote is from Jeanetta Duvall.

21. Interviews, Virginia Hampton, Mildred Varnado, Ronald Tuttle; author's conversation with Beech homecoming participants, 30 August 1998.

22. Interviews, Jeanetta Duvall and Herbert Rice.

23. Baltimore et al., *A Children's History of Roberts Settlement* (1985).

24. Ibid. [iii].

25. Interview, Ronald Tuttle.

INDEX

Note: Italicized page numbers refer to illustrations. Tables are indicated by the italicized letter t.

STEPHEN A. VINCENT is Associate Professor of History at the University of Wisconsin–Whitewater. He grew up a few miles from Roberts Settlement.